CICS made easy

Customer
Information
Control
Systems made easy

JOSEPH J. Le BERT

McGraw-Hill Book Company

New York   St. Louis   San Francisco   Auckland
Bogotá   Hamburg   Johannesburg   London
Madrid   Mexico   Montreal   New Delhi
Panama   Paris   São Paulo   Singapore
Sydney   Tokyo   Toronto

Library of Congress Cataloging-in-Publication Data

Le Bert, Joseph J.
  Customer Information Control Systems made
easy.

  Bibliography: p.
  Includes index.
  1. CICS (Computer system) I. Title.
QA76.76.T45L4   1986   005.4'3   85-18072
ISBN 0-07-036972-0

 234567890   DOC/DOC   8932109876

ISBN 0-07-036972-0

*The editors for this book were Tyler G. Hicks and Mary Ann McLaughlin,
the designer was Naomi Auerbach, and the production supervisor
was Sara L. Fliess. It was set in Century Schoolbook
by McGraw-Hill Computer Assisted Publishing.
Printed and bound by R. R. Donnelley & Sons Company.*

To my wife, Maryann, who encouraged me and my children Joseph, Dorothy, and Jean who inspired me.

CONTENTS

PREFACE

CICS Made Easy is for you if you wish to gain a strong foundation in COBOL command-level CICS (Customer Information Control System) design, coding, and concepts. Application programmers, system analysts, and project leaders should find it easy to read, as well as an ideal reference book. It can be used as a textbook in a one-semester course for business and computer science majors. Familiarity with COBOL, 3270 terminals, and data processing concepts is the only prerequisite to understanding this book. Knowledge of virtual storage access methods (VSAM) is helpful but not required.

Online systems, which send, receive, and process data via a terminal, are here to stay and will soon exceed the number of batch systems in many companies. CICS makes it easy for a programmer to code instructions which facilitate online functions. The more you learn about CICS, the better prepared you will be to play a significant role in the transition from batch to online systems.

This book takes a very simple nuts-and-bolts approach toward CICS commands and concepts. It does not attempt to convey every detail of CICS; many of these details are confusing to the beginner. I believe that once you master the material in this book, you will be prepared to develop and maintain most CICS programs. The initial foundation gained from this book will provide you with knowledge and confidence to pursue advanced studies in CICS. You will not be overwhelmed with terminology at the start—only those terms and concepts which will actually be used are introduced as needed. A person unfamiliar with CICS will benefit most from this book by reading it from start to finish. Experienced CICS programmers can read those chapters which cover the material that they wish to review.

CICS Made Easy illustrates techniques and concepts through numerous simple examples and programs. Designers and programmers using this text should become productive very quickly. The programs in the examples employ a simple structured programming style which eliminates GO TO's without confusing you with numerous nested IF statements. The examples can serve as models for future programs and should result in increased programmer productivity.

Maintenance should be reduced because most of the program code is reusable. If you have a good model to begin with, it should comprise as much as 80 percent of the code you will require for similar programs. It follows that if you start each program with a substantial percent of its code pretested, program development should be quicker and easier.

Many CICS concepts and examples in the text are associated with COBOL commands and techniques with which you are familiar. The best way to learn anything is through examples and use; you will master these principles quite easily by using them when writing and testing your own programs.

Chapter 1 defines a typical CICS system as viewed by a user and introduces basic terms and concepts.

Chapter 2 is devoted to designing maps which are easy to work with. Map design and the conversational flow from screen to screen play an important role in the success or failure of an online system. Several map design guidelines are presented to make your screen design more effective.

Pseudoconversational programming, a technique which minimizes computer main storage requirements, is explained in Chap. 3 and used for all programs throughout the text. System and programming documentation standards, discussed in Chap. 4, are essential to the success of a CICS system. Emphasis has been placed on those standards and documentation methods which are most effective and easiest to create and maintain.

Chapter 5 presents short easy-to-understand programs which build a foundation for the more comprehensive programs introduced in later chapters.

Chapter 6 on basic mapping support (BMS) explains how assembler language macros are coded in order to create maps: BMS maps are included with program examples. Chapter 7 is devoted to the use of assembled BMS maps. It is easy to create BMS maps when you have models to use for new maps, but their use can cause much difficulty if you do not understand certain fundamentals. Map attribute usage and its relation to physical and symbolic maps are covered extensively.

Program control commands, covered in Chap. 8, aid in the design of programs which communicate with one another. They are necessary in order to design effective systems and to develop efficient programming techniques. Chapter 11 on file control presents and explains all the commands that you are likely to use. File control is easier in CICS programs than is the case in a batch environment.

Chapters 9, 10, 12, 13, 14, 15, and 17 are devoted, with complete examples, to the following programs, respectively: menu, linked, inquiry, addition, change, deletion, and browse. Commands and concepts which have been presented are discussed on a section-by-section basis. All programs function as part of a simplified system, enabling you to see the relation of the parts to the whole. This should prepare designers for new system development. High-quality work is more important than ever in online systems because it is difficult to conceal poor design and programming in an online environment.

Temporary storage, for which creative programmers will find many applications, is covered in Chap. 16. Several paging techniques, which can be coded with or without using temporary storage, are discussed. The browse program uses temporary storage queues for its paging routines. Routines used to accomplish forward and backward paging are presented. Methods for resetting a browse starting point and for returning a selection to an invoking program are also explained.

Chapter 18 on debugging and testing concentrates on the execution diagnostic facility (EDF) which is available with all command level CICS systems. Techniques are explained which can decrease the amount of time required to debug CICS programs.

Online systems have been around for many years. The extent of their application over the next few years should far exceed all that has been done in the past. Without knowledgeable and competent data processing personnel and users, this transition will not occur smoothly. I hope that this book will be successful in preparing you for the role you will play in putting your company online.

Joseph J. Le Bert

ACKNOWLEDGMENTS

CICS Made Easy contains much information gathered through experience and contact with knowledgeable associates. I am grateful for help obtained from the following people: Curt Collver and Lamar McIntosh for sharing their knowledge of CICS with me and especially for their help with structured programming. My proofreaders and contributors: William L. Newmark, Judy Morenberg, Jim Lentine, Harry S. Smith, Curt Collver, Andy Jones, James Massoni, George Mendez, Keith Barnes, Art Gubitosa, Nick Alderiso, Margaret C. Hao, Lorraine Orlowski, Jim Cuffe, LeWalter Dilligard, Patricia Fisher-Olsen, Richard F. Kinsella, C. C. Laganas, Tom Peri, and Chung-Hsun Yu. I thank Guy Ciotto, Om Singhal, and Alfred Tina for allowing me to share their extensive knowledge of CICS. And finally, my appreciation to my wife, Maryann, and daughter Dorothy for typing the manuscript.

CICS made easy

1

THE USER'S VIEW OF A CICS SYSTEM

I am often asked, "What is CICS?" My answer is that CICS (Customer Information Control System) is basically an IBM teleprocessing monitor which makes it easy to send, receive, and process data through interaction with a terminal that consists of a display unit or cathode-ray tube (CRT) and a keyboard. CICS runs on IBM and IBM-compatible mainframes and provides an interface between applications programs and the computer's operating system. CICS application programmers use command-level Cobol to code easy-to-use instructions into their programs. These commands facilitate accessing and updating online database files, data entry, and display of data and other information on the CRT. Users of CICS can transmit data from their terminals to the mainframe, where the data is processed and then transmitted back to the user.

Hands-on experience is important when learning one's way around a new teleprocessing system. Since I cannot take each of you to a terminal for a demonstration, this book uses pictures called "maps" on simulated 3270 terminal screens to illustrate CICS.

CICS, like most of data processing, hasa jargon all its own; the required terms will be explained as they arise. Familiarize yourself with your terminal keyboard; most are similar to typewriter keyboards, with some models containing additional keys which are used in combination with a primary key.

Terminal Keyboard Usage

The terminal keyboard keys referred to in this book are

Attention IDentifier (AID) Keys

1. ENTER—This is the most commonly used key; it is usually pressed in order to effect the transfer of data from a terminal into a program. A

1

program can test if this key was pressed in order to control the flow of its logic.

2. CLEAR—I use this key to terminate a session on the terminal. When the terminal operator is finished, the CLEAR key is pressed causing the program to display the message SESSION COMPLETED. This is a programmer-defined action, not a standard function.

3. PFXX—Program function (PF) keys transfer data from a terminal into a program. They are signals or switches set external to the program by keys on the terminal keyboard. PF keys can be used by a program to control the sequence of its logic. There are up to 24 PF keys, designated as PF1 through PF24.

4. PAX—Program attention (PA) keys are similar to PF keys, but they do not transfer data from a terminal into a program as the ENTER and PF keys do. There are three PA keys: PA1, PA2, and PA3.

Miscellaneous Keys

1. ALT—The ALTernate or shift key is used on some keyboards in conjunction with the CLEAR, PF, or PA keys in much the same fashion as the shift key is used on a typewriter.

2. TAB—The TAB key is used to position the cursor to a specific location on the screen. It moves the cursor across the terminal screen in a left-to-right, top-to-bottom sequence, stopping at designated fields.

3. EOF—The erase-to-End-of-Field (EOF) key will erase data in a specific field on the screen, from the point of the cursor position to the end of the field.

Screen Format

Screens for the 3270 terminals used for examples in this book consist of 24 lines and 80 columns. The screen is a grid in which line 1, column 1 is referred to as screen position 1; line 1, column 2 as position 2; line 2, column 1 as position 81; line 3, column 1 as position 161, etc. Screens for 3270 terminals contain a total of 1920 positions (24 lines by 80 columns). Screen position 1920 represents line 24, column 80. Figure 1-1 shows the format used for all 3270 screen illustrations presented in this book.

Screen Classifications

Most examples in this book will be based on a simplified purchasing system. Menu programs will be discussed as will be vendor file inquiry and maintenance programs. Maintenance programs will be presented for vendor file additions, changes, and deletions. A vendor file browse program will illustrate how to scroll backward and forward through a file. You may encounter combined maintenance programs which perform all maintenance and inquiry functions. I prefer individual maintenance programs, one for each function, and I employ this approach

1...5...10...15...20...25...30...35...40...45...50...55...60...65...70...75...80

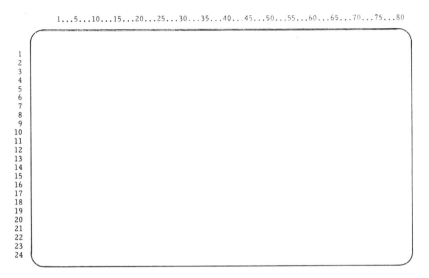

Figure 1-1 Screen Layout for 3270 Terminal.

for program examples. Your installation standards and system requirements will determine which approach you will take.

Screens used by CICS programs usually fall into one of the following categories. They are discussed in more detail later in this chapter.

1. Menu or submenu screens are selection displays used to make a choice in order to initiate a desired function. Figure 1-2 is an example of a menu screen. A submenu, shown in Fig. 1-4, takes one of the functions shown on a menu and breaks it down into subfunctions.

2. Control screens are used by the terminal operator in order to enter a record key which is used in inquiry and maintenance functions. The key entered on the control screen is used to format the detail screen, which is usually displayed next by the program. Figure 1-5 is an example of a control screen.

3. Detail screens are used to display or to facilitate the entry of data into a program during inquiry and maintenance functions. At the completion of the inquiry or maintenance function, control is passed back to the control screen. Figures 1-6 through 1-10 are typical detail screens.

4. Browse screens permit the terminal operator to view many occurrences of similar data, for instance, to scroll through a vendor file, as shown in Fig. 1-11.

The above screens are the types used by examples in this book; they are not the only types of screens you will encounter. Some designers do not use control screens; they prefer to enter the key directly on the detail screen. I prefer to use control screens and will employ them as appropriate in all programs in this book. The method you employ in your design may be determined by standards

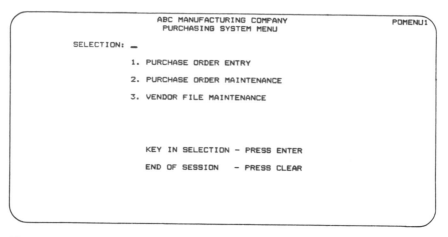

Figure 1-2 Purchasing System Menu Screen.

in effect at your installation. CICS commands and concepts are basically the same regardless of the screen design you use.

Types of CICS Systems

Most companies have two types of CICS systems, a test system and a production system.

Test System

The test system is used for development and enhancement of new and existing systems and programs. Test files contain fewer records than will actually be contained on the production system file, but they are typical of the kind expected to be on the production file. Do not rush programs through the test system without thoroughly testing them. It is difficult to explain to knowledgeable users why a program moved from the test system to the production system is not working properly.

Production System

Systems and programs which have been thoroughly tested and are error-free (hopefully) are put into the production system. This system is used for day-to-day online operations. Errors in design or programming not caught by the test system before programs are promoted to the production system can be a source of embarrassment to the data processing department.

Promotion from Test to Production

Moving or copying a program from the test to production system is often referred to as *promotion*. The interaction between the user and the system is the same for the test and production systems. This book assumes that the user utilizes the test system until convinced that a program is error-free, then signs off on the program and authorizes its promotion to the production system.

User Involvement

One major advantage of CICS is that users or user-interface personnel are required to get heavily involved in the development and testing of a system. High-quality work is essential, because, once a program is promoted, it may be accessed by users all across the country. The image of a system, or the reputation of data processing, is not enhanced if the system fails to function as expected. Batch systems, in which all data is grouped and entered into an input file before a program is run, sometimes encounter an abnormal termination (ABEND). The error can be fixed and the program rerun without the user ever knowing that a problem had existed. Depending on the system, an ABEND of an online program could trigger calls from users all across the country. The frequently heard complaint, "There is never time to do it right the first time, but always time to correct it" should never be said of the work of the online designer/programmer.

Getting on the CICS System

The procedure for logging on to a CICS system is generally similar from one installation to another. Screens displayed by the system during the log-on/sign-on procedure are not illustrated here because the procedure varies somewhat from one installation to another. To log on to the CICS system, the terminal operator presses the CLEAR key in order to clear the screen and set the cursor at position 1; keys in TESTCICS, PRODCICS, or a similar entry; then presses ENTER to get connected to the requested CICS system. An indicative message such as TEST CICS SYSTEM will be returned on the screen. Clear the screen and you are ready to sign on to CICS. Key in CSSN in screen positions 1 through 4 and press ENTER; a screen will be displayed requiring the entry of the operator's name and password (assigned by each installation). Key in these entries, which may not be displayed, and then press ENTER. A message indicating that the sign-on is complete will be displayed if the name and password keyed in match entries in the installation's sign-on table (SNT); otherwise, an error message will be displayed. Error messages usually appear when the terminal operator keys in a name or password incorrectly; if this occurs, the operator just clears the screen and enters CSSN again.

Summary of Sign-on Procedure

1. Clear the screen.
2. Key proper entry such as TESTCICS and press ENTER.
3. Clear the screen.

4. Key in CSSN.

5. Key in your name and password and press ENTER.

6. Clear the screen.

Initiating a CICS Transaction

The terminal screen is now clear, and you are ready to key in a TRANS-action IDentifier (TRANSID). The TRANSID is used as a key to search a CICS table in order to determine which program to access. Most installations have many TRANSIDs which a terminal operator can enter. A TRANSID is a one- to four-character code (usually four) which is keyed into screen positions 1 through 4 in order to start a CICS session when an AID key, generally ENTER, is pressed. This book defines a *session* as the period of time between entering a TRANSID and the point at which the terminal operator presses the CLEAR key to end the session. A session may consist of one or several programs being executed. There may be one or several sessions between the time you sign on to the CICS system and the time you log off.

Logging off CICS

When all sessions have been completed, a terminal operator is usually required to log off. This is accomplished by clearing the screen, keying CSSF LOGOFF, and pressing ENTER.

Typical CICS Session

Sign on to CICS and clear the screen; you are now ready to start a session. Key in the TRANSID POMU and press ENTER; this TRANSID initiates the program which displays the purchasing system menu map illustrated in Fig. 1-2. A map is a formatted screen identified in this book by the mapname in the upper-right corner of the screen (POMENU1 in Fig. 1-2). Maps will be explained thoroughly in future chapters.

Purchasing System Menu

Menu programs have as their primary purpose the display of two or more options on a screen from which the one desired can be selected. Typically, a selection number or letter is keyed in and ENTER is pressed to start the program associated with the selection.

The purchasing system menu (Fig. 1-2) lists three selections, numbered 1, 2, and 3. The terminal operator should enter the selection number at the cursor, which will be positioned to the right of SELECTION: (shown by an underscore in Fig. 1-2).

Erroneous Menu Entries

What would happen if the terminal operator:

1. Entered a character other than a 1, 2, or 3?
2. Pressed the CLEAR key?
3. Pressed an invalid AID key, such as a PA or PF key?
4. Pressed ENTER without keying in a selection?

The following list explains what would happen in each instance.

1. Figure 1-3 illustrates what happens if a 4 or any other invalid character is entered. A message is displayed at the bottom of the screen which is brighter than the rest of the screen's constants and data. Messages are usually displayed in a conversational fashion, notifying the operator of action taken or required. Generally map line 24 is reserved for operator-notification messages. Some applications may require more than one message line at the bottom of a map, perhaps lines 23 and 24.

2. For examples in this book, when the CLEAR key is pressed the screen will be cleared, then the message SESSION COMPLETED will be displayed starting at position 1 of the screen.

3. Pressing an invalid AID key would result in a programmer-defined highlighted message being displayed at the bottom of the screen. The message displayed on line 24 of the menu screen in examples in this book is;

ENTER AND CLEAR KEYS ARE ONLY VALID KEYS — PLEASE TRY AGAIN

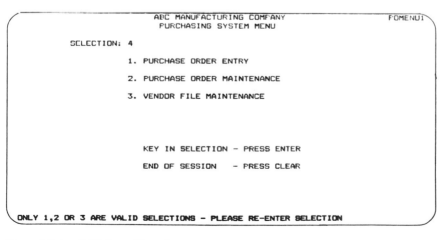

Figure 1-3 Invalid Entry on Menu Screen.

4. If ENTER is pressed without keying in a selection, the following highlighted message would appear on line 24 of the menu screen.

NO SELECTION WAS MADE — PLEASE ENTER SELECTION CODE

Valid Operator Menu Selection

Normally the terminal operator will make a valid selection and press ENTER, causing a transfer of control to the selected program. The system could be designed to display a default selection, perhaps a 1 next to SELECTION:. For our example, the terminal operator keys in a 3 next to SELECTION: and presses ENTER, causing the display shown in Fig. 1-4, the vendor file maintenance submenu screen. If the operator entered a 1 on this screen and pressed ENTER, the vendor file inquiry control screen shown in Fig. 1-5 would be displayed. The submenu shown in Fig. 1-4 could have been combined with the purchasing system menu shown in Fig. 1-2. I just want to point out options you have when designing a system. Sometimes a primary menu will have so many entries that there will not be room to include submenu fields for all items.

The cursor in Fig. 1-5 is located at the first position of the vendor code entry field, ready for the terminal operator to key in a code. The terminal operator could key in a code, for example, X-9234-1, and press the ENTER key in order to display the vendor file inquiry detail screen shown in Fig. 1-6. The message section at the bottom of the control screen (see Fig. 1-5) could show, depending on the key pressed, the following messages:

INVALID KEY PRESSED — PLEASE TRY AGAIN
VENDOR CODE MUST BE ENTERED — PLEASE KEY IN
VENDOR CODE FORMAT MUST BE: A-9999-9 — PLEASE REENTER
VENDOR RECORD NOT ON FILE

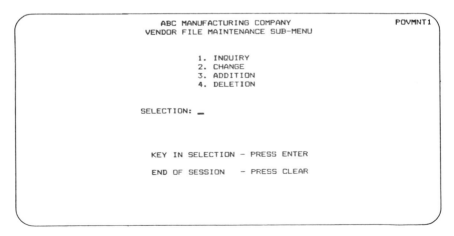

Figure 1-4 Vendor File Maintenance Submenu Screen.

```
DATE: 01/23/86            ABC MANUFACTURING COMPANY              POVMIQ1
TIME: 10.31.22            VENDOR FILE INQUIRY CONTROL



                    VENDOR CODE: X - 9234 -1



              1. FOR VENDOR FILE INQUIRY - PRESS ENTER

              2. TO BROWSE VENDOR FILE    - PRESS PF4

              3. TO RETURN TO MENU        - PRESS PF5

              4. TO END SESSION           - PRESS CLEAR
```

Figure 1-5   Vendor File Inquiry Control Screen.

Ending a Session

All programs in this book will end a CICS session by having the terminal
operator press the CLEAR key. The screen will be cleared and the message
SESSION COMPLETED displayed starting in position 1 of the screen.

A session could be terminated by leaving a cleared screen, but this sometimes leaves the terminal operator wondering if the session was ended properly.
Displaying SESSION COMPLETED leaves no doubt. It is more positive. Programs can be written to end a session based on any designated AID key being
pressed.

```
DATE: 01/23/86            ABC MANUFACTURING COMPANY              POVMIQ2
TIME: 10.32.41            VENDOR FILE INQUIRY

VENDOR CODE: X-9234-1
        NAME: XYZ INDUSTRIAL SUPPLIES     PHONE:    ( 412 ) 555 - 1000
                                          CONTACT: BILL O'BRIEN

ADDRESS - STREET: 555 MAIN STREET         DOLLARS COMMITTED:    $1,675.00
          CITY: PITTSBURGH
          STATE: PA PENNSYLVANIA
          ZIP: 15260

  TO ATTENTION OF: MARY MASSI



          1. RETURN TO INQUIRY CONTROL SCREEN   - PRESS ENTER
          2. RETURN TO MENU                     - PRESS PF5
          3. END OF SESSION                     - PRESS CLEAR
```

Figure 1-6   Vendor File Inquiry Detail Screen.

Inquiry Function

An online inquiry function refers to the act of displaying an inquiry screen which shows data contained on an individual record. If the terminal operator presses the ENTER key and the code entered in Fig. 1-5 is on the vendor file, the map named POVMIQ2 shown in Fig. 1-6 will be displayed. The map shows all significant fields in the vendor master record for vendor code X-9234-1. Remember, I am using simplified examples—your vendor master record would most likely have additional or different fields. The user can view all fields on the vendor file inquiry detail screen but cannot modify any fields on this screen. (Some systems have been designed to combine inquiry and changes.) The ability to view the current file status on line has limited the number of batch reports needed by users. Batch reports only reflect the status of a file at some point in the past. The inquiry map in Fig. 1-6 prompts you for the desired action with its instructions at the lower part of the screen. The only message likely to be displayed would appear only if an invalid key was pressed. It might read: INVALID KEY PRESSED—PLEASE TRY AGAIN. After an inquiry, the user could return to the inquiry control screen (mapname POVMIQ1, see Fig. 1-5) for entry of another code. Depending upon the AID key pressed, the program could also return to the vendor file maintenance submenu or end the session.

The inquiry function is not actually a maintenance function, but I like to include it on a maintenance control map. Some designers allow the entry of record keys on detail screens and eliminate control screens. I generally prefer to have keys entered on a control screen.

Maintenance Functions

File maintenance functions refer to the act of adding, changing, or deleting an individual record. Additions, changes, and deletions are maintenance functions which can be performed using an online system. Two types of online systems are:

1. Online real time system—In a real time system, the file being maintained is updated immediately when the change is entered by the operator.
2. Online data entry—Data is entered online but does not change a master file immediately. It is accumulated throughout the day and run through a batch program at night in order to perform file updating.

All transactions in this book will use a real time system. This system allows the user to see immediately the results of any changes made to a file, and to make corrections if required.

Permitting users to make maintenance changes directly to a file, or to enter transactions which later affect the data in that file, places the responsibility for file integrity on the user. Systems may have many users, entering data at various locations, and some files are constantly being updated. Most online files are dynamic, constantly being added to, changed, and deleted from. Online systems are usually more accurate than batch systems because

1. Transactions are usually entered by persons familiar with the input data, so there is less chance of interpretation errors.

2. Data can be updated in the desired files immediately. It is not necessary to wait until later that evening or for several days.

3. Data-entry errors are often caught by the user and corrected immediately.

4. Online systems can have many program edit checks built into them. For instance, if a vendor does not exist or is entered incorrectly, the system would detect the error and prompt the user to make a correction immediately.

Additions

Additions involve adding a new record to an existing file. On a vendor file addition control screen, similar to the inquiry control screen in Fig. 1-5, you could key in the vendor to be added and press ENTER to display the addition detail screen. The map in Fig. 1-7 would be displayed, showing the fields with underlines, into which the terminal operator will enter the required data. The underlines are not normally displayed and are only shown here to illustrate the fields and their size. The system assumes that all fields except CONTACT: and TO ATTENTION OF: require data to be entered. A program can edit each required field before it is entered into the file as an addition. Some fields need only to be checked for the presence of data. Other fields may be required to be numeric, have a valid state code, or perhaps contain a valid zip code.

Entering data on a screen. When a map such as that shown in Fig. 1-7 is displayed, the cursor is normally positioned at the first data-entry field (NAME). Pressing the TAB key will cause the cursor to move across the screen from left to right, top to bottom, stopping at the beginning of each data-entry field. After

```
DATE: 01/23/86              ABC MANUFACTURING COMPANY                    POVMAD2
TIME: 10.35.38                  VENDOR FILE ADDITION

VENDOR CODE: A-0100-1
       NAME: _____     PHONE:   ( ___ ) ___ - ____
                                         CONTACT: _____

ADDRESS - STREET: _____
            CITY: _____
           STATE: __
             ZIP: _____

TO ATTENTION OF: _____




        1. ADDITIONS, KEY-IN REQUIRED DATA        - PRESS ENTER
        2. RETURN TO ADDITION CONTROL SCREEN      - PRESS PF3
        3. RETURN TO MENU                         - PRESS PF5
        4. END OF SESSION                         - PRESS CLEAR
```

Figure 1-7 Vendor File Additions Detail Screen.

we tab to the last field, pressing the TAB key again will position the cursor at the start of the first field to be entered. Fields of fixed length, such as the PHONE, STATE, and ZIP, when completely entered, cause the cursor to skip automatically to the next field to be entered. Remember the cursor moves left to right, top to bottom when you enter data (i.e., from NAME, to PHONE, to CONTACT, to STREET, to CITY, etc.).

Data-entry error indicators. A programmer has several methods to indicate data-entry errors. Each technique listed below displays an indicative message on line 24 of the screen and positions the cursor at the first field in error.

1. Display field identifiers at a brighter intensity than those of correctly entered fields. Field identifiers as used here refer to the descriptions preceding each data-entry field, such as NAME, PHONE, and CONTACT (see Fig 1-8).

2. Display the erroneous data field itself at a brighter intensity than correctly entered fields. This method has the drawback that if failure to key in an entry is the error, there is no data to highlight. Some users of this method move asterisks to a nonentry field.

3. Display one or more messages at the bottom of the screen without any highlighting of error fields or field identifiers. The drawback to this method is that when multiple errors occur, it is not always practical to display all error messages at once.

This book will use the first technique, that of brightening all erroneous field identifiers and positioning the cursor at the start of the first incorrect field. A highlighted message will be displayed at the bottom of the screen, notifying the terminal operator to PLEASE CORRECT HIGHLIGHTED FIELDS.

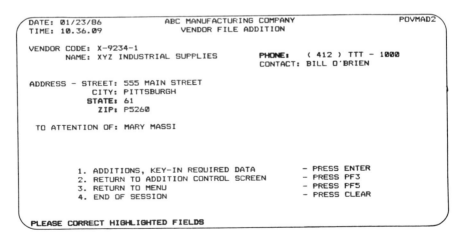

```
DATE: 01/23/86            ABC MANUFACTURING COMPANY              POVMAD2
TIME: 10.36.09                VENDOR FILE ADDITION

VENDOR CODE: X-9234-1
        NAME: XYZ INDUSTRIAL SUPPLIES        PHONE:   ( 412 ) TTT - 1000
                                             CONTACT: BILL O'BRIEN

ADDRESS - STREET: 555 MAIN STREET
            CITY: PITTSBURGH
           STATE: 61
             ZIP: P5260

TO ATTENTION OF: MARY MASSI




        1. ADDITIONS, KEY-IN REQUIRED DATA        - PRESS ENTER
        2. RETURN TO ADDITION CONTROL SCREEN      - PRESS PF3
        3. RETURN TO MENU                         - PRESS PF5
        4. END OF SESSION                         - PRESS CLEAR

PLEASE CORRECT HIGHLIGHTED FIELDS
```

Figure 1-8 Errors on Vendor File Additions Detail Screen.

Key in all required data on the screen (see Fig. 1-7), and following the instructions at the bottom of the map, press ENTER to record the addition. Assume three fields were entered incorrectly. The field identifiers of the three fields would be brightened and the message PLEASE CORRECT HIGHLIGHTED FIELDS would be displayed at the bottom of the screen as shown in Fig. 1-8.

If only two of the three errors were corrected and you pressed ENTER again, only the field identifier of the one remaining incorrect item would be highlighted. The two corrected fields will now have their field identifiers displayed at a normal intensity. The same notification message will be displayed at the bottom of the screen.

When the final error is resolved and the operator presses ENTER, the record will be added to the file and the addition control screen will be displayed. The indicative message displayed at the bottom of the control screen will be RECORD SUCCESSFULLY ADDED. The terminal operator could now perform an inquiry against the new record to see if it was added correctly. The change or delete function could be initiated if the addition was incorrect.

When entering data, sometimes an error cannot be resolved or it is decided not to add the record. If this occurs, the terminal operator has several options, as shown by the instructions at the bottom of the screen in Fig. 1-8:

1. Return to the control screen.

2. Return to the menu.

3. End the session.

Changes

In data processing there is only one thing that you can be sure of—changes! Change is a certainty; therefore, all systems, programs, files, etc. should be designed with built-in flexibility. The vendor file has an associated change function which enables a user to change any field in the record, except for vendor code and dollars committed.

After adding a vendor record, you may realize that some of the data was entered incorrectly, or that it requires a change. The vendor code would be entered on a control screen and ENTER pressed in order to display the change detail screen. The system would then display the change detail map shown in Fig. 1-9. The spaces before and after area code and other fields are actually occupied by screen attribute characters, which are discussed in Chaps. 2 and 6. The cursor would initially be located at the first position of the vendor NAME field. Press TAB to position the cursor at the start of any field requiring a change, then enter the new data. You can alter as many fields as required on the changes screen. When all changes have been entered, the instructions at the bottom of the screen direct you to press ENTER to record the change(s). The change control screen will display the notification CHANGE COMPLETED SUCCESSFULLY in the message section at the bottom of the screen, if no errors were detected. The message PLEASE CORRECT HIGHLIGHTED FIELDS would continue to appear at the bottom of the change detail screen until the

```
DATE: 01/23/86              ABC MANUFACTURING COMPANY              POVMCH2
TIME: 10.44.59                 VENDOR FILE CHANGES

VENDOR CODE: A-0100-1
        NAME: AA INDUSTRIAL SUPPLIES        PHONE:    ( 301 ) 555 - 1000
                                            CONTACT: JOHN SIMPSON OR H. JONES

ADDRESS - STREET: 555 HUDSON STREET
           CITY: NEWARK
          STATE: NJ NEW JERSEY
            ZIP: 07102

TO ATTENTION OF: PAUL ANDERSON


        1. CHANGES, KEY-IN NEW DATA          - PRESS ENTER
        2. RETURN TO CHANGES CONTROL SCREEN  - PRESS PF3
        3. RETURN TO MENU                    - PRESS PF5
        4. END OF SESSION                    - PRESS CLEAR
```

Figure 1-9 Vendor File Changes Detail Screen.

changes were made correctly or the function was ended by pressing one of the other AID keys.

Deletions

Records are sometimes added in error or become obsolete over a period of time. These records may be purged or deleted by a batch program or can be deleted online. Our system allows the online deletion of records from the vendor master file.

The code of the vendor to be deleted is entered on a control screen and ENTER is pressed to display the delete detail screen. The vendor deletion detail screen (Fig. 1-10) will be displayed. The first instruction at the lower part of

```
DATE: 01/23/86              ABC MANUFACTURING COMPANY              POVMDL2
TIME: 10.48.23                 VENDOR FILE DELETION

VENDOR CODE: A-0100-1
        NAME: AA INDUSTRIAL SUPPLIES        PHONE:    ( 301 ) 555 - 1000
                                            CONTACT: JOHN SIMPSON OR H. JONES

ADDRESS - STREET: 555 HUDSON STREET
           CITY: NEWARK
          STATE: NJ NEW JERSEY
            ZIP: 07102

TO ATTENTION OF: PAUL ANDERSON


        1. DELETIONS VERIFY DATA BEFORE DELETING  - PRESS ENTER
        2. RETURN TO DELETION CONTROL SCREEN      - PRESS PF3
        3. RETURN TO MENU                         - PRESS PF5
        4. END OF SESSION                         - PRESS CLEAR
```

Figure 1-10 Vendor File Deletions Detail Screen.

the screen directs you to verify data before deleting. When the data has been checked to verify that you have the right record, press ENTER to finalize the delete. The next display would be that of the delete control screen with the message RECORD DELETED SUCCESSFULLY displayed at the bottom of the screen.

Browse Function

The browse function, like the inquiry function, is not a maintenance function, but it is often helpful to include it on a control screen as shown in Fig. 1-5.

A browse is a sequential search of a file, starting at the key passed to the browse program. For example, if you wanted to search the vendor file for a code beginning with S, you would enter one character, an S, in the vendor code entry field on the control screen (see Fig. 1-5) and press PF4 to start the browse function. The browse will display the vendor file browse map shown in Fig. 1-11. Since you entered only one character, the browse starts its sequential search with the first vendor record beginning with an S. If you were searching for a vendor named Smith Brothers Parts, which is near the middle of the S records, it wouldn't be advisable to start your browse at the beginning of the S records. You would have to read half of the S records before reaching the one which is desired. This would not only be a waste of time, since sequential file searches are slow, but it would also tie up computer resources by requiring numerous unnecessary file reads. Try to limit the scope of browse searches. Limit your search by trial and error. For instance, when searching for Smith, enter S-5 as the first two characters on the control screen (see Fig. 1-5) before initiating the browse (S-5000-0 should be near the middle of the S records). If S-5 is much greater than or less than the code of the desired vendor, reset the browse. Key in a new start browse code, a full or partial code on the bottom of the vendor file

```
DATE: 01/23/86            ABC MANUFACTURING COMPANY                    POVMBR1
TIME: 10.51.37               VENDOR FILE BROWSE
   VENDOR CD  VENDOR NAME              STREET              CITY / STATE
01 S-0010-1  SABER SAWS & TOOLS       106 MULBERRY STREET  NEWARK           NJ
02 S-0020-1  SACRET CEMENT PRODUCTS   23 RIVER DRIVE       SCRANTON         PA
03 S-0030-1  SADLER SCRAP STEEL       1103 ESSEX STREET    PITTSBURGH       PA
04 S-0035-1  SADOR DISCOUNT EQUIPMENT 310 E MAIN AVENUE    CLEVELAND        OH
05 S-0040-1  SAFETY GLASS INSTALLERS  11 HUDSON STREET     JERSEY CITY      NJ
06 S-0050-1  SAFEWAY INDUSTRIAL TOOLS 48 BROADWAY          NEW HAVEN        CT
07 S-0060-1  SAKSON BROTHERS CHEMICALS 454 JUNCTION BLVD   PATERSON         NJ
08 S-0065-1  SALE ITEM PAINTS         1610 BLEEKER STREET  NEW YORK         NY
09 S-0070-1  SALVAGE METALS           34 UNION AVENUE      YOUNGSTOWN       OH
10 S-0070-2  SALVAGE METALS           88 BROAD STREET      BETHLEHEM        PA
11 S-0080-1  SAMPSON STEEL INC.       754 AVON STREET      PHILADELPHIA     PA
12 S-0090-1  SANDOR INDUSTRIAL ACIDS  101 MONROE STREET    HARTFORD         CT
13 S-0095-1  SANITARY CLEANSERS       33 EASTON DRIVE      SYRACUSE         NY
14 S-0100-1  SANORA RESINS            2300 BELT PARKWAY    BUFFALO          NY
15 S-0065-1  SANTOR CHEMICALS         1000 ERIE BLVD       NEW YORK         NY
   : SELECTION
   RESET VENDOR CODE:
1. PF1  - FWD      4. PF3  - KEY IN SELECTION - RETURN TO CALLING PROGRAM
2. PF2  - BWD      5. PF4  - KEY IN RESET VENDOR CODE (FULL OR PARTIAL CODE)
3. PF5  - MENU     6. CLEAR - END OF SESSION
```

Figure 1-11 Vendor File Browse Screen.

browse map (Fig. 1-11), next to the field identifier RESET VENDOR CODE:, and press PF4. For instance, try S-4, S-6, S-45, or S-55. Partial key searches of a file are referred to as *generic* searches.

After displaying a full map of vendor browse data, the terminal operator has several options corresponding to the instructions at the bottom of Fig. 1-11.

1. Press PF1, which is commonly used for forward paging, in order to display the next page of sequential vendor browse data. The display of succeeding pages of data can be continued by pressing PF1. The browse process of paging forward and backward is often referred to as *scrolling*.

2. Press PF2, which is commonly used for backward paging, to display the previous page of data. Normally you are required to scroll forward and save succeeding pages before you can page backward.

3. Return to the vendor file maintenance submenu (see Fig. 1-4).

4. Key in a selection, from 01 to 15, and return with the selected vendor to the program which initiated the browse. Some systems may be designed to have a program pass control to a browse program in order to select a code and return it to the invoking program.

5. Enter a full or partial vendor code to reset the browse, then press PF4 to continue the browse from the point of the reset code.

6. Press CLEAR to end the session.

SUMMARY

The illustrations in this chapter are typical of online functions you are likely to encounter or to design into new applications at your installation. Your company may have some variations to the material presented in this chapter, but the concepts will be basically the same. Most installations will have a sign-on procedure, start transactions with a four-character TRANSID, and display and receive maps. You will most likely have a menu program and the following functions: additions, changes, deletions, and inquiries. A browse function, which should be tailored to your accessing and file structure requirements, will probably be present in many systems.

Online systems, unlike batch systems, make it difficult to cover up poor design and programming errors. It is in the best interest of both the user and the programmer/analyst to work closely in the design and testing stages of all systems. High-quality work is more important than ever in an online environment. It can only be achieved by substantial cooperation between users and system designers. Poor design will cause more problems than any other factor in an online system. The challenge presented by online systems should be *"do it right the first time!"*

2

DESIGNING
USER-FRIENDLY MAPS

The design of user-friendly maps requires user involvement. Users have to live with the screens and the system, while data processing personnel only maintain the system. Almost any concept the user can define and convey to a programmer/analyst can be implemented. The best in-house systems (not packages) and their associated screens are developed through close cooperation and coordination between users and data processing personnel.

Data processing in its simplest form has always consisted of receiving input, processing the data, and creating some form of output. CICS is no different, although the sequence is slightly different. Generally, after initiating a transaction by entering a TRANSID, the first thing you get is output, in the form of a map, displayed on a terminal. Next, you key information on the screen and enter the input into the system, which then processes it. The design of maps, which are the major source of input and output in a CICS system, is the subject of this chapter. Later chapters will explain the coding required to generate the maps.

Designing Maps

Maps define formatted screens which are users' input and output in an online environment. The map is the user's primary aid when conveying to data processing the input and output of a system. The map is used to send information to and receive data from a screen. Users will view some maps repeatedly throughout the day. Therefore, it is in their best interest to make sure they understand the map and feel comfortable with its format. Obtain or design a form similar to Fig. 2-1, which will be used to paint a picture of a map corresponding to a terminal screen and containing 80 columns and 24 lines. Figure 2-2 shows the basic map format I recommend. Many terminals have nearby printers that can

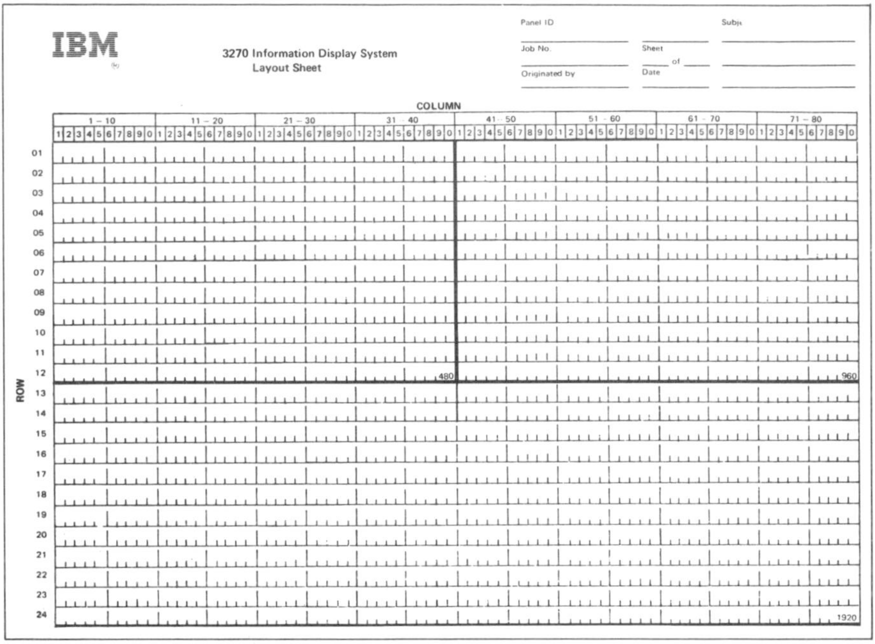

Figure 2-1 3270 Map Layout Form.

reproduce a screen image by pressing a designated key on the terminal keyboard. It is often important for future reference to know the date and time when map images were printed. I recommend putting date and time on detail and browse maps. They are optional on menu maps and control screens. These different types of maps were discussed under "Screen Classifications" in Chap. 1.

The mapname should be put on all maps; I find the upper-right-hand corner a convenient location for this. Users often have questions or recommendations pertaining to the system; it is easier to identify the map in question if it can be referred to by a common name. Occasionally a program will come to an ABEND; it is easier to identify where the problem occurred if the map which triggered the ABEND can be identified. The center of the first line of the map is a good location for company name or system name, and the map title should be centered on the second line. The last line of the map (line 24) is generally reserved for program-generated user-notification messages.

The area between the two heading lines and the message line contains the body of the map and user instructions. There are no rules for this part of the map, but the body of the map should precede the instructions. This is the area of the map where a user and an analyst can express their creativity and their good design skills. A series of maps helps develop the picture a user receives of a system. This picture can be pleasing, neutral, or irritating. How can a map be irritating? Anything which is difficult to understand, cumbersome to work

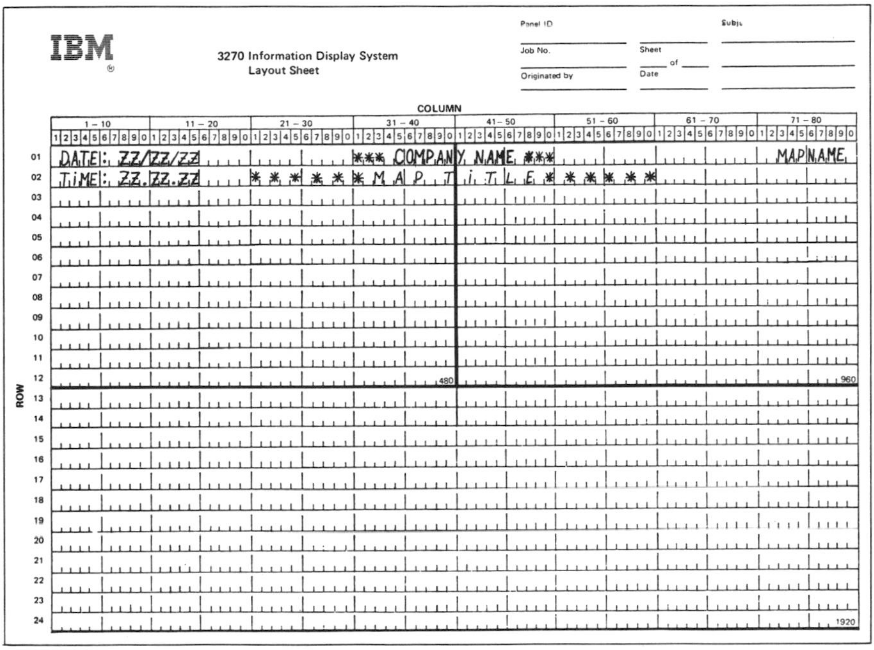

Figure 2-2 Basic Map Screen Format.

with, and causes frustration to a user is a source of irritation. Poorly planned and designed maps, as well as the sequence of map appearance in a system, can be a major irritant. Since users have to live and work with a system's screens, they should help design maps which are pleasing and logical.

I usually design and redesign a map several times before showing it to a user. The user usually offers suggestions which necessitate a few additional map alterations. This communication between screen designer and user, before programming begins, minimizes the number of changes required after a program has been written.

Map Design Guidelines

When designing maps, as in most areas of data processing, an important consideration should be, "keep it simple and straightforward" (KISS). Some guidelines I like to apply when designing a map are

1. Balance the data to be displayed. Don't cramp it all to the left and top of the map. You have 80 columns and 21 lines plus 2 header lines and a message line; don't be reluctant to use them.

2. Put date and time on detail maps.

3. Depending on company standards, display company, department, or system name, centered on line 1 of the map.

4. Always include mapname in the upper-right corner of each map.

5. Give the map a title centered on line 2 of the map.

6. Start the body of the map on line 3 or lower.

7. Indicate display-only variable data (such as date and time) by Z's and data-entry fields by X's.

8. Follow the body with instructions which will guide the terminal operator to perform the required function.

9. Number instructions when there are three or more options from which to choose.

10. Generally locate operator-notification and action-required messages on line 24 of the map. A notification message between the body and instructions is sometimes an asset, usually on control maps.

11. Brighten all messages so that they will stand out from the rest of the map.

12. Highlight the field identifiers of items which are entered incorrectly.

13. Strive for consistency of format for similar functions on different maps.

14. Reserve column 1 of all lines for map attributes (see "Map Attributes" later in this chapter). Attributes can be set in column 80 of the preceding line if you wish to display or enter data starting at column 1, but this is awkward and can lead to errors.

Consistency in Map Design

A map which is similar from one program to another is easier to reproduce and modify for new programs. Maps can be generated much more quickly for new programs if a skeleton map exists which is similar to the new map. Consistency will enable a programmer/analyst to design a prototype of a new system within a reasonable period of time using existing systems as models. Maps can generally be classified into types which have many similarities. Maps discussed in Chap. 1 which possess similarities from one system to another are

1. Menus

2. Control maps

3. Detail maps

4. Browse maps

I like to show the field identifiers for date and time. Your installation may just want to display the date and time without descriptions. Either method is acceptable, but when possible always place them in the same location on all maps. *Always* place the mapname in the same location for all maps.

Map Attributes

Each field on a map has an attribute associated with it. A field, as a user perceives it, is any displayed data or any location on a map at which data can be entered. In reality all literals, field identifiers, displayed data, and data-entry locations are map fields. Figure 2-3 shows a menu map for the purchasing system; this is the map used to format the screen shown in Fig. 1-2. There are several fields on this map, but only one in which the terminal operator is permitted to enter data—the SELECTION field.

The common attributes you should be familiar with are

1. ASKIP (Automatic SKIP)—The cursor skips over fields with this attribute.

2. UNPROT (UNPROTected)—A field the cursor will stop at so that the terminal operator can enter data.

3. BRT (BRighTer intensity)—A field displayed at a brighter intensity than normal. A BRT field may be referred to as a *highlighted* or *high-intensity* field. Messages and field identifiers of erroneous entries are highlighted in this book.

4. NORM (NORMal intensity)—The usual display for fields. When errors are corrected, their field identifiers are changed from BRT to NORM.

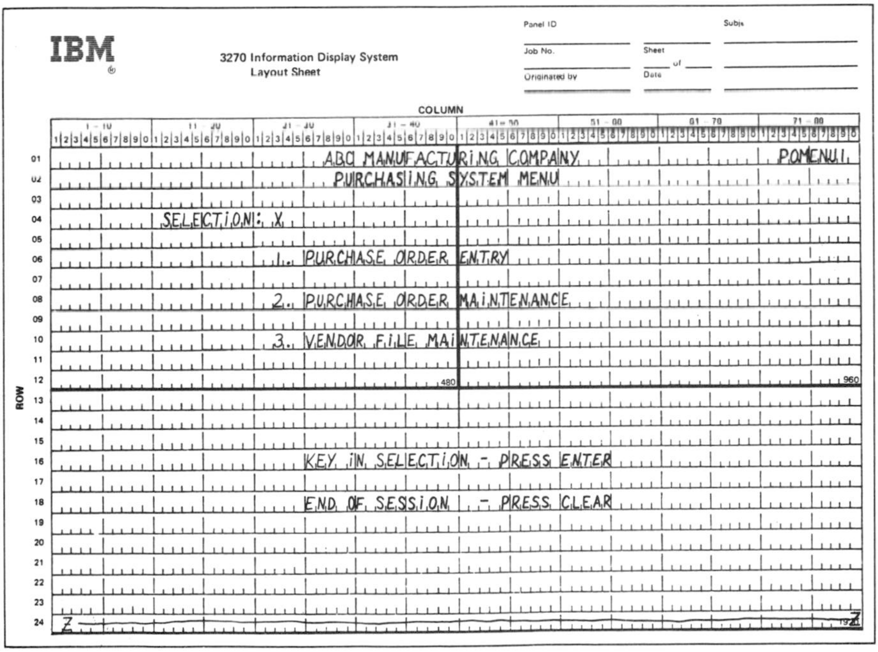

Figure 2-3 Purchasing System Menu Map.

5. DRK (DaRK intensity)—This field cannot be seen and is generally used for a password field. It is sometimes used to darken a message field on a subsequent display of the screen, when the message no longer applies.

Each attribute occupies one position on the map and controls the field which immediately follows it. All field attributes in Fig. 2-3 are defined as ASKIP, NORM initially, except the attribute for the entry of the selection. The attribute for the selection entry is UNPROT in order to allow for the entry of the selection number by the terminal operator. The UNPROT attribute occupies the screen position between SELECTION and the field to be entered (shown on the map by an X). The UNPROT attribute occupies screen location line 4, column 22; it is not visible, but it is there. An attribute immediately follows the SELECTION field; it is ASKIP and is located at screen location line 4, column 24. Without this ASKIP attribute, there would be nothing to stop the entry of data by the terminal operator. This attribute limits the operator to one digit of entry data. An ASKIP attribute following an UNPROT field is sometimes referred to as a *stopper* attribute. If there was another UNPROT field on the map, the cursor would skip to the start of that field when it encountered the ASKIP attribute. The cursor never stops at an ASKIP field. When designing a screen, just keep in mind that each UNPROT field is immediately preceded by and followed by an attribute, each of which occupies one position on the screen. ASKIP fields have only a preceding attribute which skips past the field until the next unprotected field is encountered. Note that the message line starts at line 24, column 2 because column 1 is occupied by an ASKIP attribute. A program can change this attribute from ASKIP,NORM to ASKIP,BRT to ASKIP,DRK and back again in order to highlight and "erase" messages by brightening and darkening them.

Screen or map size is 80 columns by 24 lines and contains 1920 available positions for characters and attributes. The two heading lines plus the message line take up 3 lines, or 240 of the available positions, leaving 21 lines or 1680 positions for the body and instructions of your map. Twenty-one lines are usually sufficient space for display and entry information and for instructions to the terminal operator. Two or more maps can be used in cases where one map is insufficient for a required function.

Map Body and Instructions

The body of the map is the most important part of the display screen and therefore requires the most planning; it is the area in which the designer can best express creativity. Users of the most complicated and advanced system, even if it performs every function imaginable, will think the system is poorly designed if it is difficult to understand and cumbersome to use.

The body of the purchasing system menu (see Fig. 2-3) is typical of that used for a menu program. Most menus will have more than three selections which may be indicated by numbers and/or letters. On a menu with numerous entries, you may display two or more entries per line if necessary. The operator will normally key in the number or letter and press ENTER.

The instruction section of a menu map is usually rather simple, generally consisting of two entries:

KEY IN SELECTION — PRESS ENTER

END OF SESSION   — PRESS CLEAR

I do not usually number fewer than three instructions on a map, although you may choose to do so. There is no reason a map must have instructions numbered, but doing so sometimes helps a user to remember the options by association.

Designing the Control Map

The heading and message lines of the control map are similar to those of the menu and all of the maps in this book. Date and time are the basic differences on the heading lines for the vendor file inquiry control map shown in Fig. 2-4.

Body of the Control Map

The body of a control map is generally brief, usually consisting of one or more entries which are concatenated (joined together) to develop a key for the

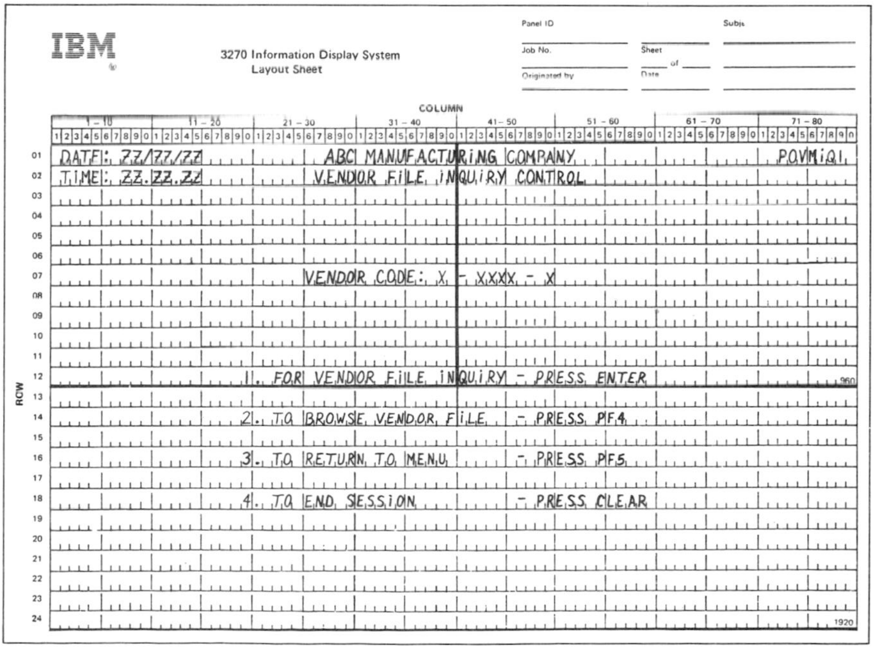

Figure 2-4 Vendor File Inquiry Control Map.

record which is to be acted upon. Figure 2-4 has just one item in the body, the vendor code. I like to have codes entered in a format to which the user is accustomed—for example, one alphabetic character followed by a four-digit sequence number and a one-digit location number. The vendor code and its associated attributes could be laid out in several different ways, as shown in Fig. 2-5. Use the structure with which the system's users are most comfortable.

Entering Data into a Key Field

Figure 2-5 shows four different ways a user can enter data into a field. The X's, indicating where data would be entered, do not actually appear on the control screen.

① Shows the field to be entered with the edit characters displayed on the screen. The cursor is initially positioned after the first UNPROT attribute to allow entry of the first character in the vendor code. After entering the first character, the ASKIP attribute causes the cursor to move to the right of the next UNPROT attribute. After the fourth digit is entered, the cursor skips to the right of the last UNPROT attribute to enable entry of the last vendor code digit. For all fields, the trailing ASKIP attribute is called a stopper attribute.

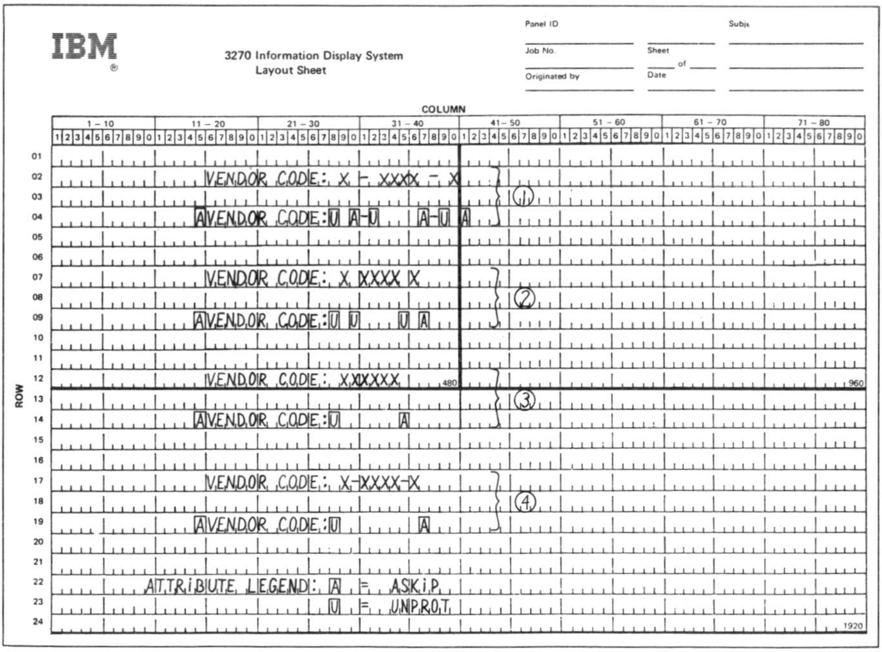

Figure 2-5 Key Field Entry Techniques.

② Leave a space between significant groupings of characters to be entered. The space actually contains an UNPROT attribute which causes the cursor to skip over the space to the start of the next significant entry field.

③ Enter the code without any editing characters displayed or implied by a space. This method becomes less effective when the size of the field to be entered increases.

④ Enter the edit characters (dashes,—) along with the key characters. This method involves additional keying (the dashes), and in general seems to cause the most problems; avoid it if possible.

Since there are many methods of entering data into a field on a terminal, understanding the various options will enable you to be more effective in your map design.

Instructions on the Control Map

Control maps are often dominated by instructions, and the vendor file inquiry control map in Fig. 2-4 is no exception. The instructions occupy the area between vendor code and the message line at the bottom of the map. Why display instructions on a map when they can be placed in a user's manual? They do occupy screen space and result in more data being transmitted to the screen, but I believe it is easier for the user to read instructions from a screen. This book is concerned with reducing maintenance and making the user and programmer more productive. It is not overly concerned with computer efficiencies and does not attempt to minimize terminal response time. I prefer to let new technology address that area.

Instructions on a control map generally list a number of functions which prompt the operator to press the appropriate key in order to invoke the desired function.

Messages Displayed on the Control Map

Normally, when a programmer writes a program, checks are made for all anticipated conditions which could create a problem, and a message is displayed notifying the terminal operator of the condition. The experienced CICS programmer/analyst who has dealt with users has an instinct for the type of messages which should be displayed. Users or user-interface personnel, when testing a system, will often offer suggestions for making the messages more meaningful. A professional programmer/analyst expects this kind of feedback from a user. Alterations of this type are not difficult to make. User representatives and data processing personnel realize that many of the messages displayed notify the terminal operator that an incorrect entry has been made. Nobody likes to be corrected in an abusive fashion or in a way that will make he or she feel foolish, so the professional will use care to soften messages. A word like "please" as part of messages of this type is usually an effective softener.

Detail Maps

A detail map is one which is displayed as a result of an entry made on a control map. Common detail map types are

1. Inquiries
2. Additions
3. Changes
4. Deletions

Inquiry Map

The inquiry detail map shown in Fig. 2-6 contains data found on the vendor master record. All attributes on the inquiry map are ASKIP,NORM. The only attribute which changes on this map is the message attribute, which can change from ASKIP,NORM to ASKIP,BRT when an error message is displayed.

The body of the report displays information from the vendor master record for the code entered on the control map. The instructions prompt you for action after viewing the map.

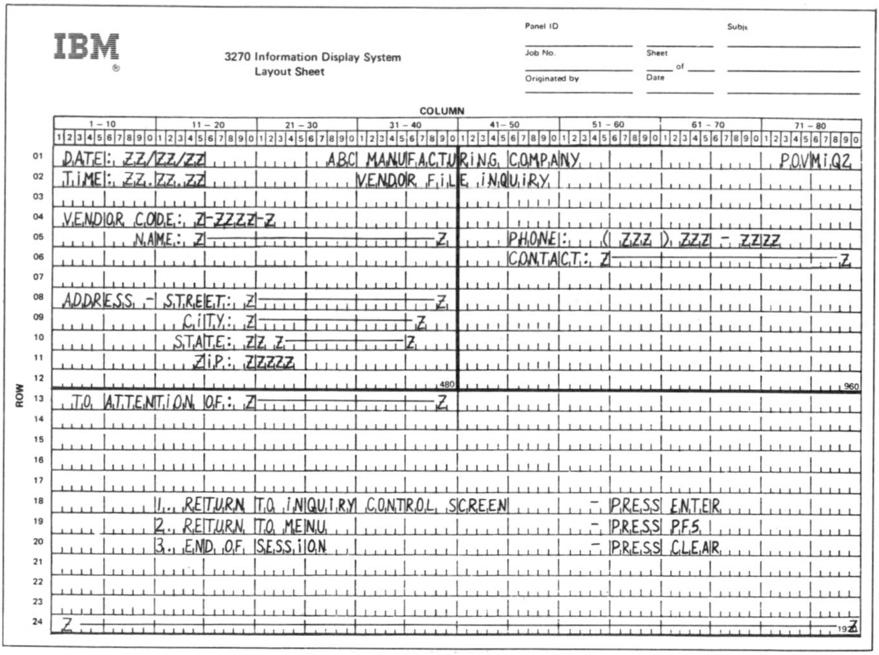

Figure 2-6 Vendor File Inquiry Detail Map.

IBM ®   3270 Information Display System
Layout Sheet

Panel ID _____ Subjx _____
Job No. _____ Sheet ___ of ___ _____
Originated by _____ Date _____

COLUMN

```
       1-10        11-20       21-30       31-40       41-50       51-60       61-70       71-80
01  DATE:, ZZ/ZZ/ZZ           ABC MANUFACTURING COMPANY                                    POVMADZ
02  TIME:, ZZ.ZZ.ZZ           VENDOR FILE ADDITION
03
04  VENDOR CODE:, Z-ZZZZ-Z
05        NAME:, X-------------------X    PHONE:, (,XXX,), XXX - XXXX
06                                        CONTACT:, X---------------------------X
07
08  ADDRESS, - STREET:, X-------------X
09          CITY:, X----------------X
10          STATE:, XX, Z---------Z
11          ZIP:, XXXXX
12                                                    480                            960
13  TO ATTENTION OF:, X-----------X
14
15
16
17
18       1., ADDITIONS, KEY iN REQUIRED DATA         - PRESS ENTER
19       2., RETURN TO ADDITION CONTROL SCREEN       - PRESS PF3
20       3., RETURN TO MENU                          - PRESS PF5
21       4., END OF SESSION                          - PRESS CLEAR
22
23
24  Z                                                                                        Z
```

Figure 2-7 Vendor File Addition Detail Map.

Addition Map

Figure 2-7 shows the format of the vendor file addition detail map. Unlike the inquiry map, all variable field attributes in the body of this map with the exception of vendor code are UNPROT. Vendor code cannot be changed, since its attribute is ASKIP,NORM. It can only be entered on the control screen.

The body of the map contains fields into which new data can be entered. The ENTER key is then pressed to effect the addition. The design of this part of the addition map must be closely coordinated with the user, since the entry of data must flow smoothly. The layout of data should correspond closely with the format of the source document used for adding a new vendor. Plan the layout of the data fields carefully; for instance, it would be awkward to put PHONE on the same line as VENDOR CODE. Remember, the cursor moves from left to right, top to bottom, stopping at UNPROT fields and skipping over ASKIP fields. Placing PHONE, which is an UNPROT field, on the same line as VENDOR CODE, an ASKIP field, would position the cursor at the first UNPROT field, which is PHONE. This seems illogical for two reasons: first, it is backward to enter the phone number before keying in the vendor's name; second, it seems more logical to have the cursor positioned initially on the left side of the screen.

Another illogical and awkward situation would arise if the fields PHONE and CONTACT were moved down opposite STREET and CITY. The terminal operator would in this case enter STREET, then PHONE, followed by CITY,

CONTACT, and STATE. On a full screen, a better alternative than breaking up an address entry in this fashion would be to design the screen with the entire address on the same line. For example,

```
STREET                    CITY               STATE   ZIP
XXXXXXXXXXXXXXXXXX XXXXXXXXXXXXXXXXX   XX    XXXXX
```

When a field is entered erroneously or inadvertently missed, the field identifier describing that field should have its attribute changed to ASKIP,BRT, which highlights the description. Field identifiers should be restored to ASKIP,NORM after their corresponding fields have been corrected and should no longer display brightly. The brightening of field identifiers is accompanied by the highlighting and display of the message field containing the message PLEASE CORRECT HIGHLIGHTED FIELDS (see Fig. 1-8).

Change Map

The vendor file change map layout is shown in Fig. 2-8. Upon the initial send of a change map, the existing record's data is displayed. Each variable data

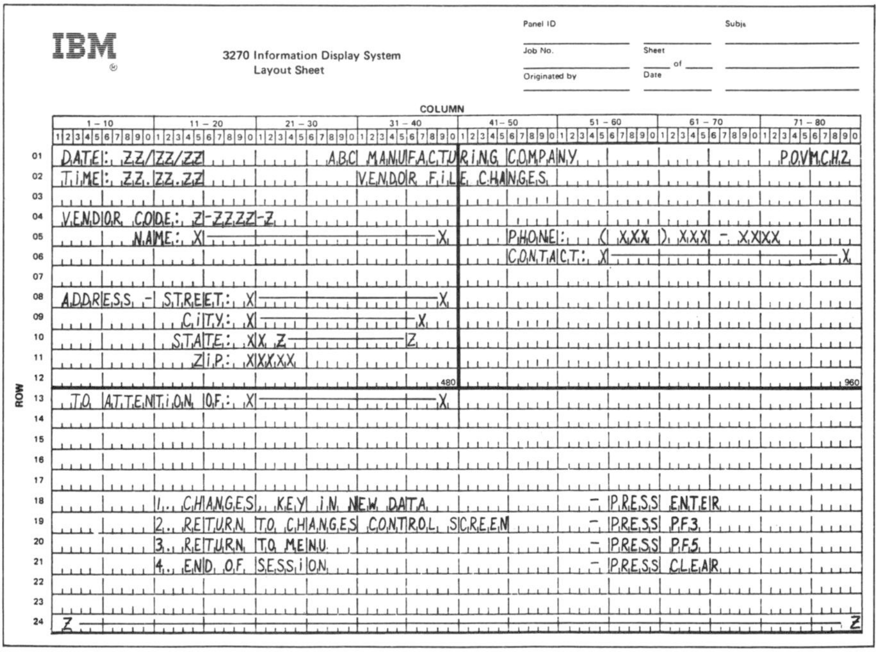

Figure 2-8   Vendor File Change Detail Map.

attribute in the body of this map is UNPROT,NORM, except for vendor code, which is ASKIP,NORM.

Changes can be keyed in over the existing data that is displayed or the terminal operator can press the EOF key to clear the field before entering the new data. The TAB key can be used to skip over fields which do not require changes. The ENTER key is pressed to update the record with the altered data. Do *not* put data in different locations on the various maintenance maps. Terminal operators become more easily accustomed to a system if similar fields are located in the same relative positions on all inquiry and maintenance screens.

Deletion Map

The deletion detail map is shown in Fig. 2-9. The fields displayed all have attributes of ASKIP,NORM. The purpose of displaying a record before deleting it is to give the terminal operator a chance to verify that the record is the proper one to be deleted before pressing ENTER. The operator could exercise one of the other options listed in the instructions if he or she did not want to delete the record. I recommend *always* displaying a record for operator verification before deleting; it takes a little longer, but the additional check is worth performing.

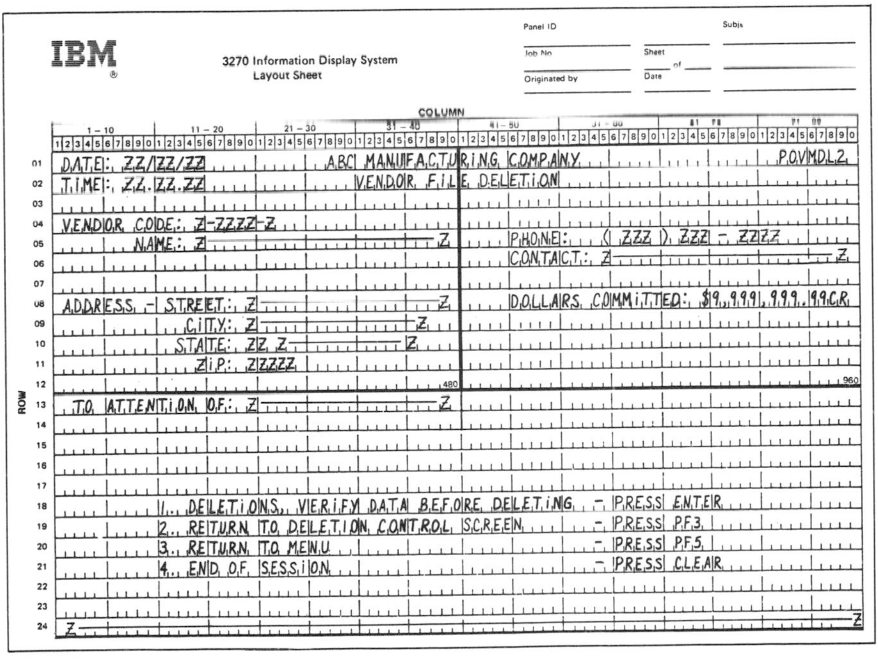

Figure 2-9 Vendor File Deletion Detail Map.

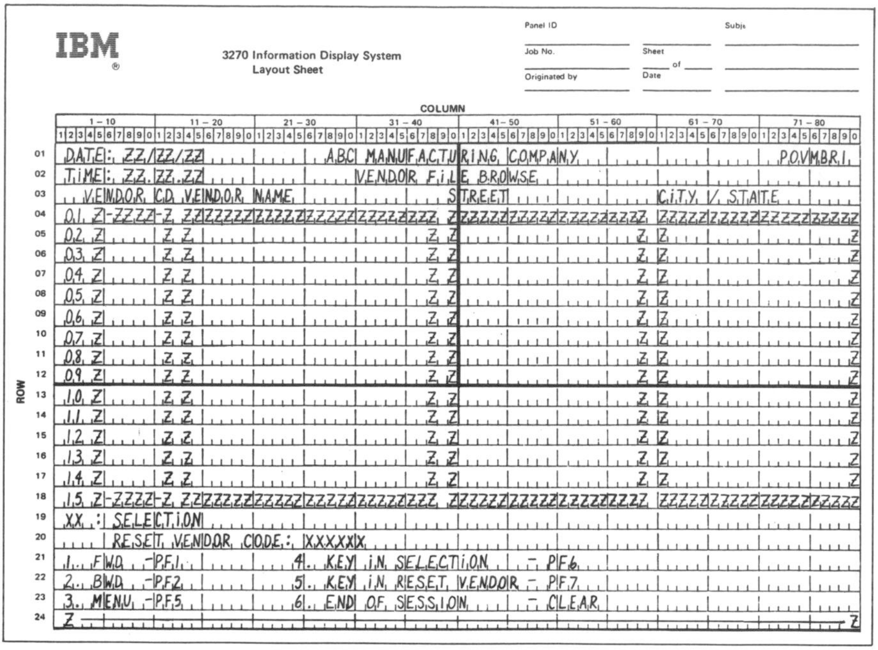

Figure 2-10 Vendor File Browse Map.

Browse Map

The browse map, shown in Fig. 2-10, contains many of the characteristics found in the other maps discussed. The headings and message lines have the same format and occupy the same line numbers as the other maps. The body follows the headings and precedes the map instructions.

The attributes for this map are all ASKIP, NORM, except for those on lines 19 and 20, the SELECTION and RESET VENDOR CODE data-entry fields, which are UNPROT. The message line attribute can be changed to brighten or darken the message.

SUMMARY

The design of user-friendly maps is best achieved through communication between users and data processing personnel. Users know their systems best and should work closely with programmer/analysts to ensure that maps and systems are designed to suit their requirements. Terminal operators frequently display and work with certain screens throughout the day. They must understand and feel comfortable with those formatted screens.

Maps can usually be broken down into header, body, instructions, and message sections. The location of certain items should be consistent from map to map.

Design maps so that they are pleasing or neutral but never irritating to work with.

Map attributes determine how screen fields are viewed and acted upon. Screen fields can be skipped over or stopped at in order to have a user enter data. These fields can be displayed at a normal or bright intensity. They can also be darkened so that they are not seen by the user. A basic understanding of map attributes will make the user more effective in working with data processing personnel in the development of maps.

Menu maps, control maps, and detail maps occur in most systems. Detail maps take many forms and cover such functions as inquiry, add, change, and delete. Browse programs are part of many systems. A professional constructs all map messages with the terminal operator's feelings in mind;—messages are often softened with words such as "please."

BACKGROUND TERMINOLOGY AND CONSIDERATIONS

Required CICS terminology and other background considerations will be introduced in this chapter. The CICS command format is presented, and pseudoconversational and conversational programming are discussed. CICS tables covered are the program-control table (PCT) and the processing program table (PPT). Multitasking and multithreading are introduced, and their use is made clear through an example. Program considerations and restrictions are discussed. System and program security for online systems is covered.

CICS programmers usually refer to the display of a map as a *send* of the map. A CICS program issues a SEND MAP command in order to display various types of maps such as menu, control, or detail maps. The design of the system will determine the types of maps to be used and the sequence in which they are to appear. The map sent will usually require data to be entered and/or an AID key to be pressed in order to initiate the receive of the map.

A CICS program obtains the information entered by a terminal operator when an AID key is pressed. The AID keys consist of ENTER, PF, CLEAR, and PA; normally only the first three AID keys are used. A CICS program issues a RECEIVE MAP command in order to initiate the action requested by the terminal operator. The action indicated by the AID key pressed will determine the type of processing to be performed.

Pseudoconversational Programming

CICS allows many users to be logged on to and to use CICS concurrently. Computer main-storage size is finite. If there are numerous users running transactions demanding main storage, a short-on-storage condition could occur, causing delays.

Pseudoconversational programming is a coding technique which results in a program being loaded into main storage when required and released when it is no longer active. For instance, when a map is displayed and the program is waiting for a user's response, the program can be released from main storage and reloaded when needed (when the user responds). CICS loads and releases application programs from main storage automatically. High-use programs are often defined as main-storage resident, and the system keeps them in main storage. Tables and maps, which are considered programs by CICS, are usually controlled by a program. Generally, when using the pseudoconversational technique of processing, pressing an AID key causes a program to be loaded if it is not already in main storage. When a program is finished with a logical segment of processing, it normally sends a map, saves required data, and returns control to CICS. This allows the release of the program from main storage if storage is needed by other programs. When an AID key is pressed, the program will be loaded into main storage if necessary, saved data will be restored, and processing will continue. Pseudoconversational programming techniques should be used whenever possible, and all program examples in this book use this technique. Pseudoconversational programming techniques are the responsibility of the application programmer.

Conversational Programming

Conversational programming is a coding technique which results in a program being loaded into and remaining in main storage until a user is finished working with the program. The program is not released from main storage when not active, as in pseudoconversational programming. For instance, a conversational program will display a map and remain in main storage while waiting for a user's response.

Conversational programming techniques usually involve the send of a map with the program remaining in main storage while the terminal operator is entering data. Unless an AID key is pressed to end the session, the program will send another map and await the terminal operator's reply, remaining all the while in main storage. The conversational technique appears the same from a terminal operator's perspective as pseudoconversational programming. Sometimes the conversational technique causes main-storage utilization problems. This occurs for many reasons such as getting a telephone call, taking a break, or engaging in conversation after starting a session. The user is generally not aware of this situation, and it is the responsibility of the programmer/analyst to design and write programs which minimize the impact of this condition. Practical applications of conversational programming are very limited and will not be covered in this book. Pseudoconversational programming is widely used and will be addressed; it eliminates many of the problems which occur when using conversational programming.

Master Terminal Commands

Master terminal commands can be issued by a programmer or a designated master terminal operator (MTO) in order to perform many functions including:

1. Place the latest load library address of a program, table, or map into the PPT (discussed later in this chapter).

2. Monitor tasks which are running (discussed later in this chapter).

3. Terminate a task.

4. Enable, disable, or inquire as to the status of programs, transactions, or files (data sets). Files can also be opened or closed.

5. Put a terminal out of service.

Master terminal commands may be entered on a cleared screen by keying in CSMT followed by the required entries. CEMT, an enhanced version of the master terminal command CSMT, is a prompting transaction which allows abbreviated keywords to be entered. Just key in CEMT and press ENTER. You can enter PRO for program, TRAN for transaction, DAT for data set, etc.

CICS Tables

Many tables are used by CICS. A few are of direct interest to the application programmer, and only they are discussed. A user initiates a compiled CICS program by clearing the screen and keying in a four-character TRANSID which directs CICS to start a program at that terminal. It is necessary to identify the TRANSID and program to CICS and to tie them together. This is accomplished by means of two tables that are very important to the CICS programmer.

Program-Control Table

The basic function of the PCT is to tie together the TRANSID entered by the terminal operator with the program name. TRANSID and PROGRAM are the PCT entries of most interest to a programmer. The terminal operator enters a TRANSID in order to start a transaction, then the TRANSID is matched against the PCT to determine if it is a valid entry. A TRANSID not in the PCT will cause an invalid TRANSID message to be displayed on the terminal. A match on TRANSID will use the associated program name to search the PPT for a match on PROGRAM. The program is loaded into main storage if it is not a main-storage resident program or already in main storage.

Processing Program Table

The PPT contains entries such as

1. Program name, language, and size

2. The main-storage address of the program (if it has been loaded)

3. A task use counter (discussed later in this chapter)

4. The load library address of the program which is to be loaded into main storage

5. An indicator as to whether the program is a main-storage resident (usually high-use) program

A PPT entry is used to locate programs which are to be loaded into main storage and is required for each program, map, and table used by the CICS system. When CICS is started up, the PPT is initialized with the address of the load module for all programs, maps, and tables. When a program is changed and compiled or assembled after CICS has been started up, it is necessary to refresh the address of the load module in the PPT. This is a normal occurrence on the test system. The new load module address can be placed into the PPT by one of the following master terminal transactions entered on a cleared screen.

CSMT NEW, PGRMID=progname
or
CEMT SET PRO (progname) NEW

Both tables contain additional entries which are usually maintained by the systems programming staff. For simplicity, assume the tables contain information of only direct importance to the applications programmer.

PCT Entries	PPT Entries
TRANSID = RECV	PROGRAM = RECEIVEP
PROGRAM = RECEIVEP	PGMLANG = COBOL

Clear the screen, key in the TRANSID RECV, and press ENTER. CICS finds the TRANSID RECV and the program name RECEIVEP in the PCT. The PCT ties the transaction to the PPT entry RECEIVEP. The PPT entry is used to locate the associated program's load module and to load it into main storage.

CICS application programmers should obtain several PCT and PPT entries through their manager and the systems programming department. These entries can be used for testing new programs until a permanent entry is assigned. All examples in this book use the following table and entries shown in Fig. 3-1 [CICS program tables and file control table (FCT) entries will be discussed later in the book].

Maps, which are generated by an assembler program, will be discussed in more detail in Chaps. 6 and 7. Maps and tables do not have TRANSIDs; they are controlled by CICS programs. The program language for all PPT entries will

* * * PCT * * * TRANSID	Program	PPT Program	PPT Map	PPT Tables	FCT DATASET
DSPL	DISPLAYP	DISPLAYP			
RECV	RECEIVEP	RECEIVEP			
POMU	POMENUPM	POMENUPM	POMENU1		
POVM	POVMAINT	POVMAINT	POVMNT1		
		JRNLPOST		T053JRSQ	JOURNAL1
POVI	POVMINQY	POVMINQY	POVMIQ1 POVMIQ2	T037STAT	VENDMAST
POVC	POVMCHGE	POVMCHGE	POVMCH1 POVMCH2	T037STAT	VENDMAST
POVA	POVMADDN	POVMADDN	POVMAD1 POVMAD2	T037STAT	VENDMAST
POVD	POVMDLET	POVMDLET	POVMDL1 POVMDL2	T037STAT	VENDMAST
POVB	POVMBROW	POVMBROW	POVMBR1		VENDMAST

Program	Description
DISPLAYP	Displays message CICS IS EASY
RECEIVEP	Receives and sends social security number
POMENUPM	Purchasing system menu
POVMAINT	Vendor file maintenance submenu
JRNLPOST	Journal file updating
POVMINQY	Vendor file inquiry
POVMCHGE	Vendor file changes
POVMADDN	Vendor file additions
POVMDLET	Vendor file deletions
POVMBROW	Vendor file browse

Figure 3-1 CICS Table Entries Used in this Book.

be PGMLANG=COBOL for all programs and PGMLANG=ASSEMBLER for all tables and maps.

Multiple PCT Entries

Multiple PCT entries are permitted to refer to the same program, but multiple programs cannot be associated with the same PCT entry.

	Valid		Invalid	
PCT	**PPT**	**PCT**	**PPT**
POVA	POVMADDN	POVA	POVMADDN
POVB	POVMADDN	POVA	POVMDLET

CICS Command Format

CICS commands have the general format

```
EXEC CICS  function
                option 1 (argument 1)
                option 2 (argument 2)
                          .
                          .
                          .
END-EXEC.
```

Function may be commands such as

```
SEND
RECEIVE
RETURN
HANDLE CONDITION
```

Options and arguments may be

```
FROM     (WS-OUTPUT)
INTO     (WS-INPUT)
LENGTH (WS-LENGTH)
ERASE
```

Options have no required sequence but must be used under the corresponding function. Many options are available for some CICS commands, but only a few may actually be required. Only options required to illustrate selected functions will be presented.

Task

A task is created for each executed TRANSID which is recognized by CICS (found in the PCT). A task can include one or several programs. A task continues until a program returns control to CICS or issues a RETURN command in a pseudoconversational program. CICS's ability to handle multiple tasks simultaneously is called *multitasking*. Different tasks can concurrently access the same program's load module which is resident in main storage; this is referred to as *multithreading*. Since a single load module in main storage may be accessed by several tasks, a program cannot have its procedure division instructions modified during a specific task. Each task obtains main storage for its unique copy of a program's working storage. Programs should be written so that their working storage is kept as small as possible. Keep constants, literals, and messages in the program's procedure division when practical.

CICS Multitasking and Multithreading

Figure 3-2 and the following table illustrate how multitasking and multithreading might utilize main storage. Four users at different terminals have entered the

	PCT			PPT Table Entries		
				Main		Load
				Storage	Use	Library
TRANSID	Program	Program		Address	Counter	Address
DSPL	DISPLAYP	DISPLAYP		2000	4	10500
RECV	RECEIVEP	RECEIVEP		3000	3	25600

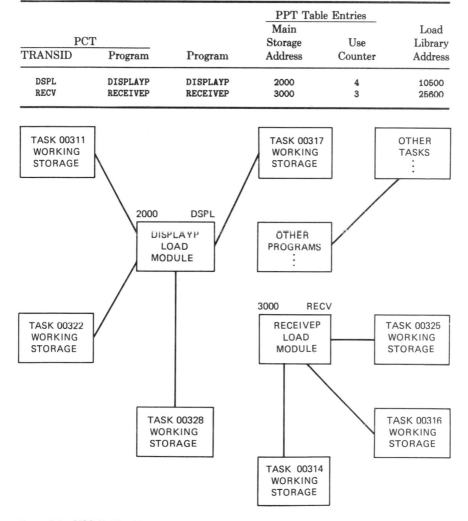

Figure 3-2 CICS Multitasking and Multithreading.

```
 INQ TAS
 STATUS:   RESULTS - OVERTYPE TO MODIFY
   TAS(00311)  TRA(DSPL)  FAC(T022)  ACT  SHO  TER
   TAS(00314)  TRA(RECV)  FAC(T014)  ACT  SHO  TER
   TAS(00316)  TRA(RECV)  FAC(T031)  ACT  SHO  TER
   TAS(00317)  TRA(DSPL)  FAC(T005)  ACT  SHO  TER
   TAS(00322)  TRA(DSPL)  FAC(T017)  ACT  SHO  TER
   TAS(00325)  TRA(RECV)  FAC(T003)  ACT  SHO  TER
   TAS(00328)  TRA(DSPL)  FAC(T027)  ACT  SHO  TER

                        .
                        .
                        .




   RESPONSE: NORMAL                    TIME:  10.16.27   DATE 86.023

   PF: 1 HELP        3 END              7 SBH 8 SFH 9 MSG 10 SB 11  SF
```

Figure 3-3   CEMT Master Terminal Display for a Task.

TRANSID DSPL and three other users have entered the TRANSID RECV, starting seven different tasks. The initial task for each TRANSID resulted in the corresponding program in the PCT obtaining the associated program's load library address for each program from the PPT. The load module was then loaded into main storage and its main-storage address moved into the PPT.

Each task for both programs obtained a copy of its own unique working storage in main storage as shown, and one was added to the program's PPT use counter. As each task completes, its use counter in the PPT is decreased by one, and its working storage can be released from main storage. When the use counter is reduced to zero, as all tasks accessing a program complete, a program may be released from main storage (if it is not defined as a resident program in the PPT) if main storage is required for another task.

Either of the following master terminal transactions will give the status of all tasks active in the CICS partition or region.

```
CSMT TAS
   or
CEMT INQ TAS
```

Entering CEMT INQ TAS at the time the tasks shown in Fig. 3-2 were active would produce a display similar to that shown in Fig. 3-3. CEMT lists all tasks active in the CICS region showing:

1. TAS (XXXXX)—TASK number

2. TRA (XXXX) —TRANSID entered

3. FAC (XXXX) —FACility, terminal at which the task was entered

4. ACT or SUS   —ACTive or SUSpended task

5. SHO or LON   —SHOrt or LONg running task

6. TER   —TERminal

Program Considerations and Restrictions

A CICS programmer needs to be aware of certain considerations and restrictions when writing programs.

Considerations

1. Must eventually return control to CICS.

2. Cannot modify procedure division instructions because CICS programs may be shared by many tasks.

3. Can modify working storage since a unique copy of working storage is created for each task.

Restrictions

1. FILE SECTION, OPEN, CLOSE, and non-CICS READ and WRITE statements are not permitted because file management is handled by CICS.

2. Many Cobol features must be avoided such as internal sorts, use of special registers, ACCEPT, DISPLAY, EXHIBIT, TRACE, STOP RUN, and GOBACK. (STOP RUN and GOBACK are sometimes included in CICS programs in order to eliminate a compiler diagnostic but are *never* executed.)

System and Program Security

Security is a major concern in the design of some online systems such as payroll and a consideration in others. The design of security techniques can be implemented at the system and/or program level. There are many security techniques that an installation can utilize. Some may require extensive user interaction; others may be less obvious to a terminal operator.

System Security

System security is important when there are applications which are restricted to certain terminals. For instance, if payroll is online, it would not be wise to allow access to these programs from every terminal in the system. Likewise, it may be necessary to limit the access or update of certain files to specific terminals. A current trend which I foresee will continue and expand is that of permitting customers and vendors to gain access to files and records, allowing them to monitor and update those files. Much as travel agents are able to access airline databases, delete stock (seats), and write out orders (tickets), I expect most major companies to partake in similar activities. A customer will be permitted to inquire as to how much stock of certain items is available for immediate delivery, then delete the stock by placing an order. Vendors will be permitted to monitor purchase orders against your files in order to determine what you actually received. Obviously it is advisable to limit customer and vendor access to certain transactions and files.

There are many software systems on the market which can restrict the use of specified transactions, programs, and files to designated terminals. Other security restrictions are possible, such as having the system restrict a terminal to certain operators and limit the time of day which a terminal can be used.

Program Security

Once the system's security has been passed and the customer or vendor is into your transaction, accessing your files, you obviously want to restrict access to specific items or purchase orders. The safest way to restrict access is by having each program check against a table of terminal identifiers and allowable passwords (see "Passwords" in Chap. 4). The table could contain authorized items, such as purchase orders and other record keys which are valid for customers or vendors to access at their terminals. A customer or vendor trying to access an item or purchase order on your system might get into your program, but an unauthorized message could be displayed if the item or purchase order was not in the table.

A situation which often occurs is that an authorized user signs on to CICS and leaves the terminal before signing off. Unauthorized personnel could use the vacated terminal. Programming techniques, not discussed in this book, are available which will force a program to terminate if an AID key is not pressed within a predetermined time interval. This technique is not often used and would be restricted to extremely sensitive transactions. A user who displays information on a terminal while on the phone with a customer would not want to be logged off CICS in the middle of a conversation.

Many of the techniques used by system security software could be coded into individual programs. Selected programs could contain routines to check a password against tables or files in order to determine file, record, transaction, program, and terminal authorization. Logic could be coded to permit or prohibit access between certain dates and times and on specified days of the week. Security violations can be written out to a file and be printed by category by a batch program. An audible alarm could be sounded at the violating terminal. All of these checks require additional program code and make programs less efficient and more complicated. Let your system security software handle as many of these checks as possible, if your installation has such software.

Program security, if planned properly and implemented correctly, can run very smoothly; if not, all types of security problems will occur. Someday, access to a system by persons outside of a company will be just as widespread as current access by company employees. This should be a major growth area for CICS usage in the years to come.

Summary

Pseudoconversational programming is a technique used to minimize computer main-storage requirements. An understanding of the advantage of this technique as opposed to conversational programming is needed in order to develop efficient systems.

The PCT and PPT were discussed. Task initiation and termination and their effects on PPT entries were covered. An example illustrated how multitasking and multithreading function. Master terminal transactions which refresh the load module address of a program in the PPT and those which list all active tasks in a CICS partition or region were discussed. CICS program considerations and restrictions were listed.

The trend toward allowing customers and vendors to access company programs and files through CICS transactions presents certain security considerations in the design of a system. Security should not be an excuse to prevent customer and vendor access to your system, but should present a challenge to plan your security system with care. Demand for system access by users has grown within companies; it will expand even further to include access by users outside the company. Companies which ignore this demand will find themselves at a competitive disadvantage in the future.

4

SYSTEM AND PROGRAMMING DOCUMENTATION STANDARDS

Standards are uniform methods of performing required functions. A standard should serve a definite purpose. The problem with standards is that few people agree about what is beneficial, and many consider documentation a wasted effort. Two excellent books which promote program standards—*How to Design and Develop COBOL Programs* and *The COBOL Programmer's Handbook*—are listed in the Bibliography. The creation and maintenance of standards often require more time than the task they support; if not kept up to date, they become useless and can actually create problems. Most data processing personnel agree that certain standards are necessary, but the fewer the better. This chapter covers what I consider to be the most worthwhile standards for use in an online environment; many can be applied also to batch systems.

System Design Standards

The best design tool and standard is perhaps one of the easiest to create and maintain—the system structure chart. A system structure chart should show at a glance the scope of a system; it should be simple, yet comprehensive. I like to work with a structure chart that shows the major functions of a system, including related PCT and PPT entries.

Structure Charts

Figure 4-1 illustrates a system structure chart which diagrams the entire purchasing system. The PCT entry, which is also referred to as the TRANSID, is shown above each block. The top section of each block contains the PPT entry; it is the program's name. Each block contains a description of the associated program. This type of structure chart requires a minimal amount of effort to

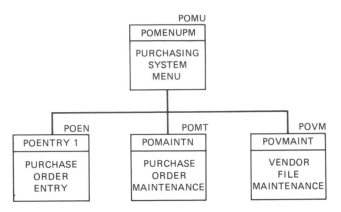

Figure 4-1 Purchasing System Structure Chart.

create and maintain, yet is an excellent planning tool and shows the scope of a project at a glance.

Once the system structure chart has been established, it is often advantageous to draw subsystem structure charts as shown in Fig. 4-2. The format of a subsystem structure chart is identical to that of a regular system structure chart. The value of both charts is twofold: they help the designer plan what functions should be contained in a system, and they also provide a picture of the scope of a system, making it easy to explain to others.

The subsystem structure chart shown in Fig. 4-2 is the structure which will be used for programs in the text. POVMAINT, referred to as the menu program, will be discussed in Chap. 9. The inquiry program POVMINQY, additions program POVMADDN, change program POVMCHGE, delete program POVMDLET, and browse program POVMBROW will be discussed in Chaps. 12, 13, 14, 15, and 17, respectively.

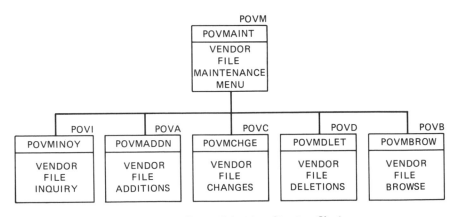

Figure 4-2 Vendor File Maintenance Menu—Subsystem Structure Chart.

Programming Standards

Program standards generally are time-consuming to create and often require considerable effort to maintain. Even in the best-documented installations, the programmer/analyst who has to maintain a program seldom uses standards as more than a general guideline as to what function a program should perform. Programs contain a tremendous amount of detail, and that detail is seldom completely and correctly reflected in program documentation. The best place for program documentation is in the program itself, by using meaningful comments. Program structure charts, program comments, and style of programming all help to determine how easy or difficult a program will be to maintain. The use of standard file layouts and of standard program routines can greatly aid the programmer in the initial writing and in future maintenance of a program. Program documentation is more of an art than a science. This chapter covers many of the techniques I employ to make a program self-documenting and easy to maintain.

Program Structure Charts

A well-designed program structure chart informs the person viewing the chart what the major functions of a program include. The structure chart for a menu program (Fig. 4-3) is rather straightforward and varies little from menu program to menu program. Fig. 4-3 lists the program section prefix at the top of each block; this prefix is usually attached to the description inside the block to form program section names. I generally prefix my mainline section with AA00 and the levels under it as B000, C000, etc. The next sublevel, if one exists, might be C100, C200, C300, etc.; sub-sublevels would be numbered C110, C120, C130, followed by C111, C112, etc., for even lower levels. If a program cannot be covered by this structure, it is probably too complicated and should be analyzed for a simpler design. I find it easier to maintain several simple programs, each of which performs one function, than one large program which performs many functions. The program structure chart, if well thought out, can be an excellent tool for the initial design and future maintenance of a program. The more functions a program contains, the more beneficial a program structure chart will be to a programmer/analyst. I like to include the program's structure as comments at the start of the procedure division of each program. I believe this technique is easier to maintain than is the block structure chart. See the menu program example in Chap. 9 for an illustration of how this is done.

Program Comments

The first place a programmer generally looks when maintaining an existing program is at the latest Cobol source program listing; often this is the only place. Time spent making this listing as readable as possible is well worth the effort. Write every program as if you will have to go through it from beginning to end 6 months after it has been written, explaining to another programmer/analyst what it is doing. You would most likely use meaningful

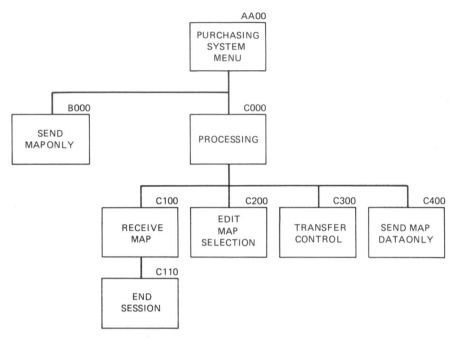

Figure 4-3   Purchasing System Menu—Program Structure Chart.

program labels which describe the function of each routine. You would include comments in the program, detailing the function of more complicated routines and clarifying others. Write all programs with ample comments; they will most likely be used as models for other programs.

Keep Programs Short and Simple

I prefer to keep programs short and simple, isolating functions into several simple programs instead of writing one large program. Maintenance functions, against the same file, usually have many common routines and use similar maps. Many designers have a tendency to put all maintenance functions into a single program. I prefer a separate program for each major function. This approach creates more PCT and PPT entry requirements for TRANSIDs, programs, and maps, but each program will be easier to write and to maintain. The trend toward sharing access to certain files and programs with customers and vendors is made easier when functions such as additions, changes, deletions, and inquiries are put into separate programs. For example, a customer may have access to inquiry and change functions, but not to add or delete functions. When each function in a system has a separate program, security is more easily maintained. Because of the trend toward sharing access to files with others outside the installation, programs should be designed to be as simple and flexible as possible. Keep it simple and straightforward—with change being inevitable, you'll be glad you did.

Different Levels of Menus

A system can be designed with many levels of menus. The purchasing system defined in Figs. 4-1 and 4-2 has two levels of menus. One menu can be displayed by entering the TRANSID POMU and the other by entering the TRANSID POVM. A system could be designed to start all installation transactions through a master menu, possibly with a TRANSID of MENU. The terminal operator could enter MENU to display the master menu, make a selection to display the purchasing system menu, make another selection to display the vendor file maintenance menu, and finally, make a selection to display an inquiry map. I am sure that you would find it cumbersome to be required to display three menus prior to the display of an inquiry map. Many systems do not require a user to go through three menus to reach an inquiry screen. The advantages of multimenus are that a user has fewer TRANSIDs to remember, and there are some security advantages to this approach. A system can be designed requiring that all programs be started by a main menu or to allow programs to be started by entering a TRANSID. The purchasing system is designed so that a program can be initiated indirectly by a menu or directly by keying the proper TRANSID. For instance, a user can key in MENU, POMU, POVM, POVI, etc. to initiate the desired function. Your installation's security requirements and design philosophy will determine which approach you will take regarding system menus. Figure 4-4 illustrates the level of menus;—any of the shown TRANSIDs will lead to the vendor file inquiry.

Passwords

Passwords provide a system with a certain degree of security because they can be used to limit system access to specific users. Personnel at a location where terminals are located must assume some responsibility for monitoring access to the system. System or program security can limit access based on specific passwords but cannot actually monitor *who* enters an authorized password. Each location should be responsible for who uses a terminal. Some users at a given location may know the passwords of other employees. Unauthorized personnel could gain access to the system by using these passwords. Passwords aid system security, but they are not foolproof. At best, passwords can restrict users at specific terminals to certain transactions, programs, or files.

Password requirements should be limited; continuous entering of passwords can make a system's operation cumbersome. Keying in of passwords, which are normally entered into nondisplay (DRK attribute) fields, should be limited to sign-on and to initial transaction entry screens. Carried to the ultimate, every display of a map could require the entry of a password, but the nuisance factor involved would far outweigh any security advantage gained. Passwords

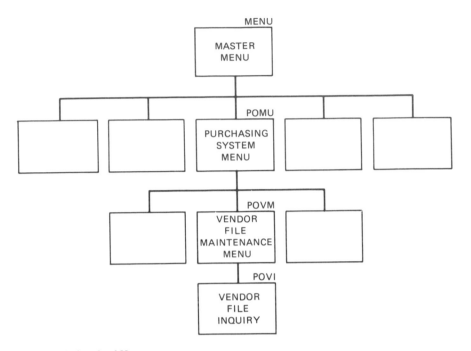

Figure 4-4 Levels of Menus.

are a necessary part of many systems, but you must plan carefully where to use them.

Message File

The use of a message file may be considered if a system is going to be adapted for use in several countries. The key to this type of a file would probably be a four-character number, the file data being the message to be displayed on the message line (line 24) of the map. A programmer would move the key of the message to be displayed to the appropriate program area, read the message file, and then move the file's message to line 24 of the map. The advantage of a message file is that the messages could be translated into the language of the country using the system. The disadvantages are that each program contains unique messages, and that a message file can grow very large. Since a read of the message file is required to fetch the proper message, program usage and maintenance of such a file can be cumbersome. It is often difficult to find an appropriate predefined message for many program conditions. When no message exists, a new message must be added to the file. Other programmer/analysts should be notified of new messages and their codes so that they will not use the same codes or create duplicate or similar messages. It is not uncommon for a program to contain dozens of messages. I recommend avoiding the use of a message file.

Program Tables

The use of tables, like the certainty of change, is inevitable in most systems. Three types of tables are commonly used, those which are

1. Defined in the program itself
2. Loaded into main storage as needed
3. Set up on a VSAM file

Tables Defined in a Program

Tables can be coded directly in a program or may be set up in a source code library, then copied into a program when it is compiled. A change to this type of table always requires programs which use the table to be recompiled. Limit the use of such tables to those which are short and unlikely to change often; otherwise you will design ongoing maintenance into your system.

Tables Loaded into Main Storage

Tables can be created and stored in a load library so that they can be loaded into main storage by a program as required, then released when the program is finished with the table. This type of table requires a PPT entry; it is the type used for large tables and for those requiring frequent maintenance. This kind of table requires an amount of main storage equal to the size of the table; it should be released, to free main storage, as soon as it is no longer needed by a program. Maintenance of such a table requires the creation of a new table load module and may require program maintenance. The table itself does require maintenance; changes can be time-consuming and the possibility of error is great on large-volume changes.

VSAM Table Files

Virtual storage access method (VSAM) is a technique for accessing and updating files randomly. An individual or general purpose VSAM file can be set up to handle each table required by the system. An advantage of individual VSAM table files is that the table can be set up to be the exact size required by the table's key plus its data. The disadvantages of individual table files are that each table has to be maintained separately and each table requires a FCT entry. A general purpose table requires only one FCT entry and can be maintained by a single program, although several programs could be used. This type of table is easy to create and maintain but has the disadvantage of wasting disk space. A general purpose table would require the key field size to be set to the largest key in the file. For instance, a table's key might consist of a four-character prefix, followed by the key itself, and then the data in the table. A two-digit state code would require the same key size as a 15-position key. The file could be set up with variable-length records so that less space would be wasted in the data portion of the file. I recommend the creation and use of a general purpose table file because it is easy to work with, flexible, and facilitates table maintenance. A general purpose file, once created, can be maintained on line by a single program or by several customized programs.

Summary

Standards should be developed with consideration given to the future maintenance of the documentation to support the standards. A worthwhile standard is the system structure chart, which shows at a glance the scope of a system. Subsystem structure charts should be used to break complicated systems into simpler segments.

Program standards should include a program structure chart; it helps a programmer/analyst design a program and serves as documentation once the program is written. Consider coding your program structure chart at the start of the procedure division to supplement or replace the block structure chart.

Keep programs simple and straightforward; they will be easier to design and maintain and will be more flexible and easier to modify. This will become more important as the trend toward sharing files with customers and vendors expands.

Programs can be designed so that they can be started only by a menu program or by individual TRANSIDs. Passwords are a necessary part of any system, but they are no guarantee that unauthorized access to a system will be prevented. Consider the creation of a general purpose VSAM table file which can be easily maintained on line.

5

BASIC PROGRAM EXAMPLES

CICS, as perceived by the applications programmer, is a collection of commands interspersed in a Cobol program. CICS commands provide the ability to send and receive terminal messages, read and write files, and perform other functions. The easiest way to learn CICS is through examples used to establish concepts the creative programmer can apply to real-life situations. Simple programs are covered here, and new commands are explained as encountered.

Send a Message to a Terminal

The program DISPLAYP shown in Fig. 5-1 is initiated by the TRANSID DSPL which is entered on a cleared screen. That's all there is to writing a CICS program which displays the message CICS IS EASY on the screen. Two commands were introduced in this program—the SEND command and the RETURN command.

SEND Command

```
EXEC CICS SEND
          FROM    (WS-MESSAGE)
          LENGTH (12)
END-EXEC.
```

The SEND command, as used in Fig. 5-1, is very similar in concept to the DISPLAY statement used in Cobol batch processing programs. WS-MESSAGE is the same as a working-storage message would be in a batch Cobol

```
0001 IDENTIFICATION DIVISION.
0002*
0003 PROGRAM-ID. DISPLAYP.
0004*
0005 REMARKS.
0006*
0007********************************************************************
0008*     THIS PROGRAM ILLUSTRATES CICS SEND AND RETURN COMMANDS.    *
0009*     A MESSAGE 'CICS IS EASY' IS DISPLAYED ON THE CRT.          *
0010********************************************************************
0011*
0012 ENVIRONMENT DIVISION.
0013*
0014 DATA DIVISION.
0015*
0016 WORKING-STORAGE SECTION.
0017*
0018 01  WS-MESSAGE            PIC X(12)     VALUE 'CICS IS EASY'.
0019*
0020 LINKAGE SECTION.
0021*
0022*
0023 PROCEDURE DIVISION.
0024*
0025* SEND CRT MESSAGE
0026     EXEC CICS SEND
0027           FROM   (WS-MESSAGE)
0028           LENGTH (12)
0029     END-EXEC.
0030*
0031* RETURN TO CICS
0032     EXEC CICS RETURN
0033     END-EXEC.
```

Figure 5-1 Program Illustrating SEND and RETURN Commands.

program. CICS requires a program to specify the length of the message being sent.

RETURN Command

```
EXEC CICS RETURN
END-EXEC.
```

The RETURN command, conceptually much like the GOBACK command in Cobol, returns control to CICS.

Compiling a CICS Program

Most data processing installations have standard job control language (JCL) set up for translating and compiling CICS programs and placing the compiled output in the appropriate CICS load library.

All CICS commands begin with EXEC CICS. The r translator recognizes this and breaks down CICS commands into call statements and prints a list of the original source program. The translated source data is then passed through a Cobol compiler which prints a second listing showing CICS commands

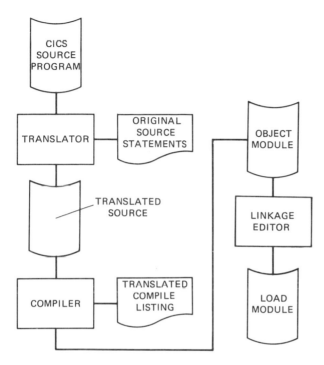

Figure 5-2 CICS Compile Procedure.

translated into move-and-call statements. Additional code is also placed into the program by the compiler. The object module created is "link-edited" to produce a load module. Figure 5-2 illustrates the CICS compile proce dure.

The translated version of the program would be similar to that shown in Fig. 5-3. A look at this version shows a field called DFHEIVAR in working storage. DFHEIVAR's subfields are copied into a program by the translator and used to hold call parameters employed by the translated version of CICS commands. CICS commands for send and return are commented out (*), and calls are generated by the translator for CICS commands, using DFHEIVAR subfields. These fields are similar to the fields shown at the top of page 57.

Translator call fields are copied into a program by the translator in order to set up Calls which effect CICS commands. These fields are of no direct interest to the application programmer and are only mentioned so that you will recognize them when they appear in your program.

The translator generates, in the linkage section, fieldsnamed DFHEIBLK, the execute interface block (EIB) (see App. A-1), and DFHCOMMAREA, the communication area. CICS creates a new version of the EIB, with its updated values, for program use each time a new task is initiated.

```
0001 IDENTIFICATION DIVISION.
0002*
0003 PROGRAM-ID. DISPLAYP.
0004*
0005 REMARKS.
0006*
0007**********************************************************************
0008*            TRANSLATED VERSION OF SAMPLE PROGRAM             *
0009*      THIS PROGRAM ILLUSTRATES CICS SEND AND RETURN COMMANDS *
0010*   THAT HAVE BEEN ALTERED AS THE FIRST STEP OF CHANGING SOURCE *
0011*   CODE INTO COMPUTER USABLE INSTRUCTIONS.                   *
0012*     A MESSAGE 'CICS IS EASY' IS DISPLAYED ON THE CRT.       *
0013**********************************************************************
0014*
0015 ENVIRONMENT DIVISION.
0016*
0017 DATA DIVISION.
0018*
0019 WORKING-STORAGE SECTION.
0020*
0021 01  WS-MESSAGE              PIC X(12)    VALUE 'CICS IS EASY'.
0022*
0023 01  DFHEIVAR   COPY   DFHEIVAR
0024*
0025*
0026 LINKAGE SECTION.
0027*
0028 01  DFHEIBLK  COPY  DFHEIBLK.
0029*      (see Appendix A-1)
0030*
0031 01  DFHCOMMAREA            PIC X.
0032*
0033 PROCEDURE DIVISION USING DFHEIBLK DFHCOMMAREA.
0034*
0035* SEND CRT MESSAGE
0036*    EXEC CICS SEND
0037*            FROM   (WS-MESSAGE)
0038*            LENGTH (12)
0039*    END-EXEC.
0040     MOVE 12 TO DFHEIV11 MOVE '           ' TO DFHEIV0
0041     CALL 'DFHEI1' USING DFHEIV0 DFHEIV99 DFHEIV98 WS-MESSAGE
0042     DFHEIV11.
0043*
0044* RETURN TO CICS
0045*    EXEC CICS RETURN
0046*    END-EXEC.
0047     MOVE '          ' TO DFHEIV0 CALL 'DFHEI1' USING DFHEIV0.
```

Figure 5-3 Translated CICS Program.

The application programmer need not be overly concerned with how the translator works; no further illustrations will be presented for the translated version of programs.

Running a Compiled Program

Once a program compiles without error, it is ready for execution (if it has the appropriate PCT and PPT entries). Refresh the PPT program address by entering CSMT NEW,PGRMID=DISPLAYP. Clear the screen to set the cursor at POS=(01,01) on the screen. Key in the TRANSID DSPL and press ENTER. The following will appear starting at POS=(01,01) of the screen:

DSPLCICS IS EASY

```
01  DFHEIVAR COPY DFHEIVAR.
    02 DFHEIV0       PIC X(26).
    02 DFHEIV1       PIC X(8).
    02 DFHEIV2       PIC X(8).
    02 DFHEIV3       PIC X(8).
    02 DFHEIV4       PIC X(6).
    02 DFHEIV5       PIC X(4).
    02 DFHEIV6       PIC X(4).
    02 DFHEIV7       PIC X(2).
    02 DFHEIV8       PIC X(2).
    02 DFHEIV9       PIC X(1).
    02 DFHEIV10      PIC S9(7)         COMP-3.
    02 DFHEIV11      PIC S9(4)         COMP.
    02 DFHEIV12      PIC S9(4)         COMP.
    02 DFHEIV13      PIC S9(4)         COMP.
    02 DFHEIV14      PIC S9(4)         COMP.
    02 DFHEIV15      PIC S9(4)         COMP.
    02 DFHEIV16      PIC S9(9)         COMP.
    02 DFHEIV17      PIC X(4).
    02 DFHEIV18      PIC X(4).
    02 DFHEIV19      PIC X(4).
    02 DFHEIV97      PIC S9(7) COMP-3  VALUE ZERO.
    02 DFHEIV98      PIC S9(4) COMP    VALUE ZERO.
    02 DFHEIV99      PIC X(1)          VALUE SPACE.
```

To display the message without DSPL, that is

CICS IS EASY

An ERASE option must be added to the SEND command:

```
EXEC CICS SEND
          FROM     (WS-MESSAGE)
          LENGTH (12)
          ERASE
END-EXEC.
```

ERASE will clear the screen and position the cursor at line 1, column 1 of the screen prior to the send. The sequence of the options following a command is not fixed. For instance, ERASE is specified last but will result in the screen's being cleared before information is sent to it.

Receive a Message

Now that you know how to send a message to the terminal, let's see how you might receive data entered by an operator. The program in Fig. 5-4 will

```
0001 IDENTIFICATION DIVISION.
0002*
0003 PROGRAM-ID. RECEIVEP.
0004*
0005 REMARKS.
0006*
0007*******************************************************************
0008*       THIS PROGRAM ILLUSTRATES THE CICS RECEIVE COMMAND       *
0009*       SOCIAL SECURITY NUMBER IS ENTERED AND THEN DISPLAYED    *
0010*       IN A DIFFERENT FORMAT                                    *
0011*******************************************************************
0012*
0013 ENVIRONMENT DIVISION.
0014*
0015 DATA DIVISION.
0016*
0017 WORKING-STORAGE  SECTION.
0018*
0019 01   WS-INPUT.
0020      05   WS-TRANSID                PIC X(4).
0021      05   FILLER                    PIC X.
0022      05   WS-INPUT-SOC-SEC-NO       PIC X(9)    VALUE ALL 'X'.
0023*
0024 01   WS-OUTPUT.
0025      05   FILLER                    PIC X(25)   VALUE
0026           'SOCIAL SECURITY NUMBER = '.
0027      05   WS-OUTPUT-SOC-SEC-NO      PIC X(9).
0028*
0029 01   WS-LENGTH                      PIC S9(4)   COMP.
0030*
0031*
0032 LINKAGE SECTION.
0033*
0034*
0035 PROCEDURE DIVISION.
0036*
0037 AA00-MAINLINE  SECTION.
0038*
0039      PERFORM B000-RECEIVE-INPUT.
0040      PERFORM C000-SEND-OUTPUT.
0041*
0042* RETURN TO CICS
0043      EXEC CICS RETURN
0044      END-EXEC.
0045 B000-RECEIVE-INPUT  SECTION.
0046      MOVE 14  TO  WS-LENGTH.
0047*
0048      EXEC CICS RECEIVE
0049               INTO   (WS-INPUT)
0050               LENGTH (WS-LENGTH)
0051      END-EXEC.
0052*
0053      MOVE WS-INPUT-SOC-SEC-NO  TO  WS-OUTPUT-SOC-SEC-NO.
0054*
0055 B000-EXIT.
0056      EXIT.
0057*
0058 C000-SEND-OUTPUT  SECTION.
0059      EXEC CICS SEND
0060               FROM   (WS-OUTPUT)
0061               LENGTH (34)
0062               ERASE
0063      END-EXEC.
0064*
0065 C000-EXIT.
0066      EXIT.
```

Figure 5-4 Program Illustrating CICS RECEIVE Command.

receive a social security number and send a message using that number. The operator keys in the TRANSID RECV, a space, and then a nine-digit social security number. The program will receive the data entered and display the message

SOCIAL SECURITY NUMBER = 999999999.

RECV 999999999   (Keyed in on first screen)

SOCIAL SECURITY NUMBER = 999999999   (Displayed on
                                                                          next screen)

The program in Fig. 5-4 illustrates several new CICS concepts plus the RE-CEIVE command. This program will receive the input message, which consists of the TRANSID, a blank, and social security number. It will then display a message containing the social security number. The new command introduced is RECEIVE. The program receives the input message, including the TRAN-SID. Note that the RECEIVE's length option is specified with an argument WS-LENGTH, which must be defined in working storage as a binary halfword. LENGTH can be hard-coded in the SEND command [i.e., LENGTH (34)]. You always receive *into* and *send* from. Basically that's all there is to the SEND and RECEIVE commands, but there are a few additional considerations when using the RECEIVE command.

The input field entered may be shorter than the specified working-storage length parameter WS-LENGTH. For instance, if only the first eight positions of a social security number were keyed in, what would happen? WS-LENGTH would be set to 13 instead of the expected 14 (TRANSID + space + social security number), and the displayed message would show an X as the last digit of the social security number. Characters keyed in are received from left to right in the input area WS-INPUT.

The input field keyed in may be greater than WS-LENGTH. What will occur if the social security number is keyed in as 10 digits in error? WS-LENGTH will be set to 15 instead of the anticipated 14 characters. Unfortunately, the output message will not display the 10-digit social security number. The program will come to an ABEND. You could probably get around this condition by making WS-INPUT-SOC-SEC-NO several digits longer than required and by adjusting WS-LENGTH accordingly, but there is a better way to handle this and similar anticipated or unexpected occurrences.

HANDLE CONDITION Commands

There is a CICS command which will handle various anticipated or unexpected CICS conditions: the CICS HANDLE CONDITION. An example of this command is

```
EXEC CICS HANDLE CONDITION
          ERROR  (ERROR-MESSAGE)
END-EXEC.
```

The ERROR option directs a program to transfer control to ERROR-MESSAGE if any unanticipated events occur which cause an ABEND. The program will transfer control to the paragraph named ERROR-MESSAGE which can display a message and cause a normal program termination. The HANDLE CONDITION command must be executed prior to the condition being encountered. CICS debugging aids, which assist CICS programmers in determining the cause of errors, will be discussed in Chap. 18.

CICS programmers can usually anticipate and handle most conditions which occur in a program. There is an option of the HANDLE CONDITION command called LENGERR which can be used to check for a length-error condition. LENGERR and other conditions which can be provided for will take precedence over the ERROR option.

```
EXEC CICS HANDLE CONDITION
          LENGERR (LENGTH-ERROR)
          ERROR    (ERROR-MESSAGE)
END-EXEC.
```

This handle condition will cause the program to branch to the paragraph named LENGTH-ERROR if the input data is longer than the anticipated working-storage length of 14.

The programmer could make the above handle condition into two separate statements as follows:

```
EXEC CICS HANDLE CONDITION
          ERROR(ERROR-MESSAGE)
END-EXEC.

EXEC CICS HANDLE CONDITION
          LENGERR (LENGTH-ERROR)
END-EXEC.
```

To make it easier for the programmer to recover from unanticipated problems, omit the ERROR option on the HANDLE CONDITION function and let the program ABEND. A program might be updating several files when an ABEND occurs. CICS has the ability to dynamically back out file updates when an ABEND occurs. The ERROR condition would prevent this back-out. Unless the program made provision for a back-out in the error message routine, files

```
0001 B000-RECEIVE-INPUT  SECTION.
0002*
0003* HANDLE LENGTH ERRORS
0004     EXEC CICS HANDLE CONDITION
0005              LENGERR (B000-LENGTH-ERROR)
0006     END-EXEC.
0007*
0008     MOVE 14  TO  WS-LENGTH.
0009*
0010     EXEC CICS RECEIVE
0011             INTO   (WS-INPUT)
0012             LENGTH (WS-LENGTH)
0013     END-EXEC.
0014*
0015     MOVE WS-INPUT-SOC-SEC-NO  TO  WS-OUTPUT-SOC-SEC-NO.
0016*
0017     GO TO  B000-EXIT.
0018*
0019 B000-LENGTH-ERROR.
0020     MOVE 'TOO MANY DIGITS ENTERED, PLEASE CLEAR SCREEN AND TRY AGAIN'
0021          TO  WS-OUTPUT.
0022*
0023 B000-EXIT.
0024     EXIT.
```

Figure 5-5 HANDLE CONDITION Command Illustration.

could get out of sync. When you maintain programs written by others, you will most likely encounter the ERROR condition. Just remember that a specific check for a condition such as LENGERR will supersede the ERROR condition if both conditions are coded.

Figure 5-5 illustrates how the procedure division of the sample program in Fig. 5-4 would appear if the HANDLE CONDITION command was added. Program examples in future chapters will contain techniques for eliminating GO TOs from similar conditions.

Note that in paragraph C000-SEND-OUTPUT, the LENGTH option is specified with a length of 58; this is to allow for the length of the larger error message. The working-storage area WS-OUTPUT in Fig. 5-4 would have a FILLER PIC X(24) added after WS-OUTPUT-SOC-SEC-NO to make the field 58 positions long.

If the operator forgot and entered dashes as part of social security number as follows:

RECV 150-22-3333

A length error would be detected because the input length would now be 16 instead of the expected length of 14. The following message would be displayed:

TOO MANY DIGITS ENTERED, PLEASE CLEAR SCREEN AND TRY AGAIN

instead of the anticipated message

SOCIAL SECURITY NUMBER = 150223333

The program could have had two separate SEND commands; one for displaying social security number and one for the length-error message. The advantage of this technique would be the ability to eliminate ERASE from the length-error send. Without ERASE, the send would keep the original entry on the screen for verification by the terminal operator. The message would be displayed from the last recognized position of the cursor as follows:

RECV 150-22-3333TOO MANY DIGITS ENTERED, PLEASE CLEAR SCREEN AND TRY AGAIN

Cursor positioning will be discussed in greater detail later in this chapter.

General Information about Handle Conditions

1. Up to 12 conditions can be handled by one command.
2. The last command encountered takes precedence when prior commands list the same option.
3. To turn off an option, list the option without an argument.

In Fig. 5-6, any length errors in HANDLE-PARAGRAPH-1 would cause a transfer of control to LENGERR-PARAGRAPH-1. Length errors in HANDLE-PARAGRAPH-2 would cause a branch to LENGERR-PARAGRAPH-2. HANDLE-PARAGRAPH-3 would turn off the LENGERR condition causing the program to default to the ERROR condition and to be directed to the paragraph ERROR-MESSAGE if a LENGERR condition occurred. If a length error occurred after HANDLE-PARAGRAPH-3 turned off the LENGERR condition and if the HANDLE ERROR condition was absent, the program would ABEND.

Cursor Position (EIBCPOSN)

CICS programs have the ability to check what the position of the cursor was when an AID key was pressed to initiate a receive. EIBCPOSN, a field in the EIB, can be tested to determine the line and column at which the cursor was positioned. The program in Fig. 5-5 could have replaced

```
        EXEC CICS HANDLE CONDITION
                    LENGERR (B000-LENGTH-ERROR)
        END-EXEC.

           by

        IF EIBCPOSN  IS GREATER THAN 14
             MOVE 'TOO MANY DIGITS ENTERED, PLEASE CLEAR SCREEN
    —          ' AND TRY AGAIN'  TO WS-OUTPUT
             GO TO  B000-EXIT.
```

```
PROCEDURE DIVISION.
    EXEC CICS HANDLE CONDITION
              ERROR (ERROR-MESSAGE)
    END-EXEC.
        .
        .
        .
HANDLE-PARAGRAPH-1.
    EXEC CICS HANDLE CONDITION
              LENGERR (LENGERR-PARAGRAPH-1)
    END-EXEC.
        .
        .
        .
HANDLE-PARAGRAPH-2.
    EXEC CICS HANDLE CONDITION
              LENGERR (LENGERR-PARAGRAPH-2)
    END-EXEC.
        .
        .
        .
HANDLE-PARAGRAPH-3.
    EXEC CICS HANDLE CONDITION
              LENGERR
    END-EXEC.
        .
        .
        .
```

Figure 5-6 HANDLE CONDITION Command Priorities.

The HANDLE CONDITION command is removed and replaced by the
EIBCPOSN check which should precede the receive, otherwise LENGERR
could occur on the receive, causing an ABEND. In this case, the paragraph
B000-LENGTH-ERROR could be eliminated.

When developing applications and writing programs, it is sometimes beneficial
to know the line and column at which the cursor is positioned. The cursor
position for line 1, column 1 is 0; for line 2, column 1, 80; for line 3, column 1,
160; etc. The last allowable cursor position is 1919. A programmer can determine
the value of EIBCPOSN for any line and column by subtracting 1 from line
number, multiplying that result by 80, and adding column number minus 1. For
example,

Line 3, column 1

$$(3-1) \times 80 + (1-1) = 160 = EIBCPOSN$$

Line 11, column 10

$$(11-1) \times 80 + (10-1) = 809 = EIBCPOSN$$

The technique of cursor positioning is sometimes used in order to select an
item, if the cursor is placed next to that item, prior to pressing a designated
AID key. Positioning the cursor anywhere on a line could be used as a signal to
delete the record displayed on that line when a designated AID key is pressed.

SUMMARY

Simplified program examples were used to present the following commands—SEND, RECEIVE, RETURN, and HANDLE CONDITION. The CICS compiler and translator were discussed and a sample program was presented in order to illustrate how the translator breaks down CICS commands.

This chapter was intended to give you an indication of how easy the use of CICS commands will be with practice. Future chapters will build on this basic knowledge by introducing more involved program examples.

6

BASIC MAPPING SUPPORT

Proper design of maps is essential to the success of a CICS system. This discussion of basic mapping support (BMS) will be limited to what you need to know in order to create usable maps; it will not cover every option and possibility. BMS maps, which are collections of assembler language macros, can create problems if not properly understood; Chap. 7 will present examples which should help to eliminate most difficulties you may encounter. The theory presented in this chapter will make more sense when it is used with the commands presented in Chap. 7.

The SEND command examples in Chap. 5 were introduced to aid in the presentation of important concepts; in reality, most terminal communication is performed through the use of maps. A map is basically an assembler program which formats terminal screens and controls the transfer of data between a terminal and CICS programs.

Map Types

The BMS map is run through an assembler program twice in order to produce two maps; the physical map and the symbolic map. A macro is an instruction which generates additional code when it is passed through an assembler program. Macros generate many statements when the BMS map is assembled; these statements result in instructions which aid in controlling physical and symbolic maps.

Physical Maps

Physical maps are assembly language programs which are created and placed in a load library. Physical maps control screen alignment plus the sending and receiving of constants and data to and from a terminal.

Symbolic Maps

Symbolic maps define map fields used to store variable data referenced in a
Cobol program. They may be placed by BMS into a copy library and included
in the Cobol program at compile time.

Format and Structure

Figure 6-1 defines a skeleton BMS map which should aid you in understanding
the format and structure of a BMS map. When BMS maps are assembled, the
macros are expanded. The application programmer is generally not interested

```
1...5...10...15...20...25...30...35...40...45...50...55...60...65...70..
          PRINT NOGEN
mapset    DFHMSD TYPE=MAP,                                              X
                 CTRL=(FREEKB,FRSET),                                   X
                 LANG=COBOL,                                            X
                 MODE=INOUT,                                            X
                 TERM=3270,                                             X
                 TIOAPFX=YES
*
mapnam1   DFHMDI LINE=01,                                              X
                 COLUMN=01,                                            X
                 SIZE=(24,80)
*
field1    DFHMDF POS=(  ,  ),                                          X
                 ATTRB=(attr1,attr2,...),                              X
                 LENGTH=99,                                            X
                 INITIAL='Map Constants'
*
          DFHMDF POS=(  ,  ),                                          X
                 ATTRB=(attr1,attr2,...),                              X
                 LENGTH=99,                                            X
                 INITIAL='Map Constants'
*
field2    DFHMDF POS=(  ,  ),                                          X
                 ATTRB=(attr1,attr2,...),                              X
                 LENGTH=99
*
                 .
                 .
                 .
*
fieldN    DFHMDF POS=(  ,  ),                                          X
                 ATTRB=(attr1,attr2,...),                              X
                 LENGTH=99
*
*
mapnam2   DFHMDI
                 .
                 .
                 .
*
field1    DFHMDF
                 .
                 .
                 .
*
fieldN    DFHMDF
                 .
                 .
                 .
*
          DFHMSD TYPE=FINAL
          END
```

Figure 6-1 BMS Map Structure.

in the listing of expanded macros. Including the statement PRINT NOGEN at the beginning of the BMS map will suppress the listing of expanded macros.

BMS Format Rules

The basic format of a BMS entry is

[Label][Macro]operand=(parameter 1, [parameter 2,. . .]),   X

Some of the rules BMS maps follow are

1. PRINT NOGEN starts in the same column as the mapset definition (DFHMSD) macro, usually column 10.
2. Mapset, mapname(s), and field name(s) start in column 1, begin with an alphabetic character, and are seven or fewer characters in length.
3. Macros such as DFHMSD, map definition for individual maps (DFHMDI) and map definition for fields (DFHMDF) usually begin in column 10 and are followed by operands and parameters.
4. Macros should be followed by one space and then an operand plus parameters such as TYPE=MAP,.
5. Additional continuation operands must start in column 16, as does CTRL=(FREEKB,FRSET),.
6. If an operand is to be continued from one line to the next, it must be followed by a comma and have a continuation character (usually an X) in column 72. Parameters plus a comma must end at column 71 or sooner. An operand to be continued must be followed by a comma; otherwise the assembler assumes it is the last operand and ignores additional operands and parameters until it encounters the next macro.
7. END usually starts in the same column as the preceding DFHMSD TYPE=FINAL macro; it signals the end of a map.
8. Multiple parameters for the same operand are enclosed in parentheses, such as CTRL=(FREEKB,FRSET).
9. The operands for all macros can be set up as shown in Fig. 6-1 or can be strung across a couple of lines, such as

```
    mapset    DFHMSD TYPE=MAP,CTRL=(FREEKB,FRSET),        X
                     LANG=COBOL,MODE=INOUT,                X
                     TERM=3270,TIOAPFX=YES
```

I recommend placing one operand per line for ease of maintenance and readability.

10. The sequence of operands is free-form.

11. An asterisk in column 1 defines the line as a comment line; its use as shown in Fig. 6-1 improves readability.

Map Structure

The BMS map structure shown in Fig. 6-1 consists of the DFHMSD, DFHMDI, and DFHMDF macros.

Mapset definition macro (DFHMSD). DFHMSD macros vary little from map to map within an installation; usually mapset name is the only difference. All maps in this book use identical DFHMSD operands and parameters; only mapset changes from map to map. This macro applies to all individual maps within a mapset; it occurs only as the first and last macro in a BMS map. Mapset is the name assigned to the BMS map.

Most installations have standards for assigning mapset names. The name assigned to mapset *must* be supported by a PPT entry; it is the label used in a SEND MAP (mapset) command, which will be discussed in the next chapter. Mapset name will be included in the physical map's load module. The DFHMSD macro follows mapset name and is preceded and followed by a space.

$$\text{TYPE} = \begin{cases} \text{MAP} \\ \text{DSECT} \\ \text{FINAL} \end{cases}$$

This operand may use one of the first two parameters listed above for the first DFHMSD macro. A BMS map is assembled twice in order to create two maps: a physical map and a symbolic map. When defined as TYPE=MAP, the physical map is created, and when TYPE=DSECT, the symbolic map is generated. Application programmers refer to the symbolic map as a DSECT. A proc or standard JCL generally handles the creation of both maps. Usually only one job is submitted and BMS ignores the operands not required for each individual map. Always assemble both maps at the same time, otherwise the physical and symbolic maps may become out of sync. Every BMS map ends with a DFHMSD TYPE=FINAL macro, followed on the last line by END.

CTRL=(FREEKB,FRSET)

The CTRL operand can contain several parameters. The most common are FREEKB, FRSET, and ALARM.

- FREEKB—This parameter FREEs the KeyBoard and permits the entry of data when a map is sent to the screen; this parameter is usually included.

- FRSET—Resets FSET attributes to OFF before the send of a map; modified data tags (MDTs), part of the attribute which were on, will be turned off.

This concept will be explained later in the chapter, under FSET. (When ON, FSET attributes result in the transfer of data from the screen into the program.)

• ALARM—Sounds an audible alarm or beep at a terminal when a map is sent.

LANG=COBOL

This statement defines the language of the source program in which the map will be used. It would only be modified if the map were to be used in a non-Cobol program. This entry generates the proper symbolic map.

MODE=INOUT

Specifies that the map will be used for both input and output operations and generates input and output symbolic map labels.

• =IN—generates an input symbolic map only

• =OUT—generates an output symbolic map only

I recommend using MODE=INOUT for all maps because it is required if you use symbolic cursor positioning, which is discussed in Chap. 7.

TERM=3270

Defines the type of terminal this map will be used with.

TIOAPFX=YES

Always include this parameter; it generates a 12-byte filler at the beginning of the symbolic map in order to skip over control characters. Failure to include this operand would cause the map to be misaligned when it is sent.

Mapset definition of individual maps (DFHMDI). DFHMDI macros, like DFHMSD macros, differ little from map to map within an installation; usually mapname is the only difference. All maps in this book use the same DFHMDI operands and parameters; only mapname varies from map to map. A mapset can have several maps associated with it as shown in Fig. 6-l; each map would have its own mapname, DFHMDI, and DFHMDF macros.

Mapname

This is the name assigned to individual maps within a mapset. This label is used in the SEND (mapname) command, which will be discussed in Chap. 7. Mapname is stored along with mapset in the physical map load module. The DFHMDI macro follows mapname and is preceded and followed by a space.

LINE=01, COLUMN=01, SIZE=(24,80)

These operands and parameters specify that the map starts at line 01, column 01 and is to be displayed on a screen 24 lines deep by 80 columns wide.

Map definition for fields (DFHMDF). DFHMDF macros, unlike DFHMSD and DFHMDI macros, vary considerably from map to map. Each field to be displayed or received through a map must be defined by a DFHMDF macro. The basic structure of the field macro is shown in Fig. 6-2; only the most commonly used operands and parameters will be discussed.

Field name

Every map field name which is to be referenced in a program must have a one- to seven-character name; this name supplies the symbolic map with a field name label. The DFHMDF macro follows field name and is preceded and followed by a space.

POS=

This refers to the position of the attribute immediately preceding a field; it is usually defined as a two-digit line and column number.

ATTRB=

This defines the attribute characteristics of a field. All attributes take up 1 byte immediately preceding the field defined. ASKIP, UNPROT, and PROT attributes define how the cursor will react to a field; they are mutually exclusive.

- ASKIP—The cursor will automatically skip over this field and stop at the next UNPROT field encountered. Remember that the cursor moves left to right, top to bottom; when it reaches the end of the map, it starts at the beginning

```
field name      DFHMDF POS=(line,column),

                         ┌ASKIP           ┌NORM
                 ATTRB= ⎨ UNPROT,   NUM, ⎨ BRT,    FSET, IC,
                         └PROT            └DRK

                 LENGTH=99,   (01 thru 256)

                 INITIAL='Map Constants',

                 PICIN='Edit Mask',

                 PICOUT='Edit Mask',

                 OCCURS=Number of Occurrences
```

Figure 6-2 DFHMDF—Macro Format.

of the map again. I usually use ASKIP as a stopper field following UNPROT fields, to skip to the next UNPROT field.

- UNPROT—The cursor will stop at the first position of each UNPROT field (just to the right of the attribute) in order to allow for the entry of data. An UNPROT field should be followed by a stopper field (ASKIP or PROT), otherwise the entry of data would be permitted to continue until the next ASKIP or PROT field was encountered.

- PROT—Data cannot be entered into a PROT field. PROT is commonly used as a stopper field following an UNPROT field, when it is important to know if too many digits were entered into a field. PROT will stop movement of the cursor in this case, whereas ASKIP would skip to the next UNPROT field and allow the entry of the excess characters into that field. PROT could also be defined for map constant fields since the cursor will bypass PROT fields and stop at the next UNPROT field. *Note*: ASKIP and PROT attributes are often used interchangeably. The major difference occurs when they are used at the end of an UNPROT field as a stopper field. PROT will stop data entry, while ASKIP will skip to the next UNPROT field and allow the continued entry of data.

- NUM—Data entered into a numeric field will be right-justified, and unfilled positions to the left will be filled with zeros. Fields not defined as NUM are left-justified and filled with spaces to the right of the last significant character entered. Unless a keyboard numeric lock feature is installed, it is possible to enter nonnumeric data into a NUM field. For instance if "A " was entered into a NUM field, it would be received as 000A. I recommend editing all input data.

- NORM—A field with this attribute is displayed at normal intensity.

- BRT—A field with bright intensity is highlighted to stand out on a screen. I normally brighten field identifiers of items which were entered incorrectly, position the cursor at the start of the first field in error, and brighten error and operator-notification messages.

- DRK—Fields with dark intensity are usually used for passwords or for information that an onlooker is not permitted to view, since data entered into a dark field cannot be seen. Dark fields are sometimes used to store data in unused positions of the screen in order to pass information to the same program or among different programs.

- FSET—When the terminal operator keys data into a field, an MDT is turned on which causes entered data to be received into a program. Fields without the MDT on are not transmitted to a program. Specifying FSET in the BMS or symbolic map will turn on the MDT. This returns data in a map field to the program on a RECEIVE MAP command, even if the operator did not key data into the field. Sometimes data sent to a screen, perhaps from a file which was read, is needed upon a succeeding receive of the map. FSET fields are turned off *before* the map is sent when FRSET is specified on the CTRL operand of the DFHMSD macro; the map being displayed then controls FSET attributes. This concept is very important and will be discussed in detail in Chap. 7.

• IC—The Insert Cursor (IC), part of an attribute, places the cursor at the first position of the map field which contains IC. Normally only the first UNPROT field on a map would contain IC; if specified for more than one field, the *last* field specified with IC would be the field at which the cursor would stop. Using symbolic cursor positioning, which will be discussed in the next chapter, the cursor would be positioned at the *first* field if multiple fields were set. The cursor will be positioned at screen position line 1, column 1 if IC is not specified and symbolic cursor positioning is not used. IC could be defined for an ASKIP or PROT field but no data could be entered into the field; this is normally not done.

ASKIP,NORM is the default if ATTRB= is not defined and UN-PROT,NORM is the default if only NUMeric and/or IC is specified.

LENGTH=field length

The valid values are 1 to 256 (characters).

INITIAL='map constants'

This gives an initial value to a constant or variable field. The DFHMDF macro should be assigned a field name if the field contents or its display intensity attribute is to be modified. INITIAL generally defines map constants which will only be displayed at a predetermined intensity, and the macro does not require a field name in this case. If the map constant exceeds one line, continue the constant to column 71 of the first line, put an X in column 72, then on the next line continue the constant starting at column 16. Quotation marks should only occur at the beginning and at the end of the map constant. The characters ' and &, if used within an initial value, must be repeated twice. For example,

'O''Rourke && Sons' displays O'Rourke & Sons. The length of the constant is 15, not 17, because the extra characters do not take up any additional space on the map.

If the number of characters defined by INITIAL exceeds the value set by the length parameter, the excess characters are truncated when the map is sent.

PICIN='edit mask'

Input symbolic map fields will be assigned a picture of X unless the PICIN (PICture IN) operand defines the picture differently. For example,

PICIN='999999'

PICOUT='edit mask'

Output symbolic map fields will be assigned a picture of X unless the PICOUT (PICture OUT) operand defines the picture differently. For example,

PICOUT='$ZZ,ZZZ.99'

OCCURS=number of occurrences

This generates a symbolic map OCCURS clause for the defined number of occurrences. This clause is most commonly used with map fields to be indexed, such as in a browse display. For example,

```
MAPDESC DFHMDF POS=(09,01),        X
               ATTRB=ASKIP,        X
               LENGTH=79,          X
               OCCURS=14
```

The above would generate 14 lines of 79 characters, each with an ASKIP attribute in column 1 of each line. A programmer could then move a 79-character working-storage field to each MAPDESCO (map-index) line.

BMS Map for a Menu

Figure 6-3 shows the vendor file maintenance submenu map and Fig. 6-4, the BMS map used to format the screen.

The first macro (DFHMSD) in Fig. 6-4 ① has a label POVMNT1, the mapset name, which must be defined in the PPT. The rest of the operands and parameters are identical to those shown in Fig. 6-1.

The second macro (DFHMDI) ② is shown with a mapname of MAPPOVM; the rest of the macro is the same as shown in Fig. 6-1. Several DFHMDI macros can be defined in one mapset. I generally limit each mapset to one map.

The last macro, DFHMSD TYPE=FINAL, followed by END ⑦ is standard for all maps. Other maps in this book will not refer to the last two entries or to the mapset and mapname macros; only mapset and mapname labels will vary from map to map.

DFHMDF Macro Usage

Figure 6-4 demonstrates the use of many of the DFHMDF parameters discussed, and a comparison with Fig. 6-3 should make the defining of BMS macros easy to understand.

③ a. Defines a map-constant field ABC MANUFACTURING COMPANY with a preceding ASKIP attribute in line 1, column 27; it is 25 characters long.

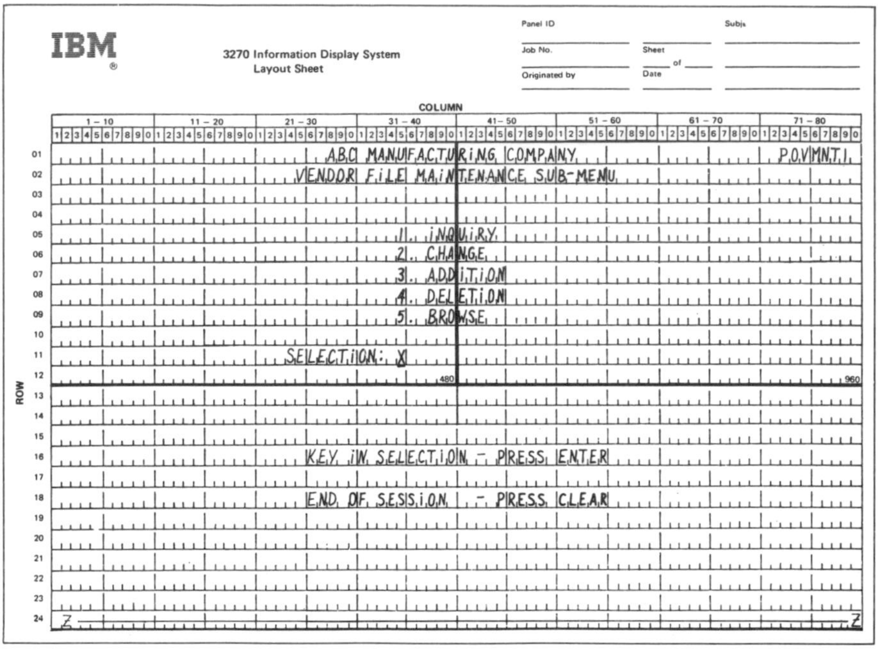

Figure 6-3   Vendor File Maintenance Submenu Map.

b. The option ATTRB=ASKIP could be omitted since it is the default; I like to include the ATTRB operand for all map fields.

c. No label is shown in columns 1 to 7; therefore no symbolic map entry will be generated. Constant fields which may be displayed with varying intensity (BRT, NORM, or DRK) require a label in order to generate a symbolic map field name.

d. LENGTH must correspond to INITIAL=map constant size.

④ a. Defines the field into which the terminal operator will make a selection. A symbolic map field name will be generated since this macro has a field name MSELECT.

b. The attribute preceding the field starts at line 11, column 34; it is one character long.

c. The attribute UNPROT will cause the cursor to stop at a field for data entry, and IC will cause the cursor to be positioned initially at the start of the field (not at the attribute) when the physical map is sent (Chap. 7 will explain this technique). This is the only UNPROT field on this map. IC alone could be entered in the ATTRB field since, in this case, UNPROT would be the default. Chapter 7 will explain symbolic cursor positioning, which allows the program to override IC on a send which includes the symbolic map.

```
          PRINT NOGEN
POVMNT1   DFHMSD TYPE=MAP,                                              X
                 CTRL=(FREEKB,FRSET),                                   X
                 LANG=COBOL,               ⎫  ①                        X
                 MODE=INOUT,               ⎬                            X
                 TERM=3270,                ⎭                            X
                 TIOAPFX=YES                                            X
*
MAPPOVM   DFHMDI LINE=01,                  ⎫  ②                        X
                 COLUMN=01,                ⎬                            X
                 SIZE=(24,80)              ⎭
*
          DFHMDF POS=(01,27),                                          X
                 ATTRB=ASKIP,                        ⎫  ③              X
                 LENGTH=25,                          ⎬                 X
                 INITIAL='ABC MANUFACTURING COMPANY' ⎭
*
          DFHMDF POS=(01,72),                                          X
                 ATTRB=ASKIP,                                          X
                 LENGTH=07,                                            X
                 INITIAL='POVMNT1'
*
          DFHMDF POS=(02,24),                                          X
                 ATTRB=ASKIP,                                          X
                 LENGTH=32,                                            X
                 INITIAL='VENDOR FILE MAINTENANCE SUB-MENU'
*
          DFHMDF POS=(05,34),                                          X
                 ATTRB=ASKIP,                                          X
                 LENGTH=10,                                            X
                 INITIAL='1. INQUIRY'
*
          DFHMDF POS=(06,34),                                          X
                 ATTRB=ASKIP,                                          X
                 LENGTH=09,                                            X
                 INITIAL='2. CHANGE'
*
          DFHMDF POS=(07,34),                                          X
                 ATTRB=ASKIP,                                          X
                 LENGTH=11,                                            X
                 INITIAL='3. ADDITION'
*
          DFHMDF POS=(08,34),                                          X
                 ATTRB=ASKIP,                                          X
                 LENGTH=11,                                            X
                 INITIAL='4. DELETION'
*
          DFHMDF POS=(09,34),                                          X
                 ATTRB=ASKIP,                                          X
                 LENGTH=09,                                            X
                 INITIAL='5. BROWSE'
*
          DFHMDF POS=(11,23),                                          X
                 ATTRB=ASKIP,                                          X
                 LENGTH=10,                                            X
                 INITIAL='SELECTION: '
*
MSELECT   DFHMDF POS=(11,34),        ⎫                                 X
                 ATTRB=(UNPROT,IC),  ⎬  ④                             X
                 LENGTH=01           ⎭
*
          DFHMDF POS=(11,36),        ⎫                                 X
                 ATTRB=PROT,         ⎬  ⑤                             X
                 LENGTH=01           ⎭
*
          DFHMDF POS=(16,25),                                          X
                 ATTRB=ASKIP,                                          X
                 LENGTH=30,                                            X
                 INITIAL='KEY IN SELECTION - PRESS ENTER'
*
          DFHMDF POS=(18,25),                                          X
                 ATTRB=ASKIP,                                          X
                 LENGTH=30,                                            X
                 INITIAL='END OF SESSION   - PRESS CLEAR'
*
MAPMESG   DFHMDF POS=(24,01),  ⎫                                       X
                 ATTRB=ASKIP,  ⎬  ⑥                                   X
                 LENGTH=79     ⎭
*
          DFHMSD TYPE=FINAL  ⎫  ⑦
          END                ⎭
```

Figure 6-4 BMS Map for Vendor File Maintenance Submenu.

d. INITIAL is often omitted for UNPROT fields unless it is desired to assign an initial default value to the field. For instance, if INQUIRY was selected much more frequently than any other item on the vendor file maintenance submenu, the DFHMDF macro would be defined as follows:

```
MSELECT DFHMDF POS=(11,34),                    X
               ATTRB=(UNPROT,FSET,IC),         X
               LENGTH=01,                      X
               INITIAL='1'
```

Note: ATTRB= now contains FSET to turn on the MDT so that when the terminal operator presses ENTER, the selection of 1 will be received by the program as if the operator had entered a 1, turning on the MDT.

⑤ a. Defines a 1-byte stopper field with an attribute of PROT; without this stopper field, the terminal operator could continue entering data into the SELECTION field. An attempt to enter more than one digit into the SELECTION field will cause the cursor to stop, the keyboard to lock, and require the terminal operator to press RESET in order to continue.

b. Generally if more than one UNPROT field exists on a map, the stopper field will contain an ATTRB=ASKIP so that when one field is entered the cursor will skip to the next UNPROT field. Setting all stopper attributes to PROT would require the terminal operator to press the TAB key each time a data field was completely filled.

⑥ a. A symbolic map field name will be generated since a field name MAPMESG is included in this field.

b. ASKIP attribute preceding this field is in line 24, column 1.

c. This field will often have its intensity changed by the program to ASKIP,BRT when operator-notification or error messages are displayed.

d. This field is sometimes defined with an initial value and ATTRB=(ASKIP,DRK), defined so that the message does not display until a program changes the attribute to ASKIP,BRT. I prefer not to assign an initial value to message fields and to let the program select the message to be displayed.

Refresh the PPT When a Map Changes

The PPT should be refreshed with the latest load library address of the physical map when it is reassembled; failure to do so can lead to unpredictable results. A map is considered a program by CICS and the PPT is updated by:

```
        CSMT NEW,PGRMID=mapset
        or
        CEMT SET PRO (mapset) NEW
```

A program almost always changes when a symbolic map is altered. Make sure the BMS map is assembled correctly before compiling the changed program to ensure that the program will have the latest version of the BMS-generated symbolic map (unless you employ user-friendly symbolic maps, discussed later in this chapter). After the program has been compiled, refresh its address in the PPT

```
        CSMT NEW,PGRMID=program
        or
        CEMT SET PRO (program) NEW
```

Command-Level Interpreter

The format of a physical map can be checked by using the command-level interpreter (CECI). CECI, a transaction identifier, initiates the command level interpreter, which is a CICS application program. CECI is a translator supplied with CICS which is useful for checking the syntax and execution of many CICS commands. The operator can clear the screen, key in CECI, and press the ENTER key in order to display a list of CICS commands. Commands can be syntax-checked and executed from this list. The complete command can be keyed in when CECI is entered, if you know the syntax and want to see the results of the execution of the command. If you do not know the syntax, just key in CECI and press ENTER and the system will prompt you for other entries.

The command-level interpreter is useful for testing new or changed BMS physical maps for format and entry of UNPROT fields. You just have to key in the following and press ENTER.

CECI SEND MAP (mapset) ERASE

The above command will display the same physical map that the SEND command in a program would. This allows you to test your physical map before it is used in a program.

The Generated Symbolic Map

The symbolic map generated by the BMS map in Fig. 6-4 would look similar to the map in Fig. 6-5. Blank (*) lines, comments, and alignment are included to improve readability; they are not found in the actual symbolic map which

```
0001*****************************************************************
0002*             SYMBOLIC MAP FOR MAPSET 'POVMNT1'                *
0003*      COMMENTS AND ASTERISKS ARE NOT GENERATED BY BMS         *
0004*        - THEY ARE INSERTED TO IMPROVE READABILITY            *
0005*****************************************************************
0006*
0007 01  MAPPOVMI.
0008     02  FILLER                    PIC X(12).
0009*
0010     02  MSELECTL                  PIC S9(4)    COMP.
0011     02  MSELECTF                  PIC X.
0012      02 FILLER  REDEFINES  MSELECTF.
0013          03  MSELECTA             PIC X.
0014     02  MSELECTI                  PIC X.
0015*
0016     02  MAPMESGL                  PIC S9(4)    COMP.
0017     02  MAPMESGF                  PIC X.
0018      02 FILLER  REDEFINES  MAPMESGF.
0019          03  MAPMESGA             PIC X.
0020     02  MAPMESGI                  PIC X(79).
0021*
0022 01  MAPPOVMO  REDEFINES  MAPPOVMI.
0023     02  FILLER                    PIC X(12).
0024*
0025     02  FILLER                    PIC X(3).
0026     02  MSELECTO                  PIC X.
0027*
0028     02  FILLER                    PIC X(3).
0029     02  MAPMESGO                  PIC X(79).
```

Figure 6-5   Symbolic Map Generated by BMS Map in Fig. 6-4.

would be generated. The symbolic map could be copied into a program by using the following COPY statement.

01 MAPPOVMI COPY POVMNT1.

Most symbolic maps will usually contain more fields than shown in Fig. 6-5, but the format of the generated symbolic map will always be the same. The first 12 bytes of the Cobol symbolic map consist of a FILLER PIC X(12). Variable fields in a map will be generated with an input (I) suffix and an output (O) suffix (such as MSELECTI and MSELECTO).

The input map MAPPOVMI contains various types of fields:

- L suffix (length field)—This field contains the length of the input field keyed in on the map by a terminal operator when the program receives the map. By moving a -1 to the length field, before issuing a SEND MAP command, the cursor is positioned at the start of that field on the screen. This is referred to as *symbolic cursor positioning* and is discussed in Chap. 7.

- F suffix (flag byte)—This field can be used by the application programmer during input procedures to test if the terminal operator has cleared a field using the EOF key on the terminal. The flag byte would contain hexadecimal 80 (X'80') if EOF had been pressed; otherwise it would equal X'00' (low-values).

- Map redefinition of this field

- A suffix (attribute field)—This field may be used during output procedures (see SEND MAP discussed in Chap. 7) to override the attribute field defined in the BMS map.

- I suffix (input field)—This field contains the data entered by the terminal operator and received into the program (see RECEIVE MAP, discussed in Chap. 7).

- MAP redefinition of this field.

- O suffix (output field)—This field is used to hold the output field for operations requiring the send of a map.

A close look at the symbolic map shows that the F (flag) and A (attribute) fields share the same storage location as do I (input) and O (output) fields. The main determinant of how these fields are referenced is whether we are receiving a map (F and I) or sending a map (A and O).

The last line of the map is usually reserved for messages sent to the terminal operator regarding conditions which may require action such as keying data into a certain field or notification of error conditions. Figure 6-5 labels this field MAPMESGO.

Creating User-Friendly Symbolic Maps

The symbolic map created by BMS is difficult to read and cumbersome to work with. Depending on your installation's standards, you may wish to create a more readable map. All Cobol symbolic maps have the same format as shown in Fig. 6-5:

1. A 12-byte filler at the beginning of the map

2. A 2-byte length field PIC S9(4) COMP for each field

3. An attribute or flag byte for each field

4. A data field for input and output

Figure 6-6 shows a user-friendly symbolic map equivalent to that shown in Fig. 6-5. All examples in this book will employ user-friendly symbolic maps.

```
0001*******************************************************************
0002*             USER FRIENDLY MENU SYMBOLIC MAP                    *
0003*******************************************************************
0004*
0005 01  MPM-MENU-MAP.
0006     05  FILLER              PIC X(12).
0007*
0008     05  MPM-L-SELECTION     PIC S9(4)    COMP.
0009     05  MPM-A-SELECTION     PIC X.
0010     05  MPM-D-SELECTION     PIC X.
0011*
0012     05  MPM-L-MESSAGE       PIC S9(4)    COMP.
0013     05  MPM-A-MESSAGE       PIC X(4).
0014     05  MPM-D-MESSAGE       PIC X(79).
```

Figure 6-6 User-Friendly Menu Symbolic Map.

SUMMARY

The creation of BMS maps, once the technique is understood, is one of the most easily utilized facets of CICS. There are two types of maps: physical maps and symbolic maps. Physical maps control map alignment and constant data on a map, while the symbolic map defines variable data. Format and structure of a BMS map was discussed, along with a detailed presentation of the DFHMSD, DFHMDI, and DFHMDF macros. BMS map attributes were discussed in detail. A simple BMS menu map was used in examples to show how it related to a screen layout and how the macros discussed were used. The command-level interpreter (CECI), which is used for checking syntax and executing CICS commands, was discussed.

A sample generated symbolic map was presented, showing how it related to the BMS map. Each field in the symbolic map was discussed, and it was shown how user-friendly symbolic maps could be created.

Most programmers I have spoken to agree that after they create a few BMS maps, the techniques given here are easy to understand and to utilize. Concentrate on the field definitions; you will find the other macros similar for most maps. More maps will be created and used in succeeding chapters. Chapter 7 will discuss the practical use of the material covered in this chapter.

7

USING ASSEMBLED BMS MAPS

Cobol CICS command-level programs are generally compiled after the BMS map has been assembled. The BMS-generated symbolic map or its user-friendly counterpart is included in the program. The symbolic map may be copied from a copy library or coded directly into the program's working storage or linkage section. Maps are either sent from or received into working storage or the linkage section of a program. This book will define its maps in working storage where they are commonly found. Conceptually, there is little difference in mapping regardless of where the map is located.

This chapter covers the SEND MAP and RECEIVE MAP commands, the use of map attributes, and cursor positioning on the map. I consider this chapter the key to mastering CICS; reread it until you thoroughly understand all concepts presented. It has been my experience that a large percentage of programming difficulty is caused by a lack of understanding of the function which map attributes perform in pseudoconversational programming.

Send Map Command

The SEND MAP command can be issued to send the physical and/or symbolic map in order to format a terminal screen. The format of the SEND MAP command is as follows; only the options you are most likely to encounter are listed.

```
EXEC CICS SEND
          MAP        (mapname)
          MAPSET     (mapset)
          FROM       (WS-MAP-AREA)
          [MAPONLY / DATAONLY]
          [ERASE /   ERASEAUP]
          [CURSOR]
          [FREEKB]
          [FRSET]
          [ALARM]
END-EXEC.
```

FREEKB, FRSET, and ALARM can be specified on the send of a map, but because I define only one map per mapset, these options, when desired, are included in the BMS map. All three options perform the same function as described under the DFHMSD CTRL= option in Chap. 6. This book will include FREEKB and FRSET in the BMS map for all examples and *not* on the SEND command. I do not use the ALARM parameter in this book.

- MAP (mapname)—The mapname from the BMS map DFHMDI label.

- MAPSET (mapset)—The mapset from the BMS map DFHMSD label; this is the PPT entry.

- FROM (WS-MAP-AREA)—A programmer-defined working-storage area from which the symbolic map is sent.

- MAPONLY—Only the physical map is to be sent.

- DATAONLY—Only the symbolic map is to be sent.

- ERASE—Clears the screen before sending the map. This option would not be used with DATAONLY because the symbolic map's data would be sent to a screen which had no constant data displayed.

- ERASEAUP—Erases all UNPROT fields; it is used only with a send of DATAONLY. ASKIP or PROT fields such as constants and message fields would not be erased by this option.

- CURSOR—This option is used with symbolic cursor positioning (discussed later in this chapter) in order to place the cursor at the start of the required field.

Types of Send Commands

The SEND MAP command is similar to the send of a message as presented in Chap. 5. There are three command types frequently selected when using the SEND MAP command: SEND MAP AND DATA, SEND MAP DATAONLY, and SEND MAP MAPONLY. The application programmer must thoroughly understand these command types in order to design and use maps properly in CICS programs.

SEND MAP AND DATA

The format of this send is

```
EXEC CICS SEND
          MAP      (mapname)
          MAPSET (mapset)
          [FROM     (WS-MAP-AREA)]
          ERASE
          [CURSOR]
END-EXEC.
```

This option will send both physical and symbolic maps, which will be merged together on the screen. Always specify ERASE with this option of SEND MAP AND DATA in order to clear the screen prior to the send. CURSOR is used with symbolic cursor positioning to set the cursor to the proper location on the screen. If CURSOR is not included on this send, the BMS map controls cursor positioning. Use this send if there is variable data on the initial send; for instance, date and time.

When FROM is omitted, the program sends its map from the working-storage symbolic map, which is generated by BMS and copied into the program at compile time. With FROM specified, the program will send its symbolic map's data from the programmer-created user-friendly symbolic map which is placed in the working-storage area WS-MAP-AREA.

SEND MAP MAPONLY

The format of this send is

```
EXEC CICS SEND
          MAP      (mapname)
          MAPSET (mapset)
          ERASE
          MAPONLY
END-EXEC.
```

It sends only the physical map and is generally used for the initial send of a map when there is no variable data to be sent to the screen. MAPONLY is also used to send informative or help screens which do not require an operator to enter data. Help screens are, in a sense, online instructions which supplement user guides. MAPONLY is usually sent only once in a program, to a cleared screen. The cursor position for this option is determined by the BMS map IC attribute. The cursor would be set at screen POS=(01,01) if the BMS map did not specify an IC attribute.

SEND MAP DATAONLY

The format of this send is

```
EXEC CICS SEND
          MAP        (mapname)
          MAPSET     (mapset)
          [FROM      (WS-MAP-AREA)]
          DATAONLY
          [CURSOR]
     END-EXEC.
```

It sends the symbolic map. This send is generally used after the physical map has been sent by one of the previously described SEND MAP commands. Only variable data has to be sent when the physical map is showing on the screen. This format of the SEND MAP command is generally used to send error and operator messages, as well as to highlight fields which contain errors. Do not specify ERASE with this option of the send, otherwise you will display a screen which contains only the variable data from the symbolic map.

Symbolic Cursor Positioning

Cursor positioning can be controlled by specifying IC in an attribute field on the BMS map and then issuing a send which includes the physical map (not DATAONLY). This method works fine if the cursor is always located at the same position, which is often not the case. On an addition or change map, a variety of fields may be entered incorrectly, and it may be desirable to position the cursor at the first field in error. Symbolic cursor positioning provides this facility. The cursor will be positioned at the start of the designated field and will override IC if specified in the BMS map. For example,

MOVE −1 TO mapfldL.

This places the cursor at the start of the map field. Sometimes multiple errors are encountered when a map's fields are edited. A −1 is moved to the length field of each item incorrectly entered. If more than one length field contains a −1, the first such field encountered controls the cursor position. The cursor is set at the start of that field when a SEND MAP command is issued.

To use symbolic cursor positioning:

1. The BMS map must specify MODE=INOUT on the DFHMSD macro.

2. CURSOR must be specified on a SEND MAP command which includes the symbolic map (not MAPONLY).

3. The program must move −1 to the symbolic map length field of the item at which the CURSOR is to be positioned, prior to issuing a SEND MAP command. If CURSOR is not specified on a DATAONLY send, the cursor will be set at POS=(01,01).

SEND MAP Transaction ABEND

During the execution of a SEND MAP command, an unanticipated condition sometimes occurs, causing a program to come to an ABEND. A message will be displayed on the screen such as:

TRANSACTION TTTT ABEND APCT IN PROGRAM MMMMMMM HH:MM:SS
TTTT = Transaction ID
APCT = ABEND Code
MMMMMMM = Program Name (mapset)
HH:MM:SS = Time of ABEND

The ABEND code APCT will be displayed if the map has not been defined in the PPT or if the map has been disabled.

Disabling a Program

Programs, maps, and tables are occasionally disabled by the use of the master terminal commands CEMT or CSMT in order to prevent the access of problem modules. A program is also disabled if no load module is found when the CICS system is started up. This condition will lead to an APCT ABEND for maps which are sent and a PGMIDERR handle condition for programs and tables which a program attempts to bring into main storage.

Low-Values Are Not Transmitted

Low-values are the characters of least value known to the computer system; they are represented by hexadecimal zeros (X'00'). Low-values are not transmitted between a program and a terminal when a map is sent or received; therefore, it is good practice to initialize symbolic maps. A program should initialize the symbolic map to low-values prior to a receive of a map and prior to formatting the map with data to be sent. A map formatted with spaces would result in the transmission of those spaces during a send operation, resulting in unnecessary traffic over transmission lines. Sometimes a field such as a message which has been displayed on the screen has to be blanked out on a subsequent send of the map. Moving low-values to the field to be blanked out will not eliminate the display of a field because low-values are not transmitted. Move spaces to any symbolic map fields which are to be blanked out by the SEND MAP command since spaces *are* transmitted.

RECEIVE MAP Command

The following RECEIVE MAP command facilitates the receive of the symbolic map into working storage.

```
EXEC CICS RECEIVE
          MAP      (mapname)
          MAPSET (mapset)
          [INTO      (WS-MAP-AREA)]
END-EXEC.
```

The program can receive the map into the working-storage area generated for the symbolic map by BMS. This area is copied into the program at compile time from a copy library. The program can also receive the map *into* a user-friendly symbolic map in working storage (WS-MAP-AREA) which can be defined by the programmer. Remember to initialize the symbolic map's working storage to low-values before issuing the RECEIVE MAP command. All fields which contain significant data (not low-values) will be received into the symbolic map when the RECEIVE MAP command is issued, provided that their MDTs are turned on (see "FSET" in Chap. 6). Remember, data may appear on the screen and *not* be returned to the program on a RECEIVE MAP command if the MDT for the field is turned off.

Map Attributes

It has been my experience that misuse of map attributes and of MDTs causes more confusion and program errors than does any other area of CICS application programming. Attributes control individual map fields on the screen. The terminal operator is given the ability to automatically skip over a field (ASKIP) or to enter data into an unprotected field (UNPROT), or is prevented from entering data into a protected field (PROT). The BMS map or program can determine the intensity at which a map field will display: BRT, NORM or DRK. A field can be received as alphanumeric data (left-justified, padded with spaces) or numeric (NUM) data (right-justified, padded with zeroes). The cursor can be set by specifying IC in the BMS map or through program symbolic cursor positioning. Specifying FSET for a field in the BMS or symbolic map will turn on its MDT when the map is sent. Symbolic map attributes override BMS map attributes. The terminal operator turns on the MDT when a map field is keyed into. Including FRSET in the CTRL operand of the BMS map's DFHMSD macro causes all MDTs to be turned off before a map is sent. The combination of all the above considerations causes the best of programmers much grief.

Standard Attribute Characters

CICS has available a list of standard attribute characters in the form of a copy book called DFHBMSCA. The standard attribute control list is a set of standard control characters used by CICS, which can be copied into a program. Many data processing departments create their own list of the more commonly used attribute characters, assigning more meaningful labels.

```
01  DFHBMSCA  COPY  DFHBMSCA.
    02  DFHBMPEM      PIC X    VALUE ' '.
    02  DFHBMPNL      PIC X    VALUE ' '.
    02  DFHBMASK      PIC X    VALUE '0'.
    02  DFHBMUNP      PIC X    VALUE ' '.
    02  DFHBMUNN      PIC X    VALUE '&'.
    02  DFHBMPRO      PIC X    VALUE '-'.
    02  DFHBMBRY      PIC X    VALUE 'H'.
    02  DFHBMDAR      PIC X    VALUE ')'.
    02  DFHBMFSE      PIC X    VALUE 'A'.
    02  DFHBMPRF      PIC X    VALUE '/'.
    02  DFHBMASF      PIC X    VALUE '1'.
    02  DFHBMASB      PIC X    VALUE '8'.
```

DFHBMSCA fields all begin with DFHBM..., and the last three characters are not very descriptive. These fields do not cover many of the attribute configurations required by the application programmer. The programmer may move the attribute character directly to the symbolic map prior to issuing a SEND MAP command. Illustrated below is the alignment of the more commonly used attribute names found in the list above (DFHBMSCA) and in App. B (STWSATTR).

DFHBMSCA	Descriptive	Value
DFHBMASK	ASKIP-NORM	'0'.
DFHBMUNP	UNPROT-NORM	SPACE.
DFHBMUNN	UNPROT-NUM	'&'.
DFHBMBRY	UNPROT-BRT	'H'.
DFHBMFSE	UNPROT-FSET	'A'.
DFHBMASF	ASKIP-FSET	'1'.
DFHBMASB	ASKIP-BRT	'8'.

The application programmer may move any of the equivalent characters, shown above, during execution of an application program, to the symbolic map's attribute field. For example,

```
MOVE DFHBMASB  TO   mapfldA.
MOVE ASKIP-BRT TO      "
MOVE '8'       TO      "
```

This book will use the attribute characters shown in App. B for all program examples. You should be aware of DFHBMSCA characters, since you may encounter them in programs which you have to maintain. I recommend using a list of characters similar to STWSATTR and making it a standard copy library member at your installation.

Changing Map Attributes

Changing the map attributes frequently causes confusion because it is often not understood how physical and symbolic maps interact. Figure 7-1 represents the interaction of the physical and symbolic maps.

Physical Map Strings

Physical maps can be visualized as a string of data consisting of control characters, a data length field, an attribute byte, and a data field. The control characters (CC) direct the positioning of data on the screen. Length (L suffix) fields determine the length of the data to be sent, as specified on the BMS map. The attribute field (A suffix) contains the attribute specified in the BMS map. The data field (D suffix) contains the *initial* value given to a field in the BMS map. If no initial value was specified, then the data field contains low-values and no data is transmitted on a send of only the physical map.

My interpretation of the physical map data string as shown in Fig. 7-1 contains three different prefix characters: C for constant, F for field, and S for stopper field. The circled physical and symbolic map letters and numbers relate to the corresponding items on the screen.

Physical map character prefix. The constant prefix C pertains to BMS map fields which are defined without a DFHMDF macro field name; therefore no symbolic map entry is generated. The screen constant ABC MANUFACTUR-ING COMPANY Ⓑ is defined without a field name in the BMS map; therefore no symbolic map entry is generated. The BMS map would normally define this field with an attribute Ⓐ of ASKIP or ASKIP,BRT, and the program could not change the attribute because no symbolic map field is generated. The constant ADDRESS: Ⓓ and its attribute Ⓒ would follow this same pattern.

Physical map field prefix. The F prefix represents items which were defined in the BMS map with a field name; these fields generate corresponding symbolic map entries. The attribute ① for the constant VENDOR CODE: ② would generally be set to ASKIP in the BMS map and could be turned on to ASKIP,BRT

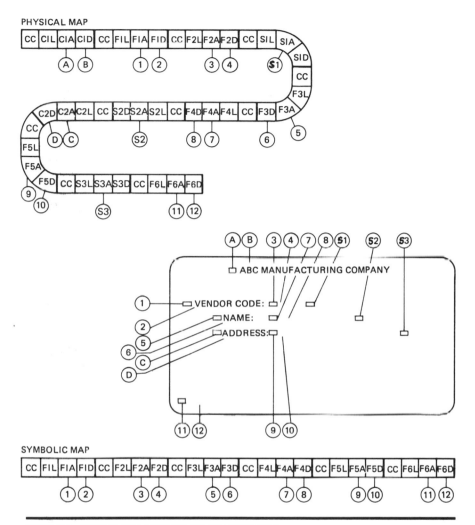

Figure 7-1 Physical Map and Symbolic Map Interaction.

through the symbolic map if the field was not entered correctly. The constant NAME: ⑥ and its attribute ⑤ would be used in a similar fashion. The attribute of a field, which contains a symbolic map entry, can be changed each time a map is sent. The attribute ③ for the data ④ to be keyed in for VENDOR CODE would most likely be UNPROT. Data-entry fields ⑧ and ⑩ would also be likely to have UNPROT attributes. The attributes ③, ⑦, and ⑨ could have some combination of UNPROT, such as UNPROT,BRT, or UNPROT,FSET.

Field ⑫ and its attribute ⑪ define the message field; this field is usually defined in the BMS map with an attribute of ASKIP. Sometimes a program detects an error condition or wants to display an operator-notification message. To highlight the message, the program sends the map with the attribute of the appropriate field in the symbolic map changed to ASKIP,BRT. The BMS map can set an initial value for the message field by defining its attribute as ATTRB=(ASKIP,DRK). When the appropriate program condition is encountered, the program highlights the message field (making it visible) by sending the symbolic map with the message field's attribute changed to ASKIP,BRT. The message can be erased on a subsequent send by changing the attribute back to ASKIP,DRK.

Physical map stopper field prefix. Stopper fields are shown with a prefix of S. Like constants, they are usually defined without a BMS map field name. The primary purpose of stopper fields is to limit the size of the preceding UNPROT data-entry field. Stopper fields (S1), (S2), and (S3) serve this purpose; they are defined in the physical map with attributes of ASKIP or PROT.

Physical Map Interaction with Symbolic Map

Figure 7-1 shows the symbolic map as a data string in which its F prefix has a one-to-one correspondence with the physical map fields. This is to be expected since these are the items which were defined with field names on the BMS map. It is important to understand how the three types of SEND MAP commands handle attributes and data fields.

SEND ONLY physical map. The SEND MAP MAPONLY command erases the screen before the send and transmits the constants and attributes defined in the BMS map to the screen. The symbolic map is never used with a MAPONLY send, therefore no variable data is transmitted. This book will refer to input data and attributes as being received from the screen and to symbolic map output data and attributes as being sent to the screen.

SEND both physical and symbolic maps. The SEND MAP AND DATA command erases the screen before sending the combined physical and symbolic maps. Visualize the physical map in Fig. 7-1 as initially being sent to the screen, then as being overlaid by corresponding attribute and data fields from the symbolic map. Remember, if the symbolic map contains low-values in any attribute or data field, then no transmission will take place for those items. On a SEND MAP AND DATA command, the physical map BMS-defined attribute will take effect if the symbolic map attribute contains low-values. When the symbolic map contains a significant attribute, it will override the physical map attribute.

SEND ONLY Symbolic Map. The SEND MAP DATAONLY command does not normally erase the screen before sending only the symbolic map. Prior to this send, one of the other two SEND MAP commands would have been executed. The prior send would have formatted the screen with constants from the BMS map and with attributes from the BMS map and/or symbolic map. The SEND

MAP AND DATA command could have sent data from the symbolic map. Once again, visualize the existing data and attributes on the screen as being overlaid by the symbolic map's data and attributes.

Manipulating MDTs

An ON MDT, which is part of the attribute byte, causes data on the screen to be returned to the program when a map is received. MDTs can be turned on by

1. Specifying FSET as part of the attribute on the BMS map, then issuing a send which includes the physical map. Do not overlay the BMS map's attribute with the symbolic map's attribute on a send of map and data. Symbolic map attributes equal to low-values will *not* overlay the BMS attributes. For example,

```
ATTRB=(ASKIP,FSET),
```

2. Moving a standard attribute which contains FSET to the symbolic map's attribute before issuing a send which includes the symbolic map, such as

```
MOVE UNPROT-FSET TO mapfldA
```

3. Keying data into an UNPROT field on the screen. Entering data into a field always turns its MDT on.

FRSET

Specifying FRSET in the BMS map (or on the SEND MAP command) will cause all MDTs on the screen to be turned off prior to sending a map. This will require the physical map field attribute or the symbolic override to control the MDT status of an attribute. An operator could key data into a field, turning on its MDT. A receive of the map and a subsequent send of the map would turn the MDT off if CTRL=FRSET was specified in the DFHMSD macro of the BMS map. If CTRL=FRSET was not specified, the MDTs would remain on.

Confusion often results when data appearing on the screen is not received into the program because its MDT is not turned on. I recommend specifying the appropriate attributes in the BMS map and in the symbolic map so that they will be properly set prior to a send. For instance, if the terminal operator enters data into a field, the MDT will be turned on. Let's suppose that the program, when it receives the map, detects an error on a different field and resends the map with an error message. The MDTs of all fields are turned off prior to the

| SEND MAP Options | Type of Map Sent | | **** Attribute Sent to Screen **** | | |
| | Symbolic | Physical | Physical Map Only | Symbolic Map Attribute Field Contains | |
				Attribute	Low Values
MAP and Data	S	P		SYM	BMS
MAPONLY		P	BMS		
DATAONLY	S			SYM	Screen

Figure 7-2   Attribute Usage Summary.

send because FRSET was specified. Correctly entered fields will not be received into the program on a subsequent receive map, even though they appear on the screen, because their MDTs have been turned off. The programmer can ensure that required fields will be returned by moving the UNPROT,FSET attribute to the appropriate symbolic map field before issuing the send. Once a field has been keyed in and verified, you may not want the operator to be allowed to change it, but it must be returned to the program on a subsequent receive. Including the attributes ASKIP,FSET in the symbolic map prior to issuing a send will ensure that the field will be returned to the program on a subsequent receive. With practice, the use of attributes and the manner in which FRSET works should become clear.

Attribute Usage Summary

Figure 7-2 and the following outlines summarize the more common attribute considerations. Control of attribute fields depends upon the type of SEND MAP command:

1. MAP AND DATA (specify ERASE)

   a. Symbolic map attributes will override the physical map attributes defined by the BMS map.

   b. Low-values in an attribute field will cause the BMS map attribute to be sent to the screen.

2. MAPONLY (specify ERASE)

   The BMS-map-defined attributes will be sent to the screen.

3. DATAONLY (omit ERASE)

   a. Attributes in the symbolic map will override existing screen attributes.

   b. Low-values in an attribute field will not change the existing attributes on the screen.

MDTs can be turned on in an attribute field by

1. The BMS map FSET parameter

2. The terminal operator's keying data into a field

3. Moving a program-defined FSET-containing attribute to a field before a send which includes the symbolic map.

Specifying FRSET in CTRL=(FREEKB,FRSET) of the BMS map DFHMSD macro turns off the attribute MDTs of all fields on the screen prior to the send of the map to the screen.

RECEIVE MAP Considerations

The RECEIVE MAP command, as presented earlier in the chapter, is easy to understand and use. However, there are additional considerations when a map is received.

1. The length of the data keyed into a map field will be received as the result of executing a RECEIVE MAP command.

2. A MAPFAIL condition will occur if no data is received from the map; if this condition is not properly handled, a program ABEND will occur.

3. The AID key pressed by the terminal operator can be tested and acted upon in several different ways.

Length Field on Map Receive

When a map is received, the symbolic map length field can be tested for two conditions:

1. If data were entered into a field

2. If the required number of characters were entered

Length field indicative of data entry. Many programs test if the symbolic map length field is greater than zero. A positive value is an indication that the terminal operator entered data into the field. For example,

```
IF mapfldL    IS GREATER THAN    ZERO
   MOVE mapfldI    TO    WS-INPUT-DATA.
```

Here, mapfldL represents a map length field and mapfldI an input field.

Monitoring number of characters entered. Sometimes a program must know the exact number of characters keyed in, for example, when a field requires a specific number of characters or digits.

MAPFAIL Conditions

A MAPFAIL, indicating that no characters were passed from the screen on a RECEIVE MAP command, occurs when

1. The CLEAR key is pressed.
2. PA1, PA2, or PA3 is pressed.
3. Any other AID key is pressed without data having been entered on the screen, and no map fields had been FSET.

MAPFAIL, which can cause a program ABEND if not provided for, can be controlled by

1. Issuing an IGNORE CONDITION MAPFAIL command before the receive. This command states that if a MAPFAIL occurs on a receive of a map, ignore the condition and continue processing. For example,

```
EXEC CICS IGNORE CONDITION
          MAPFAIL
     END-EXEC.
```

2. Issuing a HANDLE CONDITION MAPFAIL before the receive. For example,

```
EXEC CICS HANDLE CONDITION
          MAPFAIL (C100-MAPFAIL)
     END-EXEC.
```

This HANDLE CONDITION command directs that if a MAPFAIL occurs, then control is to be transferred to paragraph C100-MAPFAIL.

3. Coding a 1-byte BMS map field with an attribute of ASKIP,DRK,FSET so that at least 1 byte of data is always returned on a receive. If you specify FRSET in the BMS map, the MDTs are turned off before a SEND MAP command. If this method is employed, it is best to standardize the byte location on the screen at a position not likely to be used.
4. Executing the HANDLE AID command, discussed later in this chapter, in order to direct control to the proper routines if the CLEAR or PA key is pressed. PA keys can be handled by the ANYKEY option.
5. Testing data-entry AID keys (see below) in order to direct control to the proper routines if the CLEAR or a PA key is pressed.

It seems more logical to send a message to the terminal operator indicating that no data was keyed in (when data is required) than it is to send a message indicating that an invalid entry was made. There are situations when a receive without data having been entered is valid: for example, pressing a PF key to end an inquiry and return to a control screen. MAPFAIL sounds complicated, but it is easy to control in your program; examples which follow should help to clarify the required techniques.

Testing Data-Entry AID Keys

When the terminal operator presses an AID key, an indicator is stored in the EIB field EIBAID. The AID fields in DFHAID (see App. A-3) can be copied into working storage. They are compared against EIBAID to determine which AID key was pressed in order to determine the flow of program logic.

Valid AID keys are ENTER; CLEAR; PF1 through PF24; PA1, PA2, and PA3; and ANYKEY. DFHAID fields are DFHENTER, DFHCLEAR; DFHPF1 through DFHPF24; and DFHPA1, DFHPA2, and DFHPA3.

Options for testing EIBAID.   EIBAID can be tested in three ways:

1. Compare EIBAID against one of the DFHAID fields. For instance, to test if the AID key PF1 was pressed, code

```
IF EIBAID = DFHPF1
```

2. Execute a HANDLE AID command; for example

```
EXEC CICS HANDLE AID
    PF1 (C100-EXIT)
```

3. Test EIBAID against its actual value (see App. A-3); for example,

```
IF EIBAID = 1
```

Testing EIBAID fields against DFHAID fields.   Unlike the CICS-supplied list of standard attributes, the DFHAID fields are often used in application programs. Copy DFHAID (which is supplied with CICS) into the working-storage section of your program.

```
0001 C100-RECEIVE-CONTROL-MAP  SECTION.
0002*
0003     MOVE LOW-VALUES  TO   VM-CONTROL-MAP.
0004*
0005     IF EIBAID  =  DFHENTER    OR
0006                   DFHPF1      OR
0007                   DFHPF2      OR
0008                   DFHPF3      OR
0009                   DFHPF4
0010          MOVE 'F' TO  STATUS-OF-RECEIVE
0011*
0012          EXEC CICS HANDLE CONDITION
0013                    MAPFAIL (C100-EXIT)
0014          END-EXEC
0015*
0016          EXEC CICS RECEIVE
0017                    MAP    ('MAPPOVC')
0018                    MAPSET ('POVMNT1')
0019                    INTO   (VM-CONTROL-MAP)
0020          END-EXEC
0021*
0022          MOVE 'G' TO  STATUS-OF-RECEIVE
0023     ELSE
0024          IF EIBAID  =  DFHCLEAR
0025             PERFORM C110-END-SESSION
0026          ELSE
0027          IF EIBAID  =  DFHPF5
0028             PERFORM C120-TRANSFER-XCTL-TO-MENU
0029          ELSE
0030             MOVE 'I'      TO  STATUS-OF-RECEIVE
0031             MOVE 'INVALID KEY PRESSED - PLEASE TRY AGAIN'
0032                           TO  MVC-D-MESSAGE
0033             MOVE ASKIP-BRT TO  MVC-A-MESSAGE.
0034*
0035 C100-EXIT.
0036     EXIT.
```

Figure 7-3   Illustration of EIBAID Usage.

Any AID key pressed by the terminal operator can be tested and acted upon as soon as the program is entered. These checks can be made at the beginning of the main line of a program, before or after a receive, or almost any place in the program. For ease of maintenance, I recommend being consistent regarding where you check EIBAID against DFHAID fields. I prefer to keep these checks in the RECEIVE MAP section of my program whenever possible.

EIBAID remains unchanged throughout a program and a task until another AID key is pressed. It can be tested and used as a switch throughout the program or task. An AID key pressed prior to a receive in one program can be tested by another program in the same task [i.e., a program XCTLed or linked to (see Chap. 8, "Program Control")].

Figure 7-3 illustrates typical usage of DFHAID fields. AID keys for ENTER, PF1, PF2, PF3, and PF4 are valid data-entry keys in this example. The program will receive the map and continue processing if any of the keys are pressed. Prior to the receive, an F is moved to STATUS-OF-RECEIVE, indicating a MAPFAIL condition. If a MAPFAIL does *not* occur on the receive, a G is moved to STATUS-OF-RECEIVE after the receive is completed. STATUS-OF-RECEIVE can be tested by the routine which performed C100-RECEIVE-CONTROL-MAP.

Other valid AID keys which could have been pressed are CLEAR and PF5. All other keys would cause an I to be moved to STATUS-OF-RECEIVE and an INVALID KEY PRESSED message to be moved to the map message field.

HANDLE AID command. The HANDLE AID command is similar to the HANDLE CONDITION command discussed in Chap. 5 in format and in transfer of control. HANDLE AID is invoked upon the receive of a map. If you use this technique, I recommend placing the command in your RECEIVE MAP program section. Its basic format is

```
EXEC CICS HANDLE AID
              AID KEY    (program-paragraph)
                  .
                  .
                  .
    END-EXEC.
```

HANDLE AID considerations. The applications programmer must be aware of the following when writing a program:

1. Up to 12 AID keys can be specified on one command. Use two or more commands if required.
2. The last AID command encountered takes precedence and overrides AID keys which were specified in prior commands.
3. ANYKEY should be included to cover any key not specifically mentioned.
4. A specified AID key will override ANYKEY.
5. If ENTER is not specified in the HANDLE AID command, control will pass to the statement which follows the RECEIVE MAP command. ENTER is not included in ANYKEY.
6. AID keys listed in a HANDLE AID command without a paragraph name will fall through to the statement following a RECEIVE MAP command.
7. HANDLE AID commands take precedence over commands such as HANDLE CONDITION MAPFAIL.

HANDLE AID illustration. Figure 7-4 illustrates the use of the HANDLE AID command; it performs the same functions as the example in Fig. 7-3. AID keys ENTER, PF1, PF2, PF3, and PF4 are valid data-entry keys. Unless there is a MAPFAIL on the receive, the program will fall through to the statement following the receive. Pressing the CLEAR key always causes a MAPFAIL to occur, but since HANDLE AID takes precedence over HANDLE CONDITION, MAPFAIL will be overridden by the transfer of control to C100-END-OF-SESSION. A MAPFAIL would direct control to C100-MAPFAIL.

```
0001 C100-RECEIVE-CONTROL-MAP  SECTION.
0002*
0003      MOVE LOW-VALUES  TO  VM-CONTROL-MAP.
0004*
0005      EXEC CICS HANDLE AID
0006               PF1
0007               PF2
0008               PF3
0009               PF4
0010               PF5   (C100-RETURN-TO-MENU)
0011               CLEAR (C100-END-OF-SESSION)
0012               ANYKEY (C100-INVALID-KEY)
0013      END-EXEC.
0014*
0015      EXEC CICS HANDLE CONDITION
0016               MAPFAIL (C100-MAPFAIL)
0017      END-EXEC.
0018*
0019      EXEC CICS RECEIVE
0020               MAP    ('MAPPOVC')
0021               MAPSET ('POVMNT1')
0022               INTO   (VM-CONTROL-MAP)
0023      END-EXEC.
0024*
0025      MOVE 'G'  TO  STATUS-OF-RECEIVE.
0026*
0027* WILL REACH THIS POINT IF PF1, PF2, PF3, PF4 OR ENTER KEY PRESSED
0028*      AND DATA WAS ENTERED - OTHERWISE A MAPFAIL OCCURS
0029* PF5, CLEAR AND OTHER KEYS PASS CONTROL TO INDICATED PARAGRAPHS
0030*
0031      GO TO  C100-EXIT.
0032*
0033 C100-RETURN-TO-MENU.
0034*
0035      PERFORM C120-TRANSFER-XCTL-TO-MENU.
0036*
0037* PRECEDING PERFORM DOES NOT RETURN - IT TRANSFERS CONTROL TO MENU
0038*
0039 C100-END-SESSION.
0040*
0041      PERFORM C110-END-SESSION.
0042*
0043* PRECEDING PERFORM DOES NOT RETURN - CONTROL IS RETURNED TO CICS
0044*
0045 C100-INVALID-KEY.
0046      MOVE 'I'      TO  STATUS-OF-RECEIVE.
0047      MOVE 'INVALID KEY PRESSED - PLEASE TRY AGAIN'
0048               TO  MVC-D-MESSAGE.
0049      MOVE ASKIP-BRT  TO  MVC-A-MESSAGE.
0050      GO TO  C100-EXIT.
0051*
0052 C100-MAPFAIL.
0053      MOVE 'F'  TO  STATUS-OF-RECEIVE.
0054*
0055 C100-EXIT.
0056      EXIT.
```

Figure 7-4 Illustration of HANDLE AID Command.

PF5 is the only other valid AID key; it would override a MAPFAIL and transfer control to C100-RETURN TO MENU. For any unspecified AID key, except ENTER, ANYKEY will direct control to C100-INVALID-KEY.

Testing EIBAID against its value.   Testing EIBAID against its actual value would be handled in an identical fashion to comparing EIBAID against DFHAID fields. The only difference would be that instead of using DFHAID fields, the actual value would be used (see Fig. 7-3 for similarities).

```
IF EIBAID = QUOTE      OR
                1      OR
                2      OR
                3      OR
                4
   MOVE 'F'    TO      STATUS-OF-RECEIVE
```

SUMMARY

This chapter is the key to understanding CICS; once you master the concepts presented, CICS will be easy. Three types of SEND MAP commands were covered: SEND MAP AND DATA, SEND MAP MAPONLY, and SEND MAP DATAONLY. Symbolic cursor positioning, a technique for positioning the cursor at any field on a map, was discussed. The reasons for moving low-values to a symbolic map were explained, and the RECEIVE MAP command was introduced.

Map attributes were thoroughly explained. It was shown how you could set up a standard attribute list in your source library and how to use this list to interactively change map attributes. An illustration showed how the physical and symbolic maps interact to display data and constants and to modify map attributes. A chart was presented showing the interaction between the physical and symbolic maps and the effect of this interaction on map attributes.

MDT manipulation was discussed. It was shown how the return of data to a program occurs. The effect of FRSET on MDTs was also explained.

Considerations for the receive of a map were detailed. The functions of the AID keys, map length, and MAPFAIL were explained. Examples were presented showing two program methods for handling program AID keys: comparing EIBAID against DFHAID fields and using the HANDLE AID command.

I cannot emphasize the importance of this chapter strongly enough. Reread it now *and* again when you finish the book and are ready to start using some of the concepts you have learned.

8

PROGRAM CONTROL

Program-control commands facilitate returning control to the CICS system; passing control from one program to another; and loading and releasing programs, tables, and maps to or from main storage. An understanding of program logical levels is required in order to follow the flow of program control. A communications area is used to pass data from one program to another when using program-control commands. These commands include

1. RETURN—Return control to CICS or to an invoking program (see "LINK" below).
2. XCTL—Transfer control to another program without returning. This is conceptually similar to a GO TO statement in a Cobol program.
3. LINK—Pass control to another program which returns control to the invoking program, after performing its logic. This command is similar in concept to a PERFORM command in a Cobol program.
4. LOAD—Access and load a table, program, or map into main storage.
5. RELEASE—When a table, program, or map is no longer required, this command releases it from main storage.

Program Logical Levels

Programs of the type presented in Chap. 5 are basically started by keying in a TRANSID and pressing an AID key. CICS, which is shown at level 0 in Fig. 8-1, then passes control to the program associated with the TRANSID. A program initiated by CICS is considered to be at the highest logical level, level 1. (A program's logical level refers to its executing sequence relative to the CICS system, which is by definition at level zero.) When a

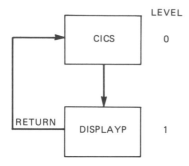

Figure 8-1 Single Program Logical Levels.

RETURN command is issued in the level 1 program, control is returned to CICS.

Transactions such as those represented in Fig. 8-1 are not as common as systems of programs which communicate with one another. Menu programs are commonly started by a TRANSID. The menu program then transfers control (XCTL) to another program at the same logical level as itself. The program transferred to can either end the session by returning to CICS or can transfer control back to the menu program. The menu program can then either return to CICS or transfer control to another program.

Programs at level 1 can always return to CICS. A program can transfer control to any program at the same level, including a program which has directly or indirectly transferred control to itself. Figure 8-2 shows this interaction.

Often a menu program will transfer control to a submenu at the same logical level. POVMAINT, a submenu program, will transfer control to individual inquiry, maintenance, and browse functions. A program to which control is transferred is always at the same logical level as the transferring program. Figure 8-3 illustrates how POMENUPM at level 1 can transfer control to three programs: POVMAINT, POMAINTN, and POENTRY1. POVMAINT

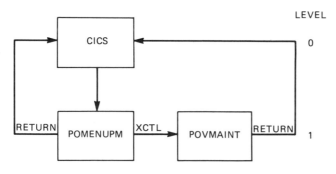

Figure 8-2 Menu Program Logical Levels.

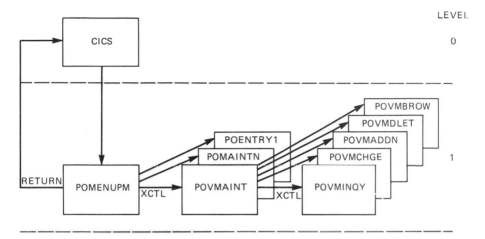

Figure 8-3   Multimenu Logical Levels—All are XCTLed to.

is shown transferring control to one of five programs, all at the same logical level. Any program shown in Fig. 8-3 at logical level 1 can return control to CICS. Each program at level 1 could be written so that it could transfer control to any other program shown at the same level. By definition, an XCTLed-to program is at the same logical level as the invoking program.

Normally an XCTLed-to program is not intended to immediately transfer control back to the invoking program. XCTL can be considered an absolute transfer of control to another program, with an option to return. Often system development requires an unconditional return from a program to which control has been passed. A change program, prior to changing a record, might write a before-journal record, and, following the change, write an after-journal record. A common program is often employed to handle such postings; our system calls this program JRNLPOST. Figure 8-4 shows how a linked program would appear at a lower logical level than the linking program.

POMENUPM is initiated by keying in the TRANSID POMU. Vendor file maintenance is selected and POMENUPM XCTLs to POVMAINT. POV-MAINT displays its submenu and the change function is selected, resulting in an XCTL to POVMCHGE. POMENUPM, POVMAINT, and POVMCHGE are all at the same logical level, level 1. The change program, POVMCHGE, needs to record the before-and-after image of all changes. This type of logic is commonly handled by a linked program. A linked program, JRNLPOST level 2, is always at a lower logical level than the invoking program, POVMCHGE level 1. When a RETURN command is issued in the linked program, control is passed back to the invoking program at the next sequential instruction following the LINK command.

The logical level structure shown in Fig. 8-4 is generally sufficient to handle most design and programming situations you will encounter. Keep your logical level structure design simple and modular; it will make maintenance easier.

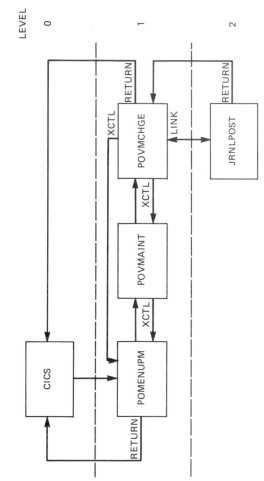

Figure 8-4 Logical Levels with LINKed-to Program.

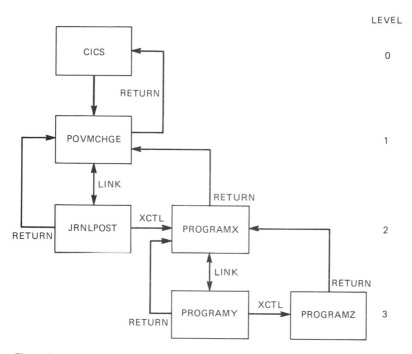

Figure 8-5   Extended Logical Level Structure.

Occasionally, a situation may arise which requires a more complicated logical level structure. Keep in mind that if a program links to another program, the linked program is always at a lower logical level. A RETURN command issued in any program at the next lower level always returns to the linking program at the next higher logical level.

Figure 8-5 illustrates how an extended logical level structure would function. POVMGHGE could be initiated by entering the TRANSID POVC. POVM-CHGE then links to JRNLPOST. After the link to JRNLPOST, several paths could be followed:

1. JRNLPOST could issue a RETURN command, which would pass control up to the next higher logical level, back to POVMCHGE.

2. JRNLPOST might XCTL to PROGRAMX. If PROGRAMX issues a RE-TURN command, control is passed up to the next higher logical level, program POVMCHGE.

3. PROGRAMX could link to PROGRAMY, which could return to PRO-GRAMX or XCTL to PROGRAMZ. A RETURN command issued in PRO-GRAMZ would pass control up to PROGRAMX. When PROGRAMX issues a RETURN command, control is passed up to the next higher logical level, to POVMCHGE.

Task Number Considerations

Each time a new transaction is initiated, a task number is assigned to the task. The task number assigned is stored in the EIB field EIBTASKN. The task number remains unchanged until a RETURN command is issued at the highest logical level, level 1.

Communications Area

A communications area (COMMAREA) is a field in working storage used for passing data from one program to another. The COMMAREA can have its length defined in working storage as a halfword binary value, thus limiting the size of COMMAREA to a maximum size of 32,768 bytes. This is not a problem, since data passed in a COMMAREA is generally small in size, often less than 100 bytes. When COMMAREA is passed to another program, the receiving program retrieves the passed data in a linkage-section field called DFHCOMMAREA.

COMMAREA can be passed between programs by using the RETURN, XCTL, and LINK commands. The COMMAREA is specified for the above commands as follows:

```
EXEC CICS . . .
            [PROGRAM   (WS-PROGRAM-NAME)]
            [TRANSID   (TRID)]
            COMMAREA (WS-COMMAREA)
            LENGTH    (WS-CA-LENGTH)       or LENGTH (15)
END-EXEC.
```

- WS-PROGRAM-NAME—The name of a linked or XCTLed-to program. Program name would not be included on a RETURN. WS-PROGRAM-NAME, or your label, could be defined in working storage as PIC X (8), or it could be hard-coded as PROGRAM ('POVMCHGE').

- TRID—The TRANSID of the next transaction to be initiated at a terminal. It is only specified on a RETURN command with a TRANSID, discussed later in this chapter.

- WS-COMMAREA—This is a data field in working storage (you can refer to this communications area by any appropriate name).

- WS-CA-LENGTH (or your label)—If this option is used, it must be defined in working storage as a halfword binary value. I prefer to include the actual length in the LENGTH option, i.e., LENGTH (15).

The program to which control is passed receives the data transferred in a linkage-section field called DFHCOMMAREA. DFHCOMMAREA should, whenever possible, be the same length as the passed data. Sometimes data of various types and lengths is passed to a program. *Avoid this if possible*: the results are unpredictable if DFHCOMMAREA is defined as being longer than the passed data *and* if your program accesses DFHCOMMAREA fields which have not been passed. You will minimize problems if the passed COMMAREA length is equal to the length of DFHCOMMAREA in the linkage section of the invoked program.

The invoked program can access passed data directly in the subfields of DFHCOMMAREA or move DFHCOMMAREA to a working-storage field. A program can determine if data has been passed to it by testing an EIB field called EIBCALEN. EIBCALEN contains the length of the COMMAREA passed by the initiating program.

EIBCALEN, the COMMAREA length, is often referred to as a *first-time switch*. A program initiated by entering a TRANSID, or one which is invoked by another program without a COMMAREA being passed to it, will have an EIBCALEN equal to 0. Subsequent entries into the program can return with a COMMAREA of length 1; COMMAREA is not required to contain any significant data. This is done so that EIBCALEN will equal the length of the COMMAREA or 1, and not 0, as it does upon initial entry. Statements similar to the following are commonly found in the main line of CICS programs:

```
IF EIBCALEN = ZERO
      PERFORM (FIRST-TIME-PROCESSING)
ELSE
      MOVE DFHCOMMAREA TO WS-COMMAREA
      PERFORM (SECOND-TIME-PROCESSING).
```

COMMAREA is sometimes used as a first-time switch or to direct the flow of program logic in pseudoconversational programs. Often a value will be moved to a WS-COMMAREA subfield; I call this field CA-SWITCH, before issuing a return to a program. The subfield will be tested upon a subsequent reentry into the program in order to determine program flow. For example,

```
IF EIBCALEN = 0
      PERFORM (FIRST-TIME-PROCESSING)
ELSE
      MOVE DFHCOMMAREA TO WS-COMMAREA
      IF CA-SWITCH = 2
            PERFORM (SECOND-TIME-PROCESSING)
      ELSE
      IF CA-SWITCH = 3
            PERFORM (THIRD-TIME-PROCESSING)
      ELSE
      IF CA-SWITCH = 4
            .
            .
            .
```

Some of these techniques will be employed in program examples in future chapters. As you work with the COMMAREA concept, you will find that it is easy to understand and master.

RETURN Command

The RETURN command, as used in the programs in Chap. 5, returned control to CICS and terminated a transaction. Most CICS systems and programs are not that simple. A program is usually initiated by a TRANSID, XCTL, or LINK command. The initiated program often sends a map upon which the terminal operator enters data. The program then executes a return to itself in order to receive and process the map's data. If invalid data has been entered, the program sends an error message, allows the terminal operator to correct the data, and issues a return to itself.

The format of the RETURN command used in previous examples to return to CICS was

```
EXEC CICS RETURN
END-EXEC.
```

This format, when issued at the highest logical level, will always terminate a task and return control to CICS. It is also the format executed at a lower logical level to return control to an invoking program which had issued a LINK command.

Return with a TRANSID

The format of the RETURN command as used in pseudoconversational programming is

```
EXEC CICS RETURN
        TRANSID    ('TRAN')
        COMMAREA (WS-COMMAREA)
        LENGTH     (WS-CA-LENGTH)
END-EXEC.
```

This format can only be issued in a program returning to CICS from the highest logical level, level 1. Using this format in a lower-logical-level program will result in the INVREQ (INValid REQuest) handle condition being invoked. Never use this option in a linked program or in programs at or below the logical level of the linked program.

This format of the RETURN command returns control back to CICS and ends the task. The program associated with the TRANSID in the RETURN command is initiated when an AID key is pressed. It is the RETURN command used to set a first-time switch. A return is issued with a one-character WS-COMMAREA and a length of 1. EIBCALEN will equal 1 when an AID key is pressed to initiate the program again. The first time the program was initiated, EIBCALEN should have been equal to 0 in order to use EIBCALEN as a first-time switch.

COMMAREA can be used to return a variety of switches and/or data to a program. A program may send a map, receive the map, and store data from the map or program in COMMAREA. When this format of the RETURN command is executed and the program is reentered, DFHCOMMAREA will contain the data returned in COMMAREA.

Transactions which are accessed frequently may use COMMAREA to store "valid" map data. If errors occur which necessitate the resend and receive of the map, the valid data saved in COMMAREA need not be retransmitted to or from the map. This is an advanced technique which will not be covered in this book.

A RETURN command with a TRANSID can be used to initiate a new program associated with the TRANSID which differs from the one which issued the return. You could design a system so that one program would send a map, then issue a return with a TRANSID in order to initiate a different program. The new program could receive and process the map and, when finished, either return with a TRANSID, which will initiate the send program again, or end the session. This technique has the advantage of using less main storage because it is more modular. I do not, however, recommend this technique because I find systems using this method more difficult to maintain. It is more logical to send and receive a map in the same program.

XCTL Command

The XCTL command is used to pass control to a program at the same logical level. Transfer is made by releasing the current program and loading the new program into main storage. Programs can be written to transfer control to another program and have the new program in turn transfer control back to the original program. This type of processing is common when a menu program transfers control to a selected program. The new program processes in the pseudoconversational mode and, when finished, transfers control back to the menu.

The format of the XCTL command is

```
EXEC CICS XCTL
          PROGRAM    (WS-PROGRAM-NAME)
          [COMMAREA (WS-COMMAREA)]
          [LENGTH     (WS-CA-LENGTH)]
    END-EXEC.
```

An XCTL command can be executed with or without COMMAREA and length being specified:

1. A program invoked without COMMAREA and LENGTH being specified on an XCTL command is similar in its initial entry to that of a program which is started by entering a TRANSID, in that EIBCALEN will equal zero.

2. If COMMAREA and LENGTH are specified on the XCTL command, EIBCALEN of the new program will be equal to the length of the COMMAREA passed to it. DFHCOMMAREA in the new program will contain the data passed from the COMMAREA of the initiating program.

The program initiated by the XCTL command can have data of varying lengths passed to it from the COMMAREA of different programs. Try to avoid this in your system design; when possible, keep the passing program's COMM-AREA the same length as the invoked program's DFHCOMMAREA. If your program attempts to access data in the linkage-section field DFHCOMMAREA which is longer than the length of the COMMAREA passed, the results are unpredictable.

The handle condition PGMIDERR (ProGraM IDentification ERRor) will occur if the XCTLed-to program is not in the PPT or if it has been disabled. I generally do not check for this condition; it should not normally occur.

LINK Command

The LINK command is similar in format to the XCTL command; however, its function is much different. A LINK command passes control to a program at a lower logical level, with the intent of returning. A RETURN command issued in a program at the next lower logical level will return to the next sequential instruction in the invoking program, immediately following the LINK command. Linking to a program is costly in terms of computer system resources which are tied up. A LINK command holds the linking program in main storage as well as the linked-to program. Figure 8-5 shows how a link could require several programs to be in main storage simultaneously. Avoid using the LINK command unless absolutely necessary because it requires more main storage and results in slower response time.

The format of the LINK command is

```
EXEC CICS LINK
        PROGRAM    (WS-PROGRAM-NAME)
        [COMMAREA (WS-COMMAREA)]
        [LENGTH    (WS-CA-LENGTH)]
END-EXEC.
```

A program which links to another program generally passes a COMM-AREA to the invoked program. There are other methods of passing data.

Actually, the address of WS-COMMAREA in the issuing program is passed to the linked program. The data passed in COMMAREA is accessed under DFHCOMMAREA in the invoked program. Any data changes made under DFHCOMMAREA in the linked program will be available under WS-COMMAREA when control is returned to the invoking program (refer to Fig. 8-5 for the following). If POVMCHGE passed a COMMAREA to JRNL-POST via a LINK command, DFHCOMMAREA in JRNLPOST would in effect point to the same address and data as WS-COMMAREA in the invoking program POVMCHGE. If JRNLPOST with COMMAREA (DFH-COMMAREA) XCTLed to PROGRAMX, DFHCOMMAREA in PROGRAMX would point to the same WS-COMMAREA in POVMCHGE. Any changes made under DFHCOMMAREA in PROGRAMX would be reflected under WS-COMMAREA in POVMCHGE, when PROGRAMX issued a RETURN command to POVMCHGE. If JRNLPOST XCTLed to PROGRAMX with COMMAREA (WS-NEW-COMMAREA), only changes made by JRNLPOST would be reflected in WS-COMMAREA of POVMCHGE when PROGRAMX issued a RETURN command. An additional new copy of COMMAREA, containing the data passed from WS-NEW-COMMAREA, would be created, and this new copy of COMMAREA would be received in DFHCOMMAREA of PROGRAMX.

When a program which has issued a LINK command is returned to, then working storage, all handle aids, handle conditions, etc., except possibly, COMMAREA, are restored to their status prior to the issue of the LINK command.

The handle condition PGMIDERR will occur if the linked-to program is not in the PPT or if it has been disabled. I generally do not check for this condition; it should not normally occur.

LOAD Command

The LOAD command is used to access and load a table, map, or program into main storage. It can be used to load program tables such as a state code table, a sales force table, or a cost table into main storage. The table accessed is addressed through a linkage-section pointer called base locator for linkage or BLL cells. The format of the LOAD command is

```
EXEC CICS LOAD
          PROGRAM (name)
          SET       (BLL-pointer)
          HOLD
END-EXEC.
```

- name—Name of the table, map, or program which is to be loaded into main storage.

- BLL-pointer—Pointer which is set to the address of the loaded program.

• HOLD—Indicates that the program is to be held in main storage, even after the task is terminated. The program will be deleted from main storage only when a RELEASE command is executed in the current or in a future task.

Chapter 10 will illustrate the load of a highly used table which is defined in the PPT as a main-storage resident table. The use of BLL-pointers for setting addressability to a table will be demonstrated.

The handle condition PGMIDERR will occur if the program to be loaded is not in the PPT or if it has been disabled. I generally do not check for this condition; it should not normally occur.

RELEASE Command

This command is issued in order to release a table, program, or map from main storage. A RELEASE command should be issued in order to free main storage as soon as the program loaded is no longer required. The format of the RELEASE command is

```
        EXEC CICS RELEASE
                    PROGRAM (name)
        END-EXEC.
```

[(name) is the name of the table, map, or program which is to be released from main storage.]

This command must be executed in order to release programs which are loaded with the HOLD option. The program loaded will be automatically released when the task is completed if hold was not specified on the LOAD command. Load tables as close as possible to their point of use; then release them as soon as they are no longer required.

The handle condition PGMIDERR can occur if the program to be released is not in the PPT or if it has been disabled. I generally do not check for this condition; it should not normally occur.

SUMMARY

An understanding of program-control commands is essential for the design of good systems and the development of efficient programming techniques. Program-control commands aid in the design of programs which communicate with one another. Communication between programs is implemented through a communications area called COMMAREA. COMMAREA passes data to the same or to another program, which receives that data in a linkage-section field called DFHCOMMAREA.

The program-control commands RETURN, XCTL, LINK, LOAD, and RE-LEASE were discussed in detail. Several diagrams were presented to convey the concept of program logical levels. EIBCALEN (COMMAREA length), often referred to as a first-time switch, was discussed, and examples of its use were included.

Program-control commands sound complicated but are reasonably easy to master. Examples in succeeding chapters should clarify their usage.

9

THE MENU PROGRAM

You have learned many important CICS concepts and commands. Practical application programs will help you pull together the theory which you have been reading. The purchase order menu program and the vendor file maintenance menu programs are similar; this chapter discusses the latter. Concepts such as pseudoconversational programming and the communications area are discussed. SEND MAP, RECEIVE MAP, and MAPFAIL commands will be used as well as the program-control commands RETURN, RETURN with a TRANSID, XCTL, and LINK.

The standard attention identifier list (DFHAID) will be used as a comparison with the EIB field EIBAID in order to determine the AID key pressed by the terminal operator. EIB fields as well as translator call fields (DFHEIVAR, see p. 57) will be copied into the linkage and working-storage sections, respectively, for all programs at compile time. COPY statements generated by the translator will accomplish this. EIB fields such as EIBCALEN are used and discussed. DFHEIVAR fields are used by the translator and are not of direct importance to the application programmer.

This chapter lays the foundation for sample programs in succeeding chapters. The explanation of the example presented is more thorough than those in following chapters, which will only detail new commands and concepts as they are encountered.

Most installations have one or more menu programs. Their basic function is to initiate other programs. A terminal operator keys in a TRANSID and presses ENTER to display a menu screen. A selection is keyed in and ENTER is pressed in order to effect the transfer of control to the chosen program.

Often a main menu cannot accommodate all the required functions. This is not the case in the purchase order system; I just want to show how it would be done. A selection of 3 entered on the purchasing system menu (Fig. 2-3) would display the submenu shown by the screen layout in Fig. 6-3.

The vendor file maintenance menu subsystem structure chart was illustrated in Fig. 4-2, and a program structure chart, which is similar for most menu programs, in Fig. 4-3. This program contains an equivalent structure chart in the form of comments at the start of the procedure division. The BMS map was shown in Fig. 6-4 and its BMS-generated symbolic map in Fig. 6-5. The user-friendly symbolic map used by this program was shown in Fig. 6-6.

Vendor File Maintenance Submenu

Figure 9-1 presents the vendor file maintenance menu program. The remarks in your CICS programs should contain sufficient information to enable someone unfamiliar with the program to understand its basic function. Be brief yet thorough; the REMARKS section of a program and a program's comments are among the first references for a maintenance programmer. Include just enough comments to make the intent of the program clear to someone unfamiliar with it. Write all of your programs as if you will have to explain them to your co-workers. All programs should be written with ease of understanding and future change in mind. Write them as if you or your fellow workers will have to make changes in them 6 months from today. You will! I like to include in the remarks the program title, the method of program initiation, and the basic program functions.

I generally start the working-storage section with the program name, i.e., POVMAINT, and if the program

1. Displays a message to end a session, the literal SESSION COMPLETED.
2. Does not end a session, for instance, a linked program—the program name and the literal START OF WS, i.e., JRNLPOST—START OF WS.

I like to end a program's working storage with a literal followed by the program's name (i.e., END WS POVMAINT). These literals often help in program debugging.

Try to be consistent from program to program in your label names. Give them meaningful names. Use your source code library to store working-storage and procedure division code that is used in more than one program. BMS-generated symbolic maps are usually copied into working storage. User-friendly symbolic maps can either be copied or hard-coded in the program's working storage.

Working-Storage Section

It is good practice to keep working storage as small as possible, since each task obtains its own unique copy of this section. Avoid unnecessarily storing literals and messages in this section; instead hard-code them in the procedure division. Fields used in this program and their meaning are as follows:

• WS-CRT-MESSAGE—Contains the literal SESSION COMPLETED, which is displayed when a program at the highest logical level returns to CICS.

Figure 9-1 Vendor File Maintenance Submenu Program.

```
0001 IDENTIFICATION DIVISION.
0002 PROGRAM-ID. POVMAINT.
0003 REMARKS.
0004****************************************************************************
0005*    VENDOR FILE MAINTENANCE SUB MENU - STARTED BY TRANSID 'POVM'    *
0006*         OR BY ANOTHER MENU        PROGRAM FUNCTIONS:               *
0007*         A) SEND MENU SCREEN                                        *
0008*         B) RECEIVE MENU MAP AND DEPENDING ON SELECTION - XCTL TO:  *
0009*            1) INQUIRY        2) CHANGE          3) ADD             *
0010*            4) DELETE         5) BROWSE                             *
0011****************************************************************************
0012 ENVIRONMENT DIVISION.
0013 DATA DIVISION.
0014*
0015 WORKING-STORAGE SECTION.
0016*
0017 01  WS-PROGRAM-FIELDS.
0018     05  FILLER              PIC X(8)     VALUE 'POVMAINT'.
0019     05  WS-CRT-MESSAGE      PIC X(17)    VALUE 'SESSION COMPLETED'.
0020     05  WS-XCTL-PROGRAM     PIC X(8)     VALUE SPACES.
0021     05  WS-COMMAREA         PIC X        VALUE SPACE.
0022*
0023 01  MPM-MENU-MAP.
0024     05  FILLER              PIC X(12).
0025     05  MPM-L-SELECTION     PIC S9(4)    COMP.
0026     05  MPM-A-SELECTION     PIC X.
0027     05  MPM-D-SELECTION     PIC X.
0028     05  MPM-L-MESSAGE       PIC S9(4)    COMP.
0029     05  MPM-A-MESSAGE       PIC X.
0030     05  MPM-D-MESSAGE       PIC X(79).
0031*
0032 01  WS-STATUS-FIELDS    COPY  STWSSTAT.
0033 01  ATTRIBUTE-LIST      COPY  STWSATTR.
0034 01  DFHAID              COPY  DFHAID.
0035*
0036 01  END-OF-WORKING-STORAGE  PIC X(15)  VALUE 'END WS POVMAINT'.
0037*
0038 LINKAGE SECTION.
0039*
0040 01  DFHCOMMAREA         PIC X.
0041*
0042 PROCEDURE DIVISION.
0043****************************************************************************
0044*              PROGRAM STRUCTURE IS:                                 *
0045*                 AA00-MAINLINE                                      *
0046*                    B000-SEND-MAPONLY                               *
0047*                    C000-PROCESSING                                 *
0048*                       C100-RECEIVE-MAP                             *
0049*                          C110-END-SESSION                         *
0050*                       C200-EDIT-MAP-SELECTION                     *
0051*                       C300-TRANSFER-CONTROL                       *
0052*                       C400-SEND-MAP-DATAONLY                      *
0053****************************************************************************
0054 AA00-MAINLINE  SECTION.
0055*
0056     IF EIBCALEN = ZERO
0057         PERFORM B000-SEND-MAPONLY
0058     ELSE
0059         PERFORM C000-PROCESSING.
0060*
0061     EXEC CICS RETURN
0062              TRANSID    ('POVM')
0063              COMMAREA   (WS-COMMAREA)
0064              LENGTH     (1)
0065     END-EXEC.
0066*
0067 B000-SEND-MAPONLY  SECTION.
0068****************************************************************************
0069*              SEND MAPONLY - PHYSICAL MAP                          *
0070*                 PERFORMED FROM:  AA00-MAINLINE                     *
0071*    ONLY PERFORMED ONCE, UPON INITIAL ENTRY WHEN EIBCALEN = 0      *
0072****************************************************************************
0073*
0074     EXEC CICS SEND
0075              MAP     ('MAPPOVM')
0076              MAPSET  ('POVMNT1')
0077              MAPONLY
0078              ERASE
0079     END-EXEC.
```

Figure 9-1 (Continued)

```
0080*
0081 B000-EXIT.
0082     EXIT.
0083*
0084 C000-PROCESSING  SECTION.
0085****************************************************************
0086*                    MAIN PROCESSING MODULE                   *
0087*              PERFORMED FROM:  AA00-MAINLINE                  *
0088*   RECEIVE AND PROCESS SELECTION SCREEN - IF VALID RECEIVE, AND *
0089*      SELECTION - TRANSFER CONTROL TO SELECTED PROGRAM ELSE  *
0090*        SEND MAP MESSAGE DEPENDING ON STATUS:                *
0091*      1) STATUS-OF-RECEIVE    = 'I'  INVALID KEY PRESSED     *
0092*      2) STATUS-OF-RECIEVE    = 'F'  MAPFAIL - NO SELECTION MADE *
0093*      3) STATUS-OF-SELECTION  = 'E'  INVALID SELECTION KEYED-IN  *
0094****************************************************************
0095*
0096     PERFORM C100-RECEIVE-MAP.
0097     IF GOOD-RECEIVE
0098        PERFORM C200-EDIT-MAP-SELECTION
0099        IF VALID-SELECTION
0100           PERFORM C300-TRANSFER-CONTROL
0101        ELSE
0102           PERFORM C400-SEND-MAP-DATAONLY
0103     ELSE
0104        IF STATUS-OF-RECEIVE  =  'F'
0105           MOVE 'NO SELECTION WAS MADE - PLEASE ENTER SELECTION'
0106                          TO  MPM-D-MESSAGE
0107           MOVE ASKIP-BRT  TO  MPM-A-MESSAGE
0108           PERFORM C400-SEND-MAP-DATAONLY
0109        ELSE
0110           PERFORM C400-SEND-MAP-DATAONLY.
0111*
0112 C000-EXIT.
0113     EXIT.
0114*
0115 C100-RECEIVE-MAP  SECTION.
0116****************************************************************
0117*              PERFORMED FROM:  C000-PROCESSING              *
0118*             ONLY ENTER AND CLEAR KEYS ARE VALID            *
0119*          OTHER CONDITIONS CHANGE STATUS-OF-RECEIVE         *
0120*   GOOD-RECEIVE = 'G'    INVALID-KEY = 'I'    MAPFAIL = 'F' *
0121****************************************************************
0122*
0123     IF EIBAID = DFHENTER
0124        MOVE 'F' TO STATUS-OF-RECEIVE
0125*
0126        EXEC CICS HANDLE CONDITION
0127                  MAPFAIL (C100-EXIT)
0128        END-EXEC
0129*
0130        EXEC CICS RECEIVE
0131             MAP    ('MAPPOVM')
0132             MAPSET ('POVMNT1')
0133             INTO   (MPM-MENU-MAP)
0134        END-EXEC
0135*
0136        MOVE 'G'  TO  STATUS-OF-RECEIVE
0137     ELSE
0138        IF EIBAID = DFHCLEAR
0139           PERFORM C110-END-SESSION
0140        ELSE
0141           MOVE 'I'  TO  STATUS-OF-RECEIVE
0142           MOVE 'ENTER AND CLEAR KEYS ARE ONLY VALID KEYS - PLEA
0143-               'SE TRY AGAIN'  TO  MPM-D-MESSAGE
0144           MOVE ASKIP-BRT  TO  MPM-A-MESSAGE
0145           MOVE UNPROT-FSET  TO  MPM-A-SELECTION.
0146*
0147 C100-EXIT.
0148     EXIT.
0149*
0150 C110-END-SESSION  SECTION.
0151****************************************************************
0152*         OPERATOR PRESSED CLEAR - END SESSION              *
0153*              PERFORMED FROM:  C100-RECEIVE-MAP            *
0154****************************************************************
```

Figure 9-1 *(Continued)*

```
0155*
0156      EXEC CICS SEND
0157               FROM   (WS-CRT-MESSAGE)
0158               LENGTH (17)
0159               ERASE
0160      END-EXEC.
0161*
0162      EXEC CICS RETURN
0163      END-EXEC.
0164*
0165 C110-EXIT.
0166      EXIT.
0167*
0168 C200-EDIT-MAP-SELECTION  SECTION.
0169*****************************************************************
0170*          EDIT SELECTION MADE BY THE CRT OPERATOR        ***
0171*          PERFORMED FROM:  C000-PROCESSING               ***
0172*****************************************************************
0173*
0174      MOVE 'G'  TO  STATUS-OF-SELECTION.
0175*
0176      IF MPM-D-SELECTION  =  '1'   MOVE 'POVMINQY'  TO  WS-XCTL-PROGRAM
0177         ELSE
0178      IF MPM-D-SELECTION  =  '2'   MOVE 'POVMCHGE'  TO  WS-XCTL-PROGRAM
0179         ELSE
0180      IF MPM-D-SELECTION  =  '3'   MOVE 'POVMADDN'  TO  WS-XCTL-PROGRAM
0181         ELSE
0182      IF MPM-D-SELECTION  =  '4'   MOVE 'POVMDLET'  TO  WS-XCTL-PROGRAM
0183         ELSE
0184      IF MPM-D-SELECTION  =  '5'   MOVE 'POVMBROW'  TO  WS-XCTL-PROGRAM
0185         ELSE
0186         MOVE 'E'      TO  STATUS-OF-SELECTION
0187         MOVE 'INVALID SELECTION - PLEASE RE-ENTER YOUR SELECTION'
0188                       TO  MPM-D-MESSAGE
0189         MOVE ASKIP-BRT  TO  MPM-A-MESSAGE.
0190*
0191 C200-EXIT.
0192      EXIT.
0193*
0194 C300-TRANSFER-CONTROL  SECTION.
0195*****************************************************************
0196*          TRANSFER CONTROL 'XCTL' TO SELECTED PROGRAM       *
0197*          PERFORMED FROM:  C000-PROCESSING                  *
0198*****************************************************************
0199*
0200      EXEC CICS XCTL
0201               PROGRAM (WS-XCTL-PROGRAM)
0202      END-EXEC.
0203*
0204 C300-EXIT.
0205      EXIT.
0206*
0207 C400-SEND-MAP-DATAONLY  SECTION.
0208*****************************************************************
0209*          SEND MAP DATAONLY - SYMBOLIC MAP                  *
0210*          PERFORMED FROM:  C000-PROCESSING                  *
0211*          WHEN INVALID CONDITIONS ARE DETECTED              *
0212*****************************************************************
0213*
0214      EXEC CICS SEND
0215               MAP     ('MAPPOVM')
0216               MAPSET  ('POVMNT1')
0217               FROM    (MPM-MENU-MAP)
0218               DATAONLY
0219      END-EXEC.
0220*
0221 C400-EXIT.
0222      EXIT.
```

- WS-XCTL-PROGRAM—Based on the selection made by the terminal operator, the program to be transferred to is moved to this field before a common XCTL command is executed.

- WS-COMMAREA—Communications area used to return with a COMMAREA and LENGTH. This is used as a first-time switch.

- MPM-MENU-MAP—Chapter 6 showed how to create user-friendly symbolic maps.

- WS-STATUS-FIELDS—Program status fields found in the copy library (see STWSSTAT in App. B). These fields contain the status of program functions such as RECEIVE MAP, SELECTION, EDIT, READ, WRITE, CHANGE, and DELETE RECORDS, etc.

- ATTRIBUTE-LIST—User-friendly standard attribute character list (see STWSATTR in App. B).

- DFHAID—AID fields (see App. A-3).

Linkage Section

The only field defined in this program's linkage section is DFHCOMMAREA (see Fig. 9-1). The translator automatically generates a 1-byte DFHCOMMAREA, even if it is not coded.

Procedure Division

The procedure division contains the program's logic and comments which assist the programmer who has to test and maintain the program.

Program comments and section-naming conventions. I recommend starting the procedure division with comments describing the program's structure. Use descriptive paragraph names, which should be the actual names used for program sections. I label my mainline section AA00-MAINLINE. All other section names begin with an alphabetic character followed by three digits and then a description of the function performed. I indent the program structure section name four spaces to reflect sections which are performed from a higher level section.

Sections which are performed or invoked from another section are listed following the literal PERFORMED FROM: or INVOKED BY:. The rest of the comment area for each section contains information which should aid somebody unfamiliar with the program to understand the intent of the section. Do not put unnecessary information in this area, just enough to clarify.

I strongly recommend using structured programming techniques. They aid in development, debugging, and maintenance. Keep your structured code straightforward and simple. KISS will make your job much easier.

AA00-MAINLINE. Many programs contain initial or first-entry processing logic which is performed only once. Succeeding entries into the program follow a different logic path.

Initial program entry. On initial entry into the vendor file maintenance menu program, EIBCALEN is equal to zero because the program is initiated either by entering the TRANSID POVM or by a transfer of control from the purchasing system menu (POMENUPM, see Fig. 2-3). EIBCALEN will always equal zero when a program is initiated by entering a TRANSID. Any program which transfers control to this program will do so without COMMAREA and LENGTH specified. This will result in EIBCALEN equaling zero on initial entry. Transferring control to this program with COMMAREA and LENGTH specified would require that the program be written differently. EIBCALEN would be greater than 0. This program could test a switch sent in the COMMAREA in order to determine program flow. It could test an EIB field EIBTRNID, the TRANSID, in order to determine how the program was initiated. The browse program in Chap. 17 will employ EIBTRNID.

When EIBCALEN equals 0, the program sends the vendor file maintenance submenu screen shown in Fig. 6-3 and returns to CICS with a TRANSID, COMMAREA, and LENGTH. Return with a TRANSID is the main technique used in pseudoconversational programming. This enables the terminal operator to initiate the next execution of the program by pressing an AID key instead of entering a TRANSID. Specifying an invalid TRANSID on a RETURN command would cause the task to ABEND with an INVALID TRANSACTION IDENTIFICATION message displayed on the screen. When a program returns with a TRANSID, the current task is terminated. The program can be released from main storage, unless the program is defined in the PPT as being main-storage resident, and storage can be used for other tasks. Each program obtains its unique copy of working storage, and when a task ends, this copy is released from main storage. Each time CICS initiates a program, working storage reverts to its initial values. For this reason a program cannot pass data from one task to another through working storage. You have so far learned two methods which can be used to transfer data between tasks: through a map and the COMMAREA. This program is not concerned with passing data through the COMMAREA. It only returns with a COMMAREA containing a space and a length of 1, in order to set EIBCALEN for succeeding entries into the program. This technique is referred to as using EIBCALEN as a first-time switch.

Second and succeeding program entries. The first entry into the program sent the initial map, MAPONLY, and returned to CICS with a TRANSID and a length of 1. On succeeding entries into the program, EIBCALEN will be equal to 1, and the program will perform C000-PROCESSING. If a RETURN command had been issued with TRANSID but without COMMAREA and LENGTH specified, EIBCALEN would equal 0 and the program would loop, performing B000-SEND-MAPONLY each time an AID key was pressed.

When a valid selection is made, control is transferred to the selected program. Invalid conditions such as pressing an invalid AID key, not entering a selection (MAPFAIL), and making an invalid selection will result in a DATAONLY map send and the execution of the return with TRANSID. The return with TRANSID, COMMAREA, and length after the send of the DATAONLY map allows the terminal operator to correct the map's data. The terminal operator reads the error message. A valid selection is keyed in. The operator presses the proper AID key (ENTER); then this program is initiated again. Upon reentry into the program, EIBCALEN equals 1 and the program will perform C000-PROCESSING again. This process is repeated as often as required until a correct selection is entered. Transfer of control will take place, or the terminal operator will press CLEAR to end the session.

An understanding of the technique presented in the menu program should aid you in learning pseudoconversational programming. Pseudoconversational programming basically involves the send of a map and the release of the program from main storage if storage is required for another task. The map can be received without having to enter a TRANSID again since the RETURN command is issued with a TRANSID. Then, if the map's data is valid, the required logic is performed. When invalid data is entered, the map is resent with an indicative message. This process continues until valid data is entered or the session is ended.

B000-SEND-MAPONLY. This section is performed only once, upon initial entry into the program, when EIBCALEN equals 0. The program specifies MAPONLY in the send because the initial map contains no variable data. Only the physical map, which contains constants, needs to be sent. Maps which contain variable data such as date and time will eliminate MAPONLY from the send and will send both map and data (physical and symbolic maps).

C000-PROCESSING. This section is executed for all entries into the program after the first time. EIBCALEN will *not* be equal to 0. Section functions are

1. Perform C100-RECEIVE-MAP—Receives the selection entered on the map.

2. Perform C200-EDIT-MAP-SELECTION—Validate the selection.

3. Perform C300-TRANSFER-CONTROL—Transfer control to the selected program if a valid selection was entered.

4. Perform C400-SEND-MAP-DATAONLY—Send only the symbolic map if any invalid conditions are encountered, such as:

   a. Invalid AID key pressed.

   b. MAPFAIL (encountered when no selection is entered).

   c. An invalid selection was entered.

C100-RECEIVE-MAP. The RECEIVE MAP section checks which AID key was pressed in order to determine a logic path to follow. The only valid AID keys are ENTER and CLEAR. Any other AID key pressed would result in an invalid key message displayed on the screen. I check which AID key was pressed by comparing the EIB field EIBAID against one of the attention identifier fields listed in App. A-3. Figure 7-4 showed an alternate method of testing which AID key was pressed; that method is used in the browse program in Chap. 17. EIBAID can be tested and used as a switch at any point in the program.

EIBAID equals DFHENTER. I move an F immediately to STATUS-OF-RECEIVE so that if a MAPFAIL occurs, the program can determine this condition by testing the status field. The HANDLE CONDITION MAPFAIL command is invoked on the receive of a map if no field is FSET. If the EOF key is pressed prior to a receive, MAPFAIL will not occur. If a MAPFAIL occurs on the receive of a map, control will pass to the section exit with an F in STATUS-OF-RECEIVE. On a good receive for which a selection has been entered, a G will be moved to STATUS-OF-RECEIVE.

The RECEIVE MAP command will receive the map into the working-storage area MPM-MENU-MAP. The flag (attribute) byte MPM-A-SELECTION can be tested for hexadecimal 80 (X'80') in order to determine if the EOF key had been pressed. In all other cases the flag byte will equal X'00' (low-values). The L suffix (length field) can be tested after a RECEIVE MAP command to determine if data has been keyed into a field. Its length will be greater than 0 if data has been entered.

EIBAID equals DFHCLEAR. If the CLEAR key is pressed, the program will perform C110-END-SESSION. The end-of-session section will send a message and return control to CICS. Any AID key(s) could have been programmed to perform this function.

EIBAID not equal to DFHENTER or DFHCLEAR. This program considers any AID key other than ENTER or CLEAR an invalid entry. An I is moved to STATUS-OF-RECEIVE and a message moved to the map output field MPM-D-MESSAGE. The attribute character ASKIP,BRT is moved to the map message attribute field MPM-A-MESSAGE. UNPROT,FSET is moved to the SELECTION field attribute MPM-A-SELECTION; otherwise the selection code would not be returned on a subsequent read of the map. The DFHMSD macro of the BMS map defines CTRL=(FREEKB,FRSET). FRSET turns off all MDTs before a map is sent. The selection would be displayed on the screen, but it would not be returned to the program when a RECEIVE MAP command was executed because its MDT was not on. Moving UNPROT,FSET to the attribute field prior to the SEND MAP DATAONLY command will turn the MDT on. This will result in the selection being returned as is if it is not changed.

C110-END-SESSION. The RECEIVE MAP section will perform the C110-END-SESSION when the terminal operator presses the CLEAR key. It will display the message SESSION COMPLETED. The length of the message (17) must be specified. ERASE clears the screen before the send. Since this program is at the highest logical level, the execution of the CICS RETURN command will return control to CICS. No TRANSID is specified on the RETURN command; therefore, if the terminal operator presses an AID key after the message is displayed, an invalid transaction message will appear on the screen.

C200-EDIT-MAP-SELECTION. The selection entered by the terminal operator will be edited in this section. The appropriate program will be moved to WS-XCTL-PROGRAM if the selection is valid. On an invalid selection, an E is placed in STATUS-OF-SELECTION. A message is then moved to the map's message field and ASKIP,BRT is moved to the map's field attribute. Unlike section C100-RECEIVE-MAP, it is *not* necessary to move UNPROT,FSET to the map's selection attribute. When an invalid selection is keyed in, it is not required to be returned on a subsequent receive of the map; the corrected selection should be entered. What do you think would happen if, after displaying the invalid selection message, the terminal operator pressed ENTER without keying in any selection? The invalid selection which was displayed on the screen would not be returned to the program since the send with FRSET turns off its MDT. Low-values would be returned. Section C000-PROCESSING would move NO SELECTION WAS MADE... to the message field and would resend the map. All the while, the invalid selection would be showing on the screen. The terminal operator might press the EOF key to erase the invalid entry and then press ENTER. This would *not* cause a MAPFAIL. Low-values would be transmitted on a RECEIVE MAP command, but the flag byte MPM-A-SELECTION would contain X'80'. In this case the selection would be treated as invalid by section C200-EDIT-MAP-SELECTION. The flag byte received would be equal to low-values (X'00') if EOF was not pressed or if a selection had been entered. The flag byte is not used often, but you may encounter it in programs which you have to maintain. Remember that the flag and attribute bytes occupy the same field. Also keep in mind that BMS map A and F suffix fields are shown only as A fields on user-friendly maps. BMS map suffix fields I and O are shown as data (D) fields on user-friendly symbolic maps.

C300-TRANSFER-CONTROL. After section C200-EDIT-MAP-SELECTION moves the selection program name to WS-XCTL-PROGRAM, this section immediately transfers control to the selected program. The new program will be loaded into main storage if necessary, and control will be transferred to that program. The menu program can be released from main storage, if it's not required by another task or if it's not defined in the PPT as a main-storage resident program. The EIB fields, task number (EIBTASKN), and TRANSID (EIB-TRNID) will remain unchanged in the new program until it issues a RETURN command at the highest logical level.

The handle condition PGMIDERR will be invoked if the program has not been defined in the PPT or if the program has been disabled. This condition generally occurs only during an initial test. I do not check for this condition; if it occurs, I let the program ABEND.

Programs initiated by this section will be entered with a communications area length (EIBCALEN) equal to 0. This program could transfer control with data, in which case the XCTL command would require the COMMAREA and LENGTH options.

C400-SEND-MAP-DATAONLY. This section is performed from C000-PROCES-SING when an invalid condition has been detected, such as invalid key pressed, MAPFAIL, or an invalid selection. This send does not include the physical map. Only the symbolic map (DATAONLY) is sent. The physical map should have been previously sent by either a SEND MAP MAPONLY command or a SEND

MAP AND DATA command. Do not specify ERASE on the DATAONLY option of the SEND MAP command because you will display variable data on a screen which has no physical constants. When the FROM option is not specified on a SEND MAP command, the output symbolic map generated by BMS, MAPPOVMO in Fig. 6-5, is the default.

If CURSOR was specified in this SEND MAP DATAONLY command, -1 would have to be moved to one of the symbolic map length field's (L suffix). The cursor would be set at map POS=(01,01) if -1 was not moved to a length field when CURSOR was specified.

SUMMARY

The best way to learn most data processing concepts is through practice and by reference to practical examples. The menu program presented in this chapter is typical of most menu programs. Many of the commands and concepts discussed so far were illustrated in the menu program. Several suggestions for program documentation and standardization were presented. I recommend comments be included as part of the program's remarks in order to make the intent of the program clear to someone unfamiliar with the system. I showed how a section reference structure chart could be included at the start of the procedure division. Comments at the start of each section should show which sections performed or invoked this logic.

Structured programming techniques, when kept simple (KISS), make program development, debugging, and maintenance easier and will be used for all program examples. As you develop your program code, keep ease of maintenance and future reusability in mind. Program code which is used in one program is often reused in others. Do not reinvent a program each time you write one!

10

THE LINKED PROGRAM

When one program links to another, the original program remains and the linked program is loaded into main storage. Since linked programs tie-up more main storage, you should limit their use. The journal-posting program discussed in this chapter is a linked program. It utilizes the COMMAREA for passing data to the linked program and for returning data to the linking program.

A couple of new commands will be introduced—ASKTIME and the file control command WRITE, which will be covered in more detail in Chap. 11. BLL pointers will be presented and explained.

Many systems require the posting of audit records when transactions change the contents of a record. Rather than having each transaction write its own audit record, one program may be designated as a journal-posting program which writes audit records for several files. Journal program JRNLPOST (Fig. 10-2) is an example of a linked program. This program will post audit transactions for the following files: vendor master, purchase order master, and item master. Programs in this book will write a before-and/or after-record for the following file maintenance transactions: changes, additions, and deletions.

Linking Routine

An audit record can be written only for designated significant field changes or whenever any field in a record changes. *All* changes, additions, and deletions in the vendor master file maintenance programs will write an audit record. Change programs will write a before-and after-record, additions an after-record, and deletions a before-record.

Figure 10-1 contains the section of program code which will be used to invoke the journal-posting program JRNLPOST. The record layout for JOURNAL-RECORD can be found in the copy library [see App. B, JRNLRECD].

```
0001 E121-POST-JOURNAL-RECORD  SECTION.
0002********************************************************************
0003*    POST JOURNAL ENTRY - LINK TO JOURNAL PROGRAM 'JRNLPOST'    *
0004********************************************************************
0005*
0006     MOVE 'VM'                  TO   JR-PREFIX.
0007     MOVE VENDOR-MASTER-RECORD  TO   JR-RECORD-DATA.
0008     MOVE SPACES                TO   JR-PASSWORD.
0009*
0010     EXEC CICS LINK
0011               PROGRAM   ('JRNLPOST')
0012               COMMAREA  (JOURNAL-RECORD)
0013               LENGTH    (524)
0014     END-EXEC.
0015*
0016 E121-EXIT.
0017     EXIT.
```

Figure 10-1 LINKing Program Section.

A B (before) is moved to JR-TYPE in JOURNAL-RECORD by maintenance programs immediately after reading a record for update and prior to a change or delete being executed. An A (after) is moved to JR-TYPE in JOURNAL-RECORD immediately after rewriting a changed record or after writing an added record to the vendor master file. Chapter 11 will discuss all file control commands. After moving an A or B to JR-TYPE, all maintenance programs perform E121-POST-JOURNAL-RECORD.

E121-POST-JOURNAL-RECORD

This section formats the journal record prior to executing a LINK command. Depending upon your installation's security requirements, a password might have to be entered on the maintenance screen or in a prior program. The password is then passed to the journal-posting program.

The LINK command invokes the program JRNLPOST, which is by definition at a lower logical level. The linking program remains in main storage while the linked program, if necessary, is loaded into main storage. Task number remains the same. JOURNAL-RECORD in COMMAREA and its length (524) are passed to JRNLPOST.

Journal-Posting Program

Figure 10-2 is the linked program JRNLPOST. The working-storage section contains the journal record layout which is found in App. B.

Linkage Section

DFHCOMMAREA is defined in the linkage section as a 524-byte field. This is the length passed by the invoking maintenance program. DFHCOMMAREA, which is moved to JOURNAL-RECORD upon entering the program, could contain subfields corresponding to JOURNAL-RECORD fields, if no data were required to be returned to the linking program. JRNLPOST issues a WRITE command from the journal record. Main storage of a record which is written from the linkage section is not available after a WRITE command is issued.

BLL Cells definition. BLL cells are pointers which must immediately follow DFHCOMMAREA in the linkage section. The filler following BLL-CELLS is automatically set to point to the BLL cell list itself. Each labeled 02 field under FILLER can be set to point to the corresponding 01 field which follows the BLL cell list. This program will set BLL-SEQ-TABLE-ADDRESS to point

Figure 10-2 LINKed Program JRNLPOST.

```
0001 IDENTIFICATION DIVISION.
0002 PROGRAM-ID. JRNLPOST.
0003 REMARKS.
0004*********************************************************************
0005*                    JOURNAL POSTING PROGRAM                       *
0006*     POST A JOURNAL RECORD FOR ITEMS PASSED TO THIS PROGRAM       *
0007*         IN THE COMMAREA BY A LINK FROM ANOTHER PROGRAM.          *
0008*********************************************************************
0009 ENVIRONMENT DIVISION.
0010 DATA DIVISION.
0011*
0012 WORKING-STORAGE SECTION.
0013*
0014 01  WS-PROGRAM-FIELDS.
0015     05  FILLER          PIC X(22)   VALUE 'JRNLPOST - START OF WS'.
0016*
0017 01  JOURNAL-RECORD   COPY   JRNLRECD.
0018*
0019 01  END-OF-WORKING-STORAGE   PIC X(15)   VALUE 'END WS JRNLPOST'.
0020*
0021 LINKAGE SECTION.
0022*
0023 01  DFHCOMMAREA           PIC X(524).
0024*
0025 01  BLL-CELLS.
0026     02  FILLER                PIC S9(8)   COMP.
0027     02  BLL-SEQ-TABLE-ADDRESS  PIC S9(8)   COMP.
0028*
0029 01  T053-SEQUENCE-TABLE.
0030     05  T053-SEQUENCE-NUMBER   PIC S9(5)   COMP-3.
0031*
0032 PROCEDURE DIVISION.
0033*********************************************************************
0034*              PROGRAM STRUCTURE IS:                               *
0035*                 AA00-MAINLINE                                    *
0036*                   B000-LOAD-SEQUENCE-TABLE                       *
0037*                   C000-FORMAT-JOURNAL-RECORD                     *
0038*                   D000-WRITE-JOURNAL-RECORD                      *
0039*********************************************************************
0040*
0041 AA00-MAINLINE  SECTION.
0042*
0043*    SERVICE RELOAD BLL-CELLS.
0044*
0045     MOVE DFHCOMMAREA  TO  JOURNAL-RECORD.
0046*
0047     PERFORM B000-LOAD-SEQUENCE-TABLE.
0048*
0049     PERFORM C000-FORMAT-JOURNAL-RECORD.
0050*
0051     PERFORM D000-WRITE-JOURNAL-RECORD.
0052*
0053     MOVE JOURNAL-RECORD  TO  DFHCOMMAREA.
0054*
0055* RETURN TO LINKED FROM PROGRAM
0056     EXEC CICS RETURN
0057     END-EXEC.
0058*
```

Figure 10-2 *(Continued)*

```
0059 B000-LOAD-SEQUENCE-TABLE  SECTION.
0060************************************************************************
0061*         SET ADDRESS OF MAIN STORAGE RESIDENT TABLE          *
0062*                 PERFORMED FROM:  AA00-MAINLINE               *
0063************************************************************************
0064*
0065     EXEC CICS LOAD
0066                 PROGRAM ('T053JRSQ')
0067                 SET     (BLL-SEQ-TABLE-ADDRESS)
0068     END-EXEC.
0069*
0070*    SERVICE RELOAD T053-SEQUENCE-TABLE.
0071*
0072 B000-EXIT.
0073     EXIT.
0074*
0075 C000-FORMAT-JOURNAL-RECORD  SECTION.
0076************************************************************************
0077*         FORMAT JOURNAL RECORD - PRIOR TO WRITING            *
0078*                 PERFORMED FROM:  AA00-MAINLINE               *
0079************************************************************************
0080*
0081     MOVE T053-SEQUENCE-NUMBER  TO  JR-SEQUENCE-NUMBER.
0082     ADD 1                      TO  T053-SEQUENCE-NUMBER.
0083*
0084     EXEC CICS ASKTIME
0085     END-EXEC.
0086*
0087     MOVE EIBDATE   TO  JR-EIBDATE.
0088     MOVE EIBTIME   TO  JR-EIBTIME.
0089     MOVE EIBTRMID  TO  JR-EIBTRMID.
0090*
0091 C000-EXIT.
0092     EXIT.
0093*
0094 D000-WRITE-JOURNAL-RECORD  SECTION.
0095************************************************************************
0096*         ADD A 'BEFORE' OR 'AFTER' JOURNAL RECORD             *
0097*                 PERFORMED FROM:  AA00-MAINLINE               *
0098*     INCLUDING SEQUENCE NUMBER AS PART OF KEY ELIMINATES      *
0099*  POSSIBILITY OF DUPREC HANDLE CONDITION ON FOLLOWING WRITE   *
0100************************************************************************
0101*
0102     EXEC CICS WRITE
0103                 DATASET ('JOURNAL1')
0104                 FROM    (JOURNAL-RECORD)
0105                 RIDFLD  (JR-KEY)
0106     END-EXEC.
0107*
0108 D000-EXIT.
0109     EXIT.
```

to T053-SEQUENCE-TABLE. BLL-cell usage will be explained further as we examine the procedure division of JRNLPOST.

Procedure Division

The program structure is defined as comments at the start of the procedure division.

AA00-MAINLINE. The SERVICE RELOAD statement must be issued at the start of the program to ensure proper linkage-section addressability if your installation uses a Cobol compiler which has the optimization feature. The SERVICE RELOAD statement should be issued whenever the address of a BLL cell is changed. The SERVICE RELOAD statement is shown commented out at points in programs where it should be included if your installation uses the optimization feature.

DFHCOMMAREA, which contains the journal record data passed from the linking program, is moved to JOURNAL-RECORD. A sequence table is loaded. The journal record is then formatted and written to the journal file. JOURNAL-RECORD is then moved to DFHCOMMAREA and a RETURN command, without TRANSID, is executed in order to return to the higher-logical-level linking program. Control will return to the statement following the LINK command (E121-EXIT) in Fig. 10-1. Any JOURNAL-RECORD fields which were changed by JRNLPOST are available in the working-storage communications area, JOURNAL-RECORD, of the linking program, *not* in DFHCOMMAREA.

B000-LOAD-SEQUENCE-TABLE. The LOAD command sets a BLL address pointer to the journal sequence table (T053JRSQ), in the linkage section. BLL-SEQ-TABLE-ADDRESS will have addressability to T053-SEQUENCE-TABLE. T053-SEQUENCE-NUMBER can be referenced and changed. The sequence table is defined in the PPT as a main-storage resident table. For nonresident tables, it is good practice to release the table as soon as it is no longer required.

The PGMIDERR handle condition will be invoked if T053JRSQ is not in the PPT or is disabled.

BLL Cells usage. BLL cells are defined, as shown in the linkage section, as binary full words. Each BLL cell can address only 4096 bytes of main storage. If a table exceeds 4096 bytes, the additional positions must be addressed in multiples of 4096, even if fewer than 4096 additional bytes are needed. Figure 10-3 illustrates how this works. Table 2 requires 9606 bytes or two full blocks of 4096 plus one partial block. Three BLL cells are required to address this table as shown. The LOAD command addresses the first 4096 bytes; then 4096 is added to the first address in order to set the address pointer to the next 4096 bytes. Finally, 4096 is added to the second address to set the address pointer to the third block of 4096. I do not show service reloads in Fig. 10-3. If your system uses the optimization feature, you would have to issue three SERVICE RELOAD commands, one after the LOAD command and one after each add of 4096 which establishes addressability.

C000-FORMAT-JOURNAL-RECORD. This section formats the journal record prior to writing it. The journal record's data is passed in DFHCOMMAREA from the linking program. When a task is initiated, the EIB is established with initial values. In a long-running task, it may be desirable to refresh the value of certain EIB fields such as EIBDATE and EIBTIME. Most likely, EIBDATE won't change, but EIBTIME might. The ASKTIME command updates the fields EIBTIME and EIBDATE when it is issued. Its format is

```
EXEC CICS ASKTIME
END-EXEC.
```

The journal record's key consists of EIBDATE, EIBTIME, and a sequence number. The sequence number is obtained from the sequence table and is incremented by 1 each time it is used. Sequence number is needed as part of the key to ensure that no multiple record keys occur. It is possible for the same task to pass the identical date and time to this program. For instance, the before- and after-record posting of a changed record could occur in a program before time had a chance to change. The EIB TeRMinal IDentification (EIBTRMID) field is moved to the journal record as a data element for audit reporting.

The journal file can be closed off line and its data written to another file by a batch program. Journal-file records can be deleted, and the next day's processing can begin with an empty file. The "stripped" journal file can be used for audit reporting and saved if required.

D000-WRITE-JOURNAL-RECORD. The journal record formatted in section C000-FORMAT-JOURNAL-RECORD is written out to a file called JOURNAL1. The WRITE command will be covered in Chap. 11, "File Control."

```
0001 LINKAGE SECTION.
0002*
0003 01  DFHCOMMAREA                         PIC X.
0004*
0005 01  BLL-CELLS.
0006     02  BLL-CELLS-ADDRESS               PIC S9(8)    COMP.
0007     02  BLL-TABLE-1-ADDRESS             PIC S9(8)    COMP.
0008     02  BLL-TABLE-2-ADDRESS-1           PIC S9(8)    COMP.
0009     02  BLL-TABLE-2-ADDRESS-2           PIC S9(8)    COMP.
0010     02  BLL-TABLE-2-ADDRESS-3           PIC S9(8)    COMP.
0011     02  BLL-TABLE-3-ADDRESS             PIC S9(8)    COMP.
0012*
0013 01  TABLE-1                             PIC X(10).
0014*
0015 01  TABLE-2                             PIC X(9606).
0016*
0017 01  TABLE-3                             PIC X(4000).
0018*
0019*
0020 PROCEDURE DIVISION.
0021        .
0022        .
0023        .
0024     EXEC CICS LOAD
0025            PROGRAM ('T002BIGT')
0026            SET     (BLL-TABLE-2-ADDRESS-1)
0027     END-EXEC.
0028*
0029     ADD 4096  BLL-TABLE-2-ADDRESS-1
0030          GIVING BLL-TABLE-2-ADDRESS-2.
0031*
0032     ADD 4096  BLL-TABLE-2-ADDRESS-2
0033          GIVING BLL-TABLE-2-ADDRESS-3.
0034        .
0035        .
0036        .
```

Figure 10-3 Establishing BLL Addressability for Large Tables.

SUMMARY

Linked programs should be used only when necessary, since they tie up more main storage than do independent programs. The journal program was presented to show how the linked program is used when required. The LINK and ASKTIME commands were used and discussed. BLL cells were used, and an illustration showed how to establish addressability to large tables.

11

FILE CONTROL

File control seems to be one of the easier concepts for CICS programmers to understand, especially those who have worked on batch systems which use virtual storage access methods (VSAM). Knowledge of VSAM is helpful but not required in order to understand this chapter. You should be familiar with the concept of random access file processing in order to gain maximum benefit from the material presented.

This chapter addresses file control using VSAM key-sequenced data sets (VSAM KSDS), the file structure used for all examples in this book. A VSAM file used for CICS must have at least one record loaded to initialize the file, even if the single record is later deleted. Files are generally opened when CICS is initialized and closed when CICS is shut down; therefore, programs do not need to open or close files. Files must *never* be opened or closed in a CICS application program. The handle condition NOTOPEN will be invoked by most file control commands if a file is closed. You can test for this condition or allow the task to ABEND if a file is not open. I generally do not test for this condition because it should not normally occur.

All CICS files must be defined in a table called the file control table (FCT). Some FCT entries are: data set name, record size, and permissible file access and update functions. The FCT eliminates the need for programmers to define those entries contained in the table. The programmer generally needs only to specify data set name, key field, and the working-storage name of a record's I/O area. For program examples, all required entries are assumed to have been made in the FCT for files containing fixed-length records. VENDMAST and JOURNAL1 are the two files which will be used, and they permit the use of all file control commands required for examples in this book. The FCT is generally maintained by the system programming staff.

Opening and Closing Files

Files used by CICS are usually opened when CICS is started up by operations personnel at the beginning of the day. CICS files must be closed if they need to be changed by a batch program since they cannot be updated by both CICS and batch systems at the same time. Occasionally users on a test system get an indicative message that files have been closed; they are most likely needed by a batch program. Whenever practical, data processing gives notice to users before closing and reopening files.

File Control Commands

The most common options used with file control commands are discussed. The commands covered are

1. READ command—Read a file for inquiry or access without update intended.
2. READ FOR UPDATE—Read a file with the intent of changing and updating a record.
3. WRITE—Write a new record to a file.
4. REWRITE—Rewrite a record read for update.
5. UNLOCK—Release a record read for update if processing indicates that updating is not required.
6. DELETE—Remove a record from the file.
7. STARTBR—Establish a starting point for a browse (sequential reads against a file).
8. READNEXT—Read the next record after a STARTBR or after a prior READNEXT command.
9. READPREV—Read the preceding record after a STARTBR or after a prior READPREV command.
10. ENDBR—Terminate a browse function initiated by the STARTBR command.
11. RESETBR—End the previous browse and start a new browse.

Options Common to Many File Control Commands

• DATASET (FCT entry)—The FCT entry uses up to seven alphanumeric characters for disk operating systems (DOS) and up to eight alphanumeric characters for operating systems (OS). Examples in this book will use eight-character FCT names. FCT entry is enclosed in single quotes, for instance, DATASET ('VENDMAST').

- INTO (WS-RECORD-I-O-AREA) / FROM (WS-RECORD-I-O-AREA)—Program-defined working-storage area used to hold your program's input and/or output area.
- RIDFLD (WS-RECORD-KEY)—RIDFLD (Record IDentification FieLD) contains the key of the record to be operated upon. This field may be defined as part of the record's key or it may be defined separately in working storage.

READ Command

The READ command reads a record into a record area defined in working storage. After a successful read, the record's data is available in working storage.
The READ command format is

```
EXEC CICS READ
        DATASET (FCT entry)
        INTO    (WS-RECORD-I-O-AREA)
        RIDFLD  (WS-RECORD-KEY)
END-EXEC.
```

- Handle Conditions—Record NOT FouND (NOTFND) is the only handle condition I generally check for when using the READ command.

WRITE Command

The WRITE command writes a record *from* an area defined in working storage. The required data must be moved to the working-storage area of the record to be added, prior to issuing a WRITE command. When a write is successful, the record will have been added to the file.
The WRITE command format is

```
EXEC CICS WRITE
        DATASET (FCT entry)
        FROM    (WS-RECORD-I-O-AREA)
        RIDFLD  (WS-RECORD-KEY)
END-EXEC.
```

- Handle Conditions—Record already exists on the file [DUPlicate RECord (DUPREC)]is the only handle condition I generally check for when using the WRITE command. NOSPACE occurs when a file to which a record is being added is full.

READ FOR UPDATE Command

The READ FOR UPDATE version of the READ command reads a record into an area defined in working storage, with the intent of updating the record. Normally, fields to be updated will have new data moved into the I/O area of the record to be changed, before the record is rewritten (see REWRITE command below). After a successful read, the record's data is available in the working-storage area (WS-RECORD-I-O-AREA).

A record READ FOR UPDATE should be read as close to the UPDATE command as possible in order to prevent file lockout of other tasks. If it is determined that a record READ FOR UPDATE will not be rewritten, issue the UNLOCK command as soon as it is determined that the record will not be rewritten (see "Exclusive Control" below).

The format of the READ FOR UPDATE option of the READ command is identical to the regular READ command, except that the option UPDATE must be specified.

```
EXEC CICS READ
          DATASET (FCT entry)
          INTO      (WS-RECORD-I-O-AREA)
          RIDFLD   (WS-RECORD-KEY)
          UPDATE
END-EXEC.
```

- Handle Conditions—NOTFND is the only handle condition I generally check for when using the READ FOR UPDATE command.

REWRITE Command

The REWRITE command writes a record *from* an area defined in working storage. Prior to issuing a REWRITE command, the required data must be moved to the working-storage area of the record to be changed. When a rewrite is successful, the record's new data replaces the old data in the designated record. A rewrite will only be successful against a record which was found when read for update.

The REWRITE command format is

```
EXEC CICS REWRITE
          DATASET (FCT entry)
          FROM      (WS-RECORD-I-O-AREA)
END-EXEC.
```

• Handle Conditions—I do not test for any handle conditions on the rewrite. The handle condition INVREQ will occur if a rewrite is attempted against a record *not* read for update.

Exclusive Control

File control gives exclusive control to the control interval which contains a record read for update. A control interval is a block of records with sequentially adjacent keys. Exclusive control prevents reading of the same record, or any record in the control interval for update, until the record read for update has been rewritten. A lockout occurs when a task tries to read another record for update or attempts to add a record before a record read for update in the same control interval is rewritten, deleted, or unlocked. Sometimes it is determined that a record which was read for update will not be changed. When the programmer can determine the point at which a record will not need to be rewritten, exclusive control should be released by issuing the UNLOCK command. Rewriting or deleting a record read for update as well as terminating a task releases exclusive control of the control interval.

Release exclusive control of a record read for update before reading another record in the same file for update. Failure to do this could cause a lockout in the same program. It is good practice to read files which may be updated in the same sequence in all programs in order to prevent a lockout from occurring between two different tasks. Try to limit the number of programs which can directly update a file.

UNLOCK Command

The UNLOCK command should be used in programs which contain much processing, after it is known that a record will not be rewritten. Exclusive control is released by issuing the UNLOCK command.

The UNLOCK command format is

```
        EXEC CICS UNLOCK
                 DATASET (FCT entry)
        END-EXEC.
```

DELETE Command

Although it is not necessary, I recommend reading a record for update prior to deletion. You might display the record in an inquiry format with a message DO YOU WISH TO DELETE THIS RECORD? To delete the record you might have the terminal operator key in YES and press a designated AID key or some similar action. The common practice is to write the record to a journal file which can be used later offline to print a batch-processing listing of transactions which updated the file. A record read prior to deletion must be read with the UPDATE option.

The format for the DELETE command when read first is

```
EXEC CICS DELETE
        DATASET (FCT entry)
END-EXEC.
```

Only the DATASET option is required when the file is read for update prior to issuing the DELETE command. If the record is *not* read prior to deletion, the RIDFLD option must be included as follows.

```
EXEC CICS DELETE
        DATASET (FCT entry)
        RIDFLD   (WS-RECORD-KEY)
END-EXEC.
```

You have to move the key of the record to be deleted to WS-RECORD-KEY prior to issuing the delete.

• Handle Conditions—I generally read a record first before deleting it and do not test for any handle conditions. INVREQ could occur on this delete if no previous read for update had been executed. NOTFND could occur for the delete without a preceding READ FOR UPDATE, if WS-RECORD-KEY was not on the file.

FILE BROWSE Commands and Considerations

Some applications require a program to start at a specified item in the file and then to display records sequentially beginning from that point. A record cannot be updated using browse commands; it must first be read for update. A vendor file could be in alphabetical sequence by vendor code prefix; assume the code is of the format A-9999-9, with the first character being A through Z. The next four digits could position the vendor alphabetically within the alphabetic prefix and the last digit might be used for vendor location. The terminal operator may want to search the file for vendors which have a name starting with the letter M. The browse could be initiated by entering vendor code M00000 or just M. The program would move the entered vendor code to WS-RECORD-KEY and issue the browse command to establish a position at that record, or at the first record with a greater key value.

STARTBR Command

The STARTBR (START Browse) command sets the beginning position for a browse. The READNEXT and READPREV commands discussed below will read records sequentially, starting at the position established by the STARTBR command. *No record is read* by the STARTBR command; a starting point in the file is established for the first READNEXT or READPREV command.

The STARTBR command format is

```
EXEC CICS STARTBR
            DATASET (FCT entry)
            RIDFLD    (WS-RECORD-KEY)
            GTEQ
END-EXEC.
```

Low-values in RIDFLD will position the browse at the beginning of the file. High-values will position it at the end of the file.

- GTEQ—The Greater Than or EQual to (GTEQ) operand of the STARTBR command specifies that if the RIDFLD record key is not found, the browse is to set the file starting point at the next sequential record. EQUAL is assumed if GTEQ is not specified.

- Handle Conditions—NOTFND will occur if GTEQ is not specified and an exact hit is not made for the record in RIDFLD. NOTFND also occurs if GTEQ is included and the record specified in RIDFLD has a key which is greater than the last key in the file. INVREQ will occur if a STARTBR command is issued against a file not defined in the FCT with the browse option.

Browse Inefficiencies

Browse operations are inefficient because many records have to be read from a file. Limit a browse by providing the ability to reset its starting key. Files which are browsed frequently should have a larger file blocking factor in order to minimize the number of required file accesses. A browse against a file with a small blocking factor will be less efficient because a greater number of accesses will be required.

READNEXT Command

The format of the READNEXT command is similar to that of the READ command. The first time READNEXT is executed following a STARTBR command, the record retrieved is the record positioned at by the STARTBR command. Succeeding READNEXT executions retrieve records sequentially from that position in the file. WS-RECORD-KEY is updated with the entire record key each time a READNEXT command is executed. Records in the file could be skipped by changing WS-RECORD-KEY to a key greater than that of the last record read. This is called "skip sequential processing" and is not frequently used.

The READNEXT command format is

```
EXEC CICS READNEXT
          DATASET    (FCT entry)
          INTO       (WS-RECORD-I-O-AREA)
          RIDFLD     (WS-RECORD-KEY)
END-EXEC.
```

- Handle Conditions—ENDFILE occurs when the end of a file is reached. NOTFND may occur if, in the same task, WS-RECORD-KEY is set to a key lower than the last key read. If this occurs, the program should execute a RESETBR or an ENDBR command (discussed later in this chapter). INVREQ occurs if no preceding STARTBR command was executed.

Generic Search

A generic (partial key) search can be used with the STARTBR command. The generic search requires the move of the generic key to the first portion of WS-RECORD-KEY and the specification of the KEYLENGTH and GENERIC options on the STARTBR command.

The format of the STARTBR command with the GENERIC option is

```
EXEC CICS STARTBR
          DATASET    (FCT entry)
          RIDFLD     (WS-RECORD-KEY)
          GTEQ
          KEYLENGTH (GENERIC-KEY-LENGTH)
          GENERIC
END-EXEC.
```

- GTEQ—This operand specifies that if the RIDFLD record key is not found, the browse is to set the file starting point at the next sequential record.
- KEYLENGTH (GENERIC-KEY-LENGTH)—This is a working-storage entry defined as a halfword binary field. The length of the portion of the key to be searched for must be moved to this field prior to execution of the GENERIC option of the STARTBR command. A generic STARTBR command will establish position at the start of the file if KEYLENGTH (0) is specified.

• GENERIC—This statement must be included along with KEYLENGTH for a generic search.

• Handle Conditions—NOTFND will occur if GTEQ is omitted and an exact hit is not made for the record in RIDFLD. NOTFND also occurs if GTEQ is included and the record specified in RIDFLD contains a key greater than the last key in the file. INVREQ will occur if a STARTBR command is issued against a file not defined in the FCT with the browse option.

READPREV Command

The READPREV command functions similarly to the READNEXT command, following the execution of a STARTBR command. The first time READPREV is executed following a STARTBR command, the record retrieved is the record at which position was established by the STARTBR command. Succeeding READPREV executions retrieve records containing keys sequentially lower than the previous record. WS-RECORD-KEY is updated with the entire record key each time a READPREV command is executed. READPREV cannot be issued following a browse initiated with the GENERIC option of the STARTBR command. If a READNEXT command is followed by a READPREV command, the READPREV reads the same record read by the READNEXT. Issue another READPREV to read the desired record. Skip sequential processing cannot be used with a backward browse.

The READPREV command format is

```
EXEC CICS READPREV
          DATASET    (FCT entry)
          INTO       (WS-RECORD-I-O-AREA)
          RIDFLD     (WS-RECORD-KEY)
END-EXEC.
```

• Handle Conditions—ENDFILE occurs when the "beginning" of the file is reached. INVREQ occurs if no preceding STARTBR command was executed or if the STARTBR command had a GENERIC option specified. NOTFND will occur if an immediately preceding STARTBR did not get an EQUAL hit.

End Browse (ENDBR) Command

The ENDBR command is issued in order to terminate a browse. Executing a new STARTBR command against the same file in a task without having ended a previous browse will result in an INVREQ handle condition. Terminate all browses with the ENDBR command as soon as possible.

The ENDBR command format is

```
EXEC CICS ENDBR
            DATASET (FCT entry)
END-EXEC.
```

- Handle Conditions—INVREQ occurs if no preceding STARTBR command was executed.

Reset Browse (RESETBR) Command

The RESETBR command resets a browse to the original or to a new browse starting point. It has the same effect as an ENDBR command followed by a STARTBR command. RESETBR commands could be used to skip sequentially through a file.

The RESETBR command format is similar to STARTBR,

```
EXEC CICS RESETBR
            DATASET (FCT entry)
            RIDFLD    (WS-RECORD-KEY)
            GTEQ
END-EXEC.
```

Low-values in RIDFLD will position the browse at the beginning of the file. High-values will position it at the end of the file.

- GTEQ—This operand of the RESETBR command specifies that if the RID-FLD record key is not found, the browse is to set the file starting point at the next sequential record. EQUAL is assumed if GTEQ is not specified.

- Handle Conditions—NOTFND will occur if GTEQ is not specified and an exact hit is not made for the record in RIDFLD. NOTFND also occurs if GTEQ is included and if the record specified in RIDFLD has a key which is greater than the last key in the file. INVREQ will occur if a RESETBR command is issued against a file not defined in the FCT with the browse option.

SUMMARY

File control commands make it easy for the application programmer to read, write, and update files in a CICS system. The commands covered were READ, WRITE, REWRITE, UNLOCK, DELETE, STARTBR, READNEXT, READ-PREV, ENDBR, and RESETBR. Programmers who have an understanding of random-access methods generally master file control commands quickly. Exclusive control was discussed, and suggestions for preventing lockout were presented.

Program examples in succeeding chapters will cover many of the commands presented and make the use of file control commands easier to understand.

12

THE INQUIRY PROGRAM

An inquiry program is one of the first programs you should write after an online file is created. This is not a maintenance program, but I include it on many maintenance menus. Inquiries generally list most fields contained on the record being displayed. Inquiry and maintenance programs are helpful during the testing stage of a system and are usually necessary once the system is running in a production environment.

Control and detail maps are used for the inquiry program. The control map, shown in Fig. 2-4, requires the terminal operator to key in a vendor code and press ENTER in order to display the inquiry detail map. The operator also has the option of transferring control to the vendor file browse program, of returning to the vendor file maintenance submenu (see Fig. 6-3), or of ending the session. The vendor file inquiry detail map shown in Fig. 2-6 is displayed when the operator enters a vendor code on the control screen and then presses ENTER. The detail screen displays all fields contained on the vendor's record. The operator can view the vendor's data and then press ENTER in order to return to the control screen. The detail screen also permits the operator to return to the submenu or to end the session.

BMS Maps

Figures 12-1 and 12-2 show the BMS maps for the control and detail maps shown in Figs. 2-4 and 2-6, respectively. The DFHMSD and DFHMDI macros are the same as those on previous maps except for the mapset and mapname labels.

BMS Control Map

All control map fields have ASKIP attributes, except for vendor code, which is UNPROT. The first vendor code entry field, MCVCOD1, has IC specified as part of its attribute. This will result in the cursor being positioned under this field if the command-level interpreter (CECI, discussed in Chap. 6) is used to test the physical map. This program specifies CURSOR as part of its SEND MAP commands and uses symbolic cursor positioning. Stopper fields are not required following BMS map labels MCVCOD1 and MCVCOD2 because the following hyphens have ASKIP attributes. MCVCOD3 is followed by a stopper field, an unlabeled 1-byte ASKIP attribute in POS=(07,51).

BMS Detail Map

All inquiry detail map attributes are defined as ASKIP. All BMS maps could be generated with ASKIP attributes defined for every field. Programs can

Figure 12-1 Vendor File Inquiry BMS Control Map.

```
           PRINT NOGEN
POVMIQ1    DFHMSD TYPE=MAP,                                          X
                  CTRL=(FREEKB,FRSET),                               X
                  LANG=COBOL,                                        X
                  MODE=INOUT,                                        X
                  TERM=3270,                                         X
                  TIOAPFX=YES
*
MAPPOVC    DFHMDI LINE=01,                                           X
                  COLUMN=01,                                         X
                  SIZE=(24,80)
*
           DFHMDF POS=(01,01),                                       X
                  ATTRB=ASKIP,                                       X
                  LENGTH=05,                                         X
                  INITIAL='DATE:'
*
MCDATE     DFHMDF POS=(01,07),                                       X
                  ATTRB=ASKIP,                                       X
                  LENGTH=08
*
           DFHMDF POS=(01,27),                                       X
                  ATTRB=ASKIP,                                       X
                  LENGTH=25,                                         X
                  INITIAL='ABC MANUFACTURING COMPANY'
*
           DFHMDF POS=(01,72),                                       X
                  ATTRB=ASKIP,                                       X
                  LENGTH=07,                                         X
                  INITIAL='POVMIQ1'
*
           DFHMDF POS=(02,01),                                       X
                  ATTRB=ASKIP,                                       X
                  LENGTH=05,                                         X
                  INITIAL='TIME:'
*
MCTIME     DFHMDF POS=(02,07),                                       X
                  ATTRB=ASKIP,                                       X
                  LENGTH=08
*
           DFHMDF POS=(02,26),                                       X
                  ATTRB=ASKIP,                                       X
                  LENGTH=27,                                         X
                  INITIAL='VENDOR FILE INQUIRY CONTROL'
*
           DFHMDF POS=(07,25),                                       X
                  ATTRB=ASKIP,                                       X
                  LENGTH=12,                                         X
                  INITIAL='VENDOR CODE:'
*
MCVCOD1    DFHMDF POS=(07,38),                                       X
                  ATTRB=(UNPROT,IC),                                 X
                  LENGTH=01
*
```

Figure 12-1 *(Continued)*

```
            DFHMDF POS=(07,40),                                        X
                   ATTRB=ASKIP,                                        X
                   LENGTH=01,                                          X
                   INITIAL='-'
*
MCVCOD2     DFHMDF POS=(07,42),                                        X
                   ATTRB=UNPROT,                                       X
                   LENGTH=04
*
            DFHMDF POS=(07,47),                                        X
                   ATTRB=ASKIP,                                        X
                   LENGTH=01,                                          X
                   INITIAL='-'
*
MCVCOD3     DFHMDF POS=(07,49),                                        X
                   ATTRB=UNPROT,                                       X
                   LENGTH=01
*
            DFHMDF POS=(07,51),                                        X
                   ATTRB=ASKIP,                                        X
                   LENGTH=01
*
            DFHMDF POS=(12,19),                                        X
                   ATTRB=ASKIP,                                        X
                   LENGTH=40,                                          X
                   INITIAL='1. FOR VENDOR FILE INQUIRY - PRESS ENTER'
*
            DFHMDF POS=(14,19),                                        X
                   ATTRB=ASKIP,                                        X
                   LENGTH=38,                                          X
                   INITIAL='2. TO BROWSE VENDOR FILE   - PRESS PF4'
*
            DFHMDF POS=(16,19),                                        X
                   ATTRB=ASKIP,                                        X
                   LENGTH=38,                                          X
                   INITIAL='3. TO RETURN TO MENU       - PRESS PF5'
*
            DFHMDF POS=(18,19),                                        X
                   ATTRB=ASKIP,                                        X
                   LENGTH=40,                                          X
                   INITIAL='4. TO END SESSION          - PRESS CLEAR'
*
MCMESSG     DFHMDF POS=(24,01),                                        X
                   ATTRB=ASKIP,                                        X
                   LENGTH=79
*
            DFHMSD TYPE=FINAL
            END
```

control attributes by modifying them prior to a send which includes the symbolic map. No IC attribute is defined on the BMS map because when the map is sent, the cursor is to be set at POS=(01,01). The cursor defaults to this position when the map is sent, unless CURSOR is specified on a send which includes the symbolic map, and −1 is moved to a map length field.

User-Friendly Symbolic Maps

User-friendly symbolic maps which correspond to the BMS-generated maps are shown in the copy library (App. B, members MAPVMCTL and MAPVDTL1). Each field defined on the BMS map has a corresponding user-friendly map field (see Chap. 6).

Figure 12-2　Vendor File Inquiry BMS Detail Map.

```
             PRINT NOGEN
POVMIQ2      DFHMSD TYPE=MAP,                                              X
                    CTRL=(FREEKB,FRSET),                                   X
                    LANG=COBOL,                                            X
                    MODE=INOUT,                                            X
                    TERM=3270,                                             X
                    TIOAPFX=YES
*
MAPPOVD      DFHMDI LINE=01,                                               X
                    COLUMN=01,                                             X
                    SIZE=(24,80)
*
             DFHMDF POS=(01,01),                                          X
                    ATTRB=ASKIP,                                          X
                    LENGTH=05,                                            X
                    INITIAL='DATE:'
*
MDDATE       DFHMDF POS=(01,07),                                          X
                    ATTRB=ASKIP,                                          X
                    LENGTH=08
*
             DFHMDF POS=(01,27),                                          X
                    ATTRB=ASKIP,                                          X
                    LENGTH=25,                                            X
                    INITIAL='ABC MANUFACTURING COMPANY'
*
             DFHMDF POS=(01,72),                                          X
                    ATTRB=ASKIP,                                          X
                    LENGTH=07,                                            X
                    INITIAL='POVMIQ2'
*
             DFHMDF POS=(02,01),                                          X
                    ATTRB=ASKIP,                                          X
                    LENGTH=05,                                            X
                    INITIAL='TIME:'
*
MDTIME       DFHMDF POS=(02,07),                                          X
                    ATTRB=ASKIP,                                          X
                    LENGTH=08
*
             DFHMDF POS=(02,30),                                          X
                    ATTRB=ASKIP,                                          X
                    LENGTH=19,                                            X
                    INITIAL='VENDOR FILE INQUIRY'
*
             DFHMDF POS=(04,01),                                          X
                    ATTRB=ASKIP,                                          X
                    LENGTH=12,                                            X
                    INITIAL='VENDOR CODE:'
*
MDVNDCD      DFHMDF POS=(04,14),                                          X
                    ATTRB=ASKIP,                                          X
                    LENGTH=08
*
             DFHMDF POS=(05,08),                                          X
                    ATTRB=ASKIP,                                          X
                    LENGTH=05,                                            X
                    INITIAL='NAME:'
*
MDVNDNM      DFHMDF POS=(05,14),                                          X
                    ATTRB=ASKIP,                                          X
                    LENGTH=25
*
             DFHMDF POS=(05,45),                                          X
                    ATTRB=ASKIP,                                          X
                    LENGTH=06,                                            X
                    INITIAL='PHONE:'
*
             DFHMDF POS=(05,54),                                          X
                    ATTRB=ASKIP,                                          X
                    LENGTH=01,                                            X
                    INITIAL='('
*
MDAREAC      DFHMDF POS=(05,56),                                          X
                    ATTRB=ASKIP,                                          X
                    LENGTH=03
*
             DFHMDF POS=(05,60),                                          X
                    ATTRB=ASKIP,                                          X
                    LENGTH=01,                                            X
                    INITIAL=')'
```

Figure 12-2 *(Continued)*

```
*
MDPHON1     DFHMDF POS=(05,62),                                        X
                   ATTRB=ASKIP,                                        X
                   LENGTH=03
*
            DFHMDF POS=(05,66),                                        X
                   ATTRB=ASKIP,                                        X
                   LENGTH=01,                                          X
                   INITIAL='-'
*
MDPHON2     DFHMDF POS=(05,68),                                        X
                   ATTRB=ASKIP,                                        X
                   LENGTH=04
*
            DFHMDF POS=(06,45),                                        X
                   ATTRB=ASKIP,                                        X
                   LENGTH=08,                                          X
                   INITIAL='CONTACT:'
*
MDCONTA     DFHMDF POS=(06,54),                                        X
                   ATTRB=ASKIP,                                        X
                   LENGTH=25
*
            DFHMDF POS=(08,01),                                        X
                   ATTRB=ASKIP,                                        X
                   LENGTH=17,                                          X
                   INITIAL='ADDRESS - STREET:'
*
MDSTRET     DFHMDF POS=(08,19),                                        X
                   ATTRB=ASKIP,                                        X
                   LENGTH=20
*
            DFHMDF POS=(08,45),                                        X
                   ATTRB=ASKIP,                                        X
                   LENGTH=18,                                          X
                   INITIAL='DOLLARS COMMITTED:'
*
MDDLRSC     DFHMDF POS=(08,64),                                        X
                   ATTRB=ASKIP,                                        X
                   LENGTH=15,                                          X
                   PICOUT='$$,$$$,$$$.99CR'
*
            DFHMDF POS=(09,13),                                        X
                   ATTRB=ASKIP,                                        X
                   LENGTH=05,                                          X
                   INITIAL='CITY:
*
MDCITY      DFHMDF POS=(09,19),                                        X
                   ATTRB=ASKIP,                                        X
                   LENGTH=18
*
            DFHMDF POS=(10,12),                                        X
                   ATTRB=ASKIP,                                        X
                   LENGTH=06,                                          X
                   INITIAL='STATE:'
*
MDSTATE     DFHMDF POS=(10,19),                                        X
                   ATTRB=ASKIP,                                        X
                   LENGTH=02
*
MDSTANM     DFHMDF POS=(10,22),                                        X
                   ATTRB=ASKIP,                                        X
                   LENGTH=14
*
            DFHMDF POS=(11,14),                                        X
                   ATTRB=ASKIP,                                        X
                   LENGTH=04,                                          X
                   INITIAL='ZIP:'
*
MDZIP       DFHMDF POS(11,19),                                         X
                   ATTRB=ASKIP,                                        X
                   LENGTH=05
*
            DFHMDF POS=(13,02),                                        X
                   ATTRB=ASKIP,                                        X
                   LENGTH=16,                                          X
                   INITIAL='TO ATTENTION OF:'
```

Figure 12-2   *(Continued)*

```
*
MDATTOF    DFHMDF POS=(13,19),                                            X
                  ATTRB=ASKIP,                                            X
                  LENGTH=20
*
           DFHMDF POS=(18,10),                                            X
                  ATTRB=ASKIP,                                            X
                  LENGTH=56,                                              X
                  INITIAL='1. RETURN TO INQUIRY CONTROL SCREEN     - PRX
                  ESS ENTER'
*
           DFHMDF POS=(19,10),                                            X
                  ATTRB=ASKIP,                                            X
                  LENGTH=54,                                              X
                  INITIAL='2. RETURN TO MENU                      - PRX
                  ESS PF5'
*
           DFHMDF POS=(20,10),                                            X
                  ATTRB=ASKIP,                                            X
                  LENGTH=56,                                              X
                  INITIAL='3. END OF SESSION                      - PRX
                  ESS CLEAR'
*
MDMESSG    DFHMDF POS=(24,01),                                            X
                  ATTRB=ASKIP,                                            X
                  LENGTH=79
*
           DFHMSD TYPE=FINAL
           END
```

Inquiry Program Source Code

The inquiry program source code shown in Fig. 12-3 follows the format used in previous examples. I will only discuss sections which contain new commands and concepts or those which need reinforcement.

Working-Storage Section

Copy library members, for all program examples, are found in the copy library (App. B). DFHAID can be found in App. A-3.

Linkage Section

The BLL cells in this program are used to establish addressability to two fields, the common work area (CWA) and state code table. The CWA is a system area common to all command-level CICS programs. It can be initialized by a system initiator program which is run on a daily basis. Member STLNKCWA in App. B contains a typical group of fields you might find in the CWA. The only CWA field that program examples in this book refer to is CWA-CURRENT-DATE. The CWA and state table will be discussed in more detail in the procedure division.

Procedure Division

The program structure for all sample programs is shown at the start of the procedure division. I find this format an acceptable and easier-to-maintain

Figure 12-3   Vendor File Inquiry Program Source Code.

```
0001 IDENTIFICATION DIVISION.
0002 PROGRAM-ID. POVMINQY.
0003 REMARKS.
0004*******************************************************************
0005*            PURCHASING SYSTEM - VENDOR FILE INQUIRY              *
0006*     - STARTED BY PURCHASING SYSTEM SUB-MENU PROGRAM 'POVMAINT'  *
0007*          COULD ALSO BE STARTED BY TRANSID 'POVI'                *
0008*******************************************************************
0009 ENVIRONMENT DIVISION.
0010 DATA DIVISION.
0011*
0012 WORKING-STORAGE  SECTION.
0013*
0014 01  WS-PROGRAM-FIELDS.
0015     05  FILLER            PIC X(8)      VALUE 'POVMINQY'.
0016     05  WS-CRT MESSAGE    PIC X(17)     VALUE 'SESSION COMPLETED'.
0017*
0018 01  VENDOR-MASTER-RECORD          COPY    VENDMAST.
0019 01  WS-COMMAREA                   COPY    POWSVMCA.
0020 01  WS-STATUS-FIELDS              COPY    STWSSTAT.
0021 01  VM-CONTROL-MAP                COPY    MAPVMCTL.
0022 01  VM-DETAIL-MAP                 COPY    MAPVDTL1.
0023 01  WS-DATE-AND-TIME              COPY    STWSDTTM.
0024 01  WS-STATE-CODE-SEARCH-ENTRIES  COPY    STWST037.
0025 01  ATTRIBUTE-LIST               COPY    STWSATTR.
0026 01  DFHAID                        COPY    DFHAID.
0027*
0028 01  END-OF-WORKING-STORAGE  PIC X(15)    VALUE 'END WS POVMINQY'.
0029*
0030 LINKAGE SECTION.
0031*
0032 01  DFHCOMMAREA                          PIC X(8).
0033*
0034 01  BLL-CELLS.
0035     05  FILLER                    PIC S9(8)    COMP.
0036     05  BLL-CWA-ADDRESS           PIC S9(8)    COMP.
0037     05  BLL-T037-STATE-TABLE-ADDRESS PIC S9(8) COMP.
0038*
0039 01  CWA-DATA         COPY    STLNKCWA.
0040 01  T037-STATE TABLE COPY    T037STAT.
0041*
0042 PROCEDURE DIVISION.
0043*******************************************************************
0044*    PROGRAM STRUCTURE IS:                                        *
0045*        AA00-MAINLINE                                            *
0046*           B000-INITIAL-ENTRY                                    *
0047*               B100-SEND-CONTROL-MAP-AND-DATA                    *
0048*                   B110-GET-DATE-AND-TIME                        *
0049*                                                                 *
0050*           C000-PROCESS-CONTROL-MAP                              *
0051*               C100-RECEIVE-CONTROL-MAP                          *
0052*                   C110-END-SESSION                              *
0053*                   C120-TRANSFER-XCTL-TO-MENU                    *
0054*                   C130-TRANSFER-XCTL-TO-BROWSE                  *
0055*               C200-VERIFY-VENDOR-FORMAT                         *
0056*               C400-VERIFY-VENDOR-FILE-STATUS                    *
0057*                   C410-READ-VENDOR-FILE                         *
0058*               C500-SEND-DETAIL-MAP-AND-DATA                     *
0059*                   B110-GET-DATE-AND-TIME                        *
0060*                   C530-FORMAT-DETAIL-MAP                        *
0061*                       C531-GET-STATE-NAME                       *
0062*               C600-SEND-CONTROL-MAP-DATAONLY                    *
0063*                                                                 *
0064*           D000-INQUIRY-PROCESSING                               *
0065*               D100-RECEIVE-DETAIL-MAP                           *
0066*                   C110-END-SESSION                              *
0067*                   C120-TRANSFER-XCTL-TO-MENU                    *
0068*               B100-SEND-CONTROL-MAP-AND-DATA                    *
0069*               D200-SEND-DETAIL-MAP-DATAONLY                     *
0070*******************************************************************
```

Figure 12-3 *(Continued)*

```
0071*
0072 AA00-MAINLINE  SECTION.
0073*
0074*     SERVICE RELOAD BLL-CELLS.
0075*
0076      IF EIBCALEN = 0
0077          PERFORM B000-INITIAL-ENTRY
0078      ELSE
0079          MOVE DFHCOMMAREA  TO  WS-COMMAREA
0080          IF CA-RECEIVE-CTL-MAP
0081              PERFORM C000-PROCESS-CONTROL-MAP
0082          ELSE
0083              PERFORM D000-INQUIRY-PROCESSING.
0084*
0085      EXEC CICS RETURN
0086              TRANSID  ('POVI')
0087              COMMAREA (WS-COMMAREA)
0088              LENGTH   (8)
0089      END-EXEC.
0090*
0091 B000-INITIAL-ENTRY  SECTION.
0092*********************************************************************
0093*         INITIAL ENTRY INTO PROGRAM - ONLY EXECUTED ONCE       *
0094*                  PERFORMED FROM:  AA00-MAINLINE                *
0095*********************************************************************
0096*
0097      MOVE LOW-VALUES  TO  VM-CONTROL-MAP.
0098      PERFORM B100-SEND-CONTROL-MAP-AND-DATA.
0099*
0100 B000-EXIT.
0101      EXIT.
0102*
0103 B100-SEND-CONTROL-MAP-AND-DATA  SECTION.
0104*********************************************************************
0105*         SEND CONTROL MAP - SYMBOLIC AND PHYSICAL MAPS         *
0106*              PERFORMED FROM:  B000-INITIAL-ENTRY               *
0107*                               D000-INQUIRY-PROCESSING          *
0108*********************************************************************
0109*
0110      PERFORM B110-GET-DATE-AND-TIME.
0111      MOVE WS-CURRENT-DATE  TO  MVC-D-DATE.
0112      MOVE WS-MAP-TIME      TO  MVC-D-TIME.
0113*
0114      MOVE -1   TO  MVC-L-VEND-CD-1.
0115      MOVE '1'  TO  CA-MAP-CONTROL.
0116*
0117      EXEC CICS SEND
0118              MAP     ('MAPPOVC')
0119              MAPSET  ('POVMIQ1')
0120              FROM    (VM-CONTROL-MAP)
0121              ERASE
0122              CURSOR
0123      END-EXEC.
0124*
0125 B100-EXIT.
0126      EXIT.
0127*
0128 B110-GET-DATE-AND-TIME  SECTION  COPY  STPDDTTM.
0129*********************************************************************
0130*         STPDDTTM - OBTAIN DATE FROM CWA AND FORMAT TIME       *
0131*         PERFORMED FROM:  B100-SEND-CONTROL-MAP-AND-DATA        *
0132*                          C500-SEND-DETAIL-MAP-AND-DATA         *
0133*********************************************************************
0134*
0135 B110-EXIT.
0136      EXIT.
0137*
0138 C000-PROCESS-CONTROL-MAP  SECTION.
0139*********************************************************************
0140*                  PERFORMED FROM:  AA00-MAINLINE                *
0141*         PROCESS CONTROL MAP - IF VALID SEND DETAIL MAP        *
0142*              ELSE SEND CONTROL MAP WITH INVALID MESSAGE:       *
0143*  1) STATUS-OF-RECEIVE  =  'I'   INVALID KEY PRESSED           *
0144*  2) STATUS-OF-RECEIVE  =  'M'   MAPFAIL - NO DATA ENTERED     *
0145*  3) STATUS-OF-FORMAT   =  'E'   INVALID VENDOR KEYED FORMAT   *
0146*  4) STATUS-OF-VERIFY   =  'E'   VENDOR FILE STATUS ERROR      *
0147*********************************************************************
```

Figure 12-3 *(Continued)*

```
0148*
0149      PERFORM C100-RECEIVE-CONTROL-MAP.
0150      IF GOOD-RECEIVE
0151          PERFORM C200-VERIFY-VENDOR-FORMAT
0152          IF VALID-FORMAT
0153              PERFORM C400-VERIFY-VENDOR-FILE-STATUS
0154              IF GOOD-VERIFY
0155                  PERFORM C500-SEND-DETAIL-MAP-AND-DATA
0156              ELSE
0157                  PERFORM C600-SEND-CONTROL-MAP-DATAONLY
0158          ELSE
0159              PERFORM C600-SEND-CONTROL-MAP-DATAONLY
0160      ELSE
0161          IF MAPFAIL-ON-RECEIVE
0162              MOVE 'VENDOR CODE MUST BE ENTERED - PLEASE KEY-IN'
0163                              TO MVC-D-MESSAGE
0164              MOVE ASKIP-BRT  TO MVC-A-MESSAGE
0165              PERFORM C600-SEND-CONTROL-MAP-DATAONLY
0166          ELSE
0167              PERFORM C600-SEND-CONTROL-MAP-DATAONLY.
0168*
0169 C000-EXIT.
0170      EXIT.
0171*
0172 C100-RECEIVE-CONTROL-MAP  SECTION.
0173*******************************************************************
0174*         PERFORMED FROM:  C000-PROCESS-CONTROL-MAP         *
0175*             ENTER IS ONLY VALID DATA ENTRY KEY            *
0176*  CLEAR KEY - ENDS TERMINAL SESSION    PF5 - RETURNS TO MENU  *
0177*                                       PF4 - XCTL TO BROWSE    *
0178*             ALL OTHER AID KEYS ARE INVALID               *
0179*      STATUS-OF-RECEIVE  =  'G'  =  GOOD RECEIVE           *
0180*                            'M'  =  MAPFAIL                *
0181*                            'I'  =  INVALID KEY PRESSED    *
0182*******************************************************************
0183*
0184      MOVE LOW-VALUES  TO  VM-CONTROL-MAP.
0185*
0186      IF EIBAID  =  DFHENTER
0187          MOVE 'M' TO  STATUS OF RECEIVE
0188*
0189          EXEC CICS HANDLE CONDITION
0190                    MAPFAIL (C100-EXIT)
0191          END-EXEC
0192*
0193          EXEC CICS RECEIVE
0194                    MAP    ('MAPPOVC')
0195                    MAPSET ('POVMIQ1')
0196                    INTO   (VM-CONTROL-MAP)
0197          END-EXEC
0198*
0199          MOVE 'G' TO  STATUS-OF-RECEIVE
0200      ELSE
0201          IF EIBAID  =  DFHCLEAR
0202              PERFORM C110-END-SESSION
0203          ELSE
0204          IF EIBAID  =  DFHPF5
0205              PERFORM C120-TRANSFER-XCTL-TO-MENU
0206          ELSE
0207          IF EIBAID  =  DFHPF4
0208              PERFORM C130-TRANSFER-XCTL-TO-BROWSE
0209          ELSE
0210              MOVE 'I'        TO  STATUS-OF-RECEIVE
0211              MOVE 'INVALID KEY PRESSED - PLEASE TRY AGAIN'
0212                              TO  MVC-D-MESSAGE
0213              MOVE ASKIP-BRT  TO  MVC-A-MESSAGE.
0214*
0215 C100-EXIT.
0216      EXIT.
0217*
0218 C110-END-SESSION  SECTION.
0219*******************************************************************
0220*  CRT OPERATOR PRESSED CLEAR KEY TO END TERMINAL SESSION   *
0221*         PERFORMED FROM:  C100-RECEIVE-CONTROL-MAP         *
```

Figure 12-3 *(Continued)*

```
0222*                        D100-RECEIVE-DETAIL-MAP                      *
0223*******************************************************************
0224*
0225      EXEC CICS SEND
0226               FROM    (WS-CRT-MESSAGE)
0227               LENGTH (17)
0228               ERASE
0229      END-EXEC.
0230*
0231      EXEC CICS RETURN
0232      END-EXEC.
0233*
0234 C110-EXIT.
0235      EXIT.
0236*
0237 C120-TRANSFER-XCTL-TO-MENU  SECTION.
0238*******************************************************************
0239*         OPERATOR PRESSED PF5 TO RETURN TO MENU PROGRAM         *
0240*            PERFORMED FROM:  C100-RECEIVE-CONTROL-MAP           *
0241*                        D100-RECEIVE-DETAIL-MAP                 *
0242*******************************************************************
0243*
0244      EXEC CICS XCTL
0245               PROGRAM ('POVMAINT')
0246      END-EXEC.
0247*
0248 C120-EXIT.
0249      EXIT.
0250*
0251 C130-TRANSFER-XCTL-TO-BROWSE  SECTION.
0252*******************************************************************
0253*      OPERATOR PRESSED PF4 TO TRANSFER CONTROL TO BROWSE       *
0254*            PERFORMED FROM:  C100-RECEIVE-CONTROL-MAP          *
0255*******************************************************************
0256*
0257      MOVE LOW-VALUES  TO  WS-COMMAREA.
0258      MOVE 'I'         TO  CA-FUNCTION-CODE.
0259*
0260      EXEC CICS XCTL
0261               PROGRAM  ('POVMBROW')
0262               COMMAREA (WS-COMMAREA)
0263               LENGTH   (8)
0264      END-EXEC.
0265*
0266 C130-EXIT.
0267      EXIT.
0268*
0269 C200-VERIFY-VENDOR-FORMAT  SECTION.
0270*******************************************************************
0271*        VERIFY FORMAT OF VENDOR CODE KEYED-IN = A-9999-9        *
0272*            PERFORMED FROM:  C000-PROCESS-CONTROL-MAP           *
0273*    IF VALID FORMAT - MOVE CODE TO WS-COMMAREA FIELDS (CA- )    *
0274*******************************************************************
0275*
0276      IF (MVC-D-VENDOR-CD-1  IS  ALPHABETIC
0277               AND
0278        MVC-D-VENDOR-CD-1  IS NOT = SPACE)
0279        AND
0280        MVC-D-VENDOR-CD-2  IS  NUMERIC
0281        AND
0282        MVC-D-VENDOR-CD-3  IS  NUMERIC
0283        MOVE MVC-D-VEND-CD-1  TO  CA-VEND-1
0284        MOVE MVC-D-VEND-CD-2  TO  CA-VEND-2
0285        MOVE MVC-D-VEND-CD-3  TO  CA-VEND-3
0286        MOVE 'G'              TO  STATUS-OF-FORMAT
0287      ELSE
0288        MOVE 'E'      TO  STATUS-OF-FORMAT
0289        MOVE 'VENDOR CODE FORMAT MUST BE: A-9999-9 - PLEASE RE-EN
0290-             'TER'   TO  MVC-D-MESSAGE
0291        MOVE ASKIP-BRT  TO  MVC-A-MESSAGE.
0292*
0293 C200-EXIT.
0294      EXIT.
0295*
0296 C400-VERIFY-VENDOR-FILE-STATUS  SECTION.
0297*******************************************************************
0298*           PERFORMED FROM:  C000-PROCESS-CONTROL-MAP           *
0299*           MUST BE A VENDOR RECORD FOR INQUIRIES              *
0300*******************************************************************
```

Figure 12-3 (*Continued*)

```
0301*
0302      MOVE 'G'  TO  STATUS-OF-VERIFY.
0303*
0304      PERFORM C410-READ-VENDOR-FILE.
0305*
0306      IF RECORD-NOT-FOUND
0307          MOVE 'E'        TO  STATUS-OF-VERIFY
0308          MOVE 'VENDOR RECORD NOT ON FILE'
0309                          TO  MVC-D-MESSAGE
0310          MOVE ASKIP-BRT  TO  MVC-A-MESSAGE.
0311*
0312 C400-EXIT.
0313      EXIT.
0314*
0315 C410-READ-VENDOR-FILE  SECTION.
0316****************************************************************
0317*        PERFORMED FROM:  C400-VERIFY-VENDOR-FILE-STATUS      *
0318****************************************************************
0319*
0320      MOVE 'E'  TO  STATUS-OF-READ.
0321*
0322      EXEC CICS HANDLE CONDITION
0323                NOTFND  (C410-EXIT)
0324      END-EXEC.
0325*
0326      EXEC CICS READ
0327                DATASET  ('VENDMAST')
0328                INTO     (VENDOR-MASTER-RECORD)
0329                RIDFLD   (CA-VENDOR-CODE)
0330      END-EXEC.
0331*
0332      MOVE 'G'  TO  STATUS-OF-READ.
0333*
0334 C410-EXIT.
0335      EXIT.
0336*
0337 C500-SEND-DETAIL-MAP-AND-DATA  SECTION.
0338****************************************************************
0339*        SEND DETAIL MAP - PHYSICAL AND SYMBOLIC MAPS        *
0340*             PERFORMED FROM:  C000-PROCESS-CONTROL-MAP       *
0341*   SENT WHEN ALL VALIDATION AND EDIT CONDITIONS HAVE BEEN MET *
0342****************************************************************
0343*
0344      MOVE LOW-VALUES  TO  VM-DETAIL-MAP.
0345*
0346      PERFORM B110-GET-DATE-AND-TIME.
0347      MOVE WS-CURRENT-DATE  TO  MVD-D-DATE.
0348      MOVE WS-MAP-TIME      TO  MVD-D-TIME.
0349*
0350      PERFORM C530-FORMAT-DETAIL-MAP.
0351*
0352      MOVE '2'  TO  CA-MAP-CONTROL.
0353*
0354      EXEC CICS SEND
0355                MAP     ('MAPPOVD')
0356                MAPSET  ('POVMIQ2')
0357                FROM    (VM-DETAIL-MAP)
0358                ERASE
0359      END-EXEC.
0360*
0361 C500-EXIT.
0362      EXIT.
0363*
0364 C530-FORMAT-DETAIL-MAP  SECTION.
0365****************************************************************
0366*        PERFORMED FROM:  C500-SEND-DETAIL-MAP-AND-DATA       *
0367****************************************************************
0368*
0369* FORMAT VENDOR CODE: A-9999-9    WS- FIELDS ARE AT END OF VENDMAST
0370      MOVE CA-VEND-1          TO  WS-VENDOR-CD-1.
0371      MOVE CA-VEND-2          TO  WS-VENDOR-CD-2.
0372      MOVE CA-VEND-3          TO  WS-VENDOR-CD-3.
0373      MOVE WS-VENDOR-CODE     TO  MVD-D-VENDOR-CODE.
0374*
0375      MOVE VM-AREA-CD         TO  MVD-D-PHONE-AREA-CODE.
0376      MOVE VM-PHONE-1-3       TO  MVD-D-PHONE-1.
0377      MOVE VM-PHONE-4-7       TO  MVD-D-PHONE-2.
0378      MOVE VM-VENDOR-NAME     TO  MVD-D-VENDOR-NAME.
0379      MOVE VM-CONTACT         TO  MVD-D-CONTACT.
0380      MOVE VM-STREET-ADDRESS  TO  MVD-D-STREET.
0381      MOVE VM-CITY            TO  MVD-D-CITY.
0382      MOVE VM-STATE           TO  MVD-D-STATE-CODE.
```

Figure 12-3 *(Continued)*

```
0383*
0384       MOVE VM-STATE                    TO   WS-STATE-CODE.
0385       PERFORM C531-GET-STATE-NAME.
0386       MOVE WS-STATE-NAME               TO   MVD-D-STATE-NAME.
0387*
0388       MOVE VM-ZIP-CODE                 TO   MVD-D-ZIP-CODE.
0389       MOVE VM-TO-ATTN-OF               TO   MVD-D-ATTENTION-OF.
0390       MOVE VM-DOLLARS-COMMITTED        TO   MVD-D-DLRS-COMMITTED.
0391*
0392 C530-EXIT.
0393       EXIT.
0394*
0395 C531-GET-STATE-NAME  SECTION   COPY   STPDT037.
0396*********************************************************************
0397*                LOAD AND SEARCH STATE CODE TABLE               *
0398*         PERFORMED FROM:  C530-SEND-DETAIL-MAP-AND-DATA         *
0399*********************************************************************
0400*
0401 C531-EXIT.
0402       EXIT.
0403*
0404 C600-SEND-CONTROL-MAP-DATAONLY  SECTION.
0405*********************************************************************
0406*         SEND CONTROL MAP DATAONLY - SYMBOLIC MAP              *
0407*         PERFORMED FROM:  C000-PROCESS-CONTROL-MAP             *
0408*                SENT FOR INVALID CONDITIONS                    *
0409*********************************************************************
0410*
0411       MOVE '1'  TO  CA-MAP-CONTROL.
0412       MOVE -1   TO  MVC-L-VEND-CD-1.
0413*
0414       MOVE UNPROT-FSET TO  MVC-A-VEND-CD-1
0415                            MVC-A-VEND-CD-2
0416                            MVC-A-VEND-CD-3.
0417*
0418       EXEC CICS SEND
0419               MAP       ('MAPPOVC')
0420               MAPSET    ('POVMIQ1')
0421               FROM      (VM-CONTROL-MAP)
0422               DATAONLY
0423               CURSOR
0424       END-EXEC.
0425*
0426 C600-EXIT.
0427       EXIT.
0428*
0429 D000-INQUIRY-PROCESSING  SECTION.
0430*********************************************************************
0431*                PERFORMED FROM:  AA00-MAINLINE                 *
0432*         DETAIL MAP IS SENT IF AN INVALID KEY WAS PRESSED      *
0433*********************************************************************
0434*
0435       PERFORM D100-RECEIVE-DETAIL-MAP.
0436*
0437       IF GOOD-RECEIVE
0438           PERFORM B100-SEND-CONTROL-MAP-AND-DATA
0439       ELSE
0440           PERFORM D200-SEND-DETAIL-MAP-DATAONLY.
0441*
0442 D000-EXIT.
0443       EXIT.
0444*
0445 D100-RECEIVE-DETAIL-MAP  SECTION.
0446*********************************************************************
0447*         PERFORMED FROM:  D000-INQUIRY-PROCESSING              *
0448* ENTER - RETURN TO CONTROL SCREEN      CLEAR - ENDS SESSION    *
0449*                              PF5    - RETURN TO MENU          *
0450*                ALL OTHER KEYS ARE INVALID                     *
0451*         STATUS-OF-RECEIVE  =  'G'  =  GOOD RECEIVE            *
0452*                               'I'  =  INVALID KEY PRESSED     *
0453*********************************************************************
0454*
0455       MOVE LOW-VALUES  TO  VM-DETAIL-MAP.
0456*
0457       IF EIBAID  =  DFHENTER
0458*
0459           EXEC CICS IGNORE CONDITION
0460                   MAPFAIL
0461           END-EXEC
```

Figure 12-3 *(Continued)*

```
0462*
0463          EXEC CICS RECEIVE
0464                    MAP      ('MAPPOVD')
0465                    MAPSET   ('POVMIQ2')
0466                    INTO     (VM-DETAIL-MAP)
0467          END-EXEC
0468*
0469          MOVE 'G' TO STATUS-OF-RECEIVE
0470     ELSE
0471          IF EIBAID = DFHCLEAR
0472              PERFORM C110-END-SESSION
0473          ELSE
0474          IF EIBAID = DFHPF5
0475              PERFORM C120-TRANSFER-XCTL-TO-MENU
0476          ELSE
0477              MOVE 'I'      TO STATUS-OF-RECEIVE
0478              MOVE 'INVALID KEY PRESSED - PLEASE TRY AGAIN'
0479                            TO MVD-D-MESSAGE
0480              MOVE ASKIP-BRT TO MVD-A-MESSAGE.
0481*
0482 D100-EXIT.
0483     EXIT.
0484*
0485 D200-SEND-DETAIL-MAP-DATAONLY  SECTION.
0486******************************************************************
0487*          SEND DETAIL MAP DATA ONLY - SYMBOLIC MAP           *
0488*       PERFORMED FROM:  D000-INQUIRY-PROCESSING              *
0489*  SENT IF INVALID KEY IS PRESSED ON A RECEIVE OF THE DETAIL MAP *
0490******************************************************************
0491*
0492     MOVE '2' TO CA-MAP-CONTROL.
0493*
0494     EXEC CICS SEND
0495               MAP      ('MAPPOVD')
0496               MAPSET   ('POVMIQ2')
0497               FROM     (VM-DETAIL-MAP)
0498               DATAONLY
0499     END-EXEC.
0500*
0501 D200-EXIT.
0502     EXIT.
```

substitute for a drawn block program structure chart. Even this form of the program structure chart requires maintenance. You might want to write a program which will generate the program structure and print it in this format. As you develop or enhance your standards, you will have to decide on the level of documentation you want to maintain.

AA00-MAINLINE.   This section is similar to that of previously discussed programs. On the first entry into the program, EIBCALEN is equal to 0 and the program performs B000-INITIAL-ENTRY. On succeeding entries EIBCALEN equals 8 (see the RETURN command) and DFHCOMMAREA will be moved to WS-COMMAREA. The contents of the COMMAREA field CA-MAP-CONTROL (see App. B, POWSVMCA) will be used as a switch to determine whether the program will receive the control or detail map. The program issues a RETURN command, with a TRANSID of POVI and a COMMAREA 8 bytes long. When the terminal operator presses an AID key, this program will be initiated again.

B100-SEND-CONTROL-MAP-AND-DATA.   Issues a PERFORM command to obtain date and time and then moves them to the control map. A 1 is moved to

CA-MAP-CONTROL. This is a signal on a subsequent entry into the program that the control map is to be received. A −1 is moved to the map's vendor code length field in order to set the cursor at the first position of that field on the SEND MAP command which contains the symbolic map and the CURSOR option.

B110-GET-DATE-AND-TIME.   The get-date-and-time routine is found in the copy library (App. B, member STPDDTTM). Two new CICS commands are introduced: the ASSIGN and ADDRESS commands. The ASSIGN command allows a program to access values outside the program. The most commonly accessed value is the length of the CWA. The CWA, as mentioned earlier in the chapter, is an area used by the system to pass common data to a program. Before attempting to establish addressability and access CWA data, it is good practice to make sure the CWA is available to CICS. The copy library member used for the CWA should be the proper length.

```
EXEC CICS ASSIGN
            CWALENG (WS-CWA-LENGTH)
END-EXEC.
```

Execution of this command makes the length of the CWA available in a working-storage field WS-CWA-LENGTH, which must be defined as a halfword binary value.

The ADDRESS command is used to establish addressability to the CWA and other system areas. It is similar in effect to the LOAD command in that it sets the address so that the BLL cell points to the CWA. Once addressability has been established, the program can access all data defined in the CWA.

```
EXEC CICS ADDRESS
            CWA (BLL-CWA-ADDRESS)
END-EXEC.
```

The execution of this command will set the linkage-section pointer BLL-CWA-ADDRESS to the address of CWA-DATA and make the CWA data available to the program.

Time is obtained from the EIB field EIBTIME and formatted to HH.MM.SS.

C000-PROCESS-CONTROL-MAP.   This section, which is similar for all maintenance functions, receives the control map, then verifies the format of vendor code. The status of the vendor file is checked to make sure a record is available to display; if so, a formatted detail map is sent. Invalid conditions, which prevent the display of the detail map, will result in the control map's being sent with an appropriate highlighted ASKIP,BRT message displayed.

C100-RECEIVE-CONTROL-MAP. This section receives the symbolic map into the working-storage area VM-CONTROL-MAP and can invoke the end-of-session or the transfer of control to the submenu or to the browse program.

C120-TRANSFER-XCTL-TO-MENU. This section transfers control back to the vendor file maintenance submenu, program POVMAINT (see Fig. 6-3).

C130-TRANSFER-XCTL-TO-BROWSE. This section transfers control to the vendor file browse program POVMBROW, which is discussed in Chap. 17. This program could pass an entered vendor code to POVMBROW. For simplicity, the code will be entered in the browse program. An I moved to CA-FUNCTION-CODE signals the browse program that control was transferred to POVMBROW by the inquiry program POVMINQY. This code will be used by the browse program to signal a return of control to POVMINQY if desired. The addition, change, and delete programs will, respectively, move an A, C, or D to CA-FUNCTION-CODE.

C200-VERIFY-VENDOR-FORMAT. This section verifies that the keyed-in vendor code is of the proper format A-9999-9. If the format is correct, the vendor code is moved to the working-storage area WS-COMMAREA; otherwise an error message and indicator are returned.

C400-VERIFY-VENDOR-FILE-STATUS. This section performs a read of the vendor file to make sure the vendor entered is on the file. If the vendor is not on the file, an error indicator is set and an error message returned.

C410-READ-VENDOR-FILE. In this section an E is moved immediately to STATUS-OF-READ, prior to executing the READ command for the vendor file. If the record is on the file, it is read into the working-storage area VENDOR-MASTER-RECORD, and a G is moved to STATUS-OF-READ. RIDFLD was set in section C200-VERIFY-VENDOR-FORMAT.

C500-SEND-DETAIL-MAP-AND-DATA. This section performs a format of the detail map and moves a 2 to CA-MAP-CONTROL, so that on a succeeding entry into this program the detail map will be received. Physical and symbolic maps are sent; the symbolic map is located in the working-storage area VM-DETAIL-MAP.

C530-FORMAT-DETAIL-MAP. This section moves vendor master file data to the appropriate map fields.

C531-GET-STATE-NAME. Logic for obtaining state name is found in the copy library (App. B, member STPDT037). This logic is included in the system in order to demonstrate the use of a nonresident table which is released from main storage as soon as it is no longer required.

```
EXEC CICS LOAD
          PROGRAM ('T037STAT')
          SET       (BLL-T037-STATE-TABLE-ADDRESS)
END-EXEC.
```

This LOAD command establishes addressability to the state code table. The state name obtained is moved to the working-storage field WS-STATE-NAME. If a state is not found, all * are moved to WS-STATE-NAME.

After the search of the state table is complete, the following command releases the state table from main storage.

```
EXEC CICS RELEASE
          PROGRAM ('T037STAT')
END-EXEC.
```

C600-SEND-CONTROL-MAP-DATAONLY. This is performed when an invalid condition occurs. UNPROT,FSET attributes are moved to the map's vendor code fields so that if vendor code was entered correctly, it will be returned on a subsequent receive of the map. FRSET on the BMS map's DFHMSD parameter turns off all MDTs prior to a send; −1 is moved to the symbolic map's length field. CURSOR is specified on the send in order to set the cursor at the first position of vendor code.

D100-RECEIVE-DETAIL-MAP. This section receives the detail map and, if the ENTER key was pressed, returns to the invoking section. The IGNORE command is used as follows:

```
EXEC CICS IGNORE CONDITION
          MAPFAIL
END-EXEC.
```

This command directs that if the specified condition (in this case MAPFAIL) occurs, the condition should be ignored. MAPFAIL is a common occurrence on many types of maps which do not require the entry of data. This command permits program logic to fall through to the MOVE command following the receive. The same result would be achieved on a MAPFAIL if a HANDLE CONDITION command directed control as follows:

```
        EXEC CICS   HANDLE CONDITION
                    MAPFAIL (D100-MOVE-G-TO-STATUS)
        END-EXEC.
            .
            .
            .
        D100-MOVE-G-TO-STATUS.
            MOVE 'G'   TO    STATUS-OF-RECEIVE.
```

If the CLEAR key or PF5 key is pressed, this section directs control to C110-END-SESSION or C120-TRANSFER-XCTL-TO-MENU, respectively. Any other key would result in an invalid key message being displayed on the detail map.

D200-SEND-DETAIL-MAP-DATAONLY.   If an invalid key was pressed prior to the receive of the detail map, this section sends the detail symbolic map only. A 2 is moved to CA-MAP-CONTROL so that the mainline section AA00-MAINLINE will direct control to the receive of the detail map on a subsequent entry into this program.

SUMMARY

The inquiry program presented here can be used as a model for most inquiry programs you will have to write. Several of the commands explained in preceding chapters were used, and a few new commands introduced. The COMMAREA contents were used in order to determine whether to receive the control or detail map. The SEND MAP AND DATA command was used, as was the READ file command. Other new commands presented were ASSIGN and ADDRESS. The maintenance programs presented in the next three chapters are very similar in format to the inquiry program.

13

THE ADDITION PROGRAM

After a file has been created and an inquiry program written to check the status of various fields, it is often necessary to make new additions to the file. The addition program is discussed in this chapter.

Control and detail maps are used for the addition program. The control map shown in Fig. 13-1 requires the terminal operator to key in a vendor code and to press ENTER in order to display the addition detail map. The operator also has the option of transferring control to the vendor file browse, returning to the vendor file maintenance submenu (see Fig. 6-3), or ending the session. The vendor file addition detail screen is defined by the map shown in Fig. 2-7. It is displayed when the operator keys in a vendor code on the control screen, which is not currently on the vendor file. The detail map shows as X's all fields which can be added to the vendor's record. This map permits the operator to key in the vendor's data and then press ENTER in order to add the record. The detail map gives an operator the option of returning to the addition control screen without adding the record, returning to the submenu, or ending the session.

BMS Maps

Figures 13-2 and 13-3 show the BMS maps for the control and detail maps shown in Figs. 13-1 and 2-7, respectively.

BMS Control Map

Only the differences between this map and the BMS control map for the inquiry program (see Fig. 12-1) are shown in Fig. 13-2. Keeping fields in the same position for similar maps makes the creation of new maps easy. An existing map serves as a model for others.

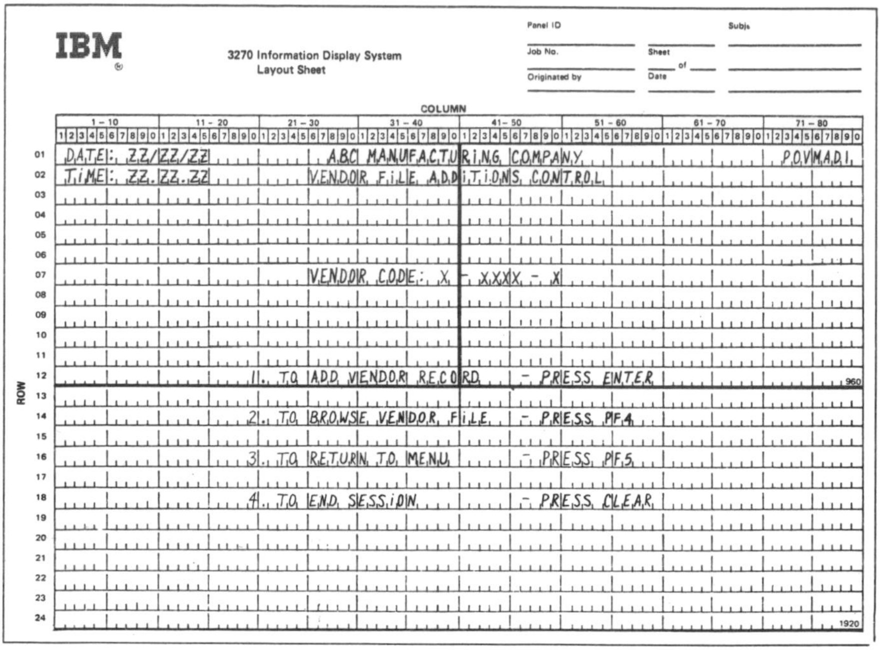

Figure 13-1 Vendor File Additions Control Map.

BMS Detail Map

All addition detail map attributes could be defined as ASKIP. The program could then control the attributes by modifying them prior to a send which includes the symbolic map. I have defined data-entry fields as UNPROT because this makes the initial testing of the map's format easier. The data-entry fields can be checked by using the command-level interpreter (CECI) discussed in Chap. 6 to display the map and check its format. All UNPROT fields have either a trailing ASKIP field or a following stopper field to limit the size of the data-entry field. Fields which require data to be entered on an addition screen have field names assigned. For instance, NAME:, a required field, is assigned a field name MDCVMNM. This will result in a symbolic map label being generated when the BMS map is assembled. Include user-friendly symbolic map entries for all field identifiers of items which will be referenced. For instance, see user-friendly map label MVD-C-A-VENDOR-NAME for member MAPVDTL2 in App. B. The program has the ability to brighten and darken field identifiers as required when testing for the entry of valid data. No IC attribute is defined on this map because the program sets the cursor by moving −1 to the appropriate length field in the symbolic map. The map is then sent with CURSOR specified.

```
          PRINT NOGEN
POVMAD1   DFHMSD TYPE=MAP,                                        X
                .
                .
          DFHMDF POS=(01,72),                                     X
                 ATTRB=ASKIP,                                     X
                 LENGTH=07,                                       X
                 INITIAL='POVMAD1'
                .
                .
          DFHMDF POS=(02,25),                                     X
                 ATTRB=ASKIP,                                     X
                 LENGTH=29,                                       X
                 INITIAL='VENDOR FILE ADDITIONS CONTROL'
                .
                .
          DFHMDF POS=(12,19),                                     X
                 ATTRB=ASKIP,                                     X
                 LENGTH=40,                                       X
                 INITIAL='1. TO ADD VENDOR RECORD    - PRESS ENTER'
                .
                .
                .
```

Figure 13-2 Vendor File Additions BMS Control Map.

User-Friendly Symbolic Maps

User-friendly symbolic maps created to correspond to generated BMS maps are shown in the copy library (App. B, members MAPVMCTL and MAPVDTL2). Note the inclusion of additional names for the field identifiers on the detail symbolic map. They are used by the addition program to highlight field identifiers of incorrectly entered items.

Addition Program Source Code

The addition program source code shown in Fig. 13-4 follows the format used in previous examples. I will discuss only sections which differ from previous examples.

Procedure Division

AA00-MAINLINE. This section is similar to that of the inquiry program in Chap. 12 except that the perform E000-ADDITION-PROCESSING replaces D000-INQUIRY-PROCESSING and TRANSID POVA replaces POVI.

C400-VERIFY-VENDOR-FILE-STATUS. This section performs a read of the vendor file to make sure that the vendor to be added is not already on the file. If the vendor is on the file, an error indicator is set and an error message is returned.

C410-READ-VENDOR-FILE. An E is moved immediately to STATUS-OF-READ prior to executing the READ command for the vendor file. If the record is on

Figure 13-3   Vendor File Additions BMS Detail Map.

```
          PRINT NOGEN
POVMAD2   DFHMSD TYPE=MAP,                                        X
                 CTRL=(FREEKB,FRSET),                             X
                 LANG=COBOL,                                      X
                 MODE=INOUT,                                      X
                 TERM=3270,                                       X
                 TIOAPFX=YES
*
MAPPOVD   DFHMDI LINE=01,                                         X
                 COLUMN=01,                                       X
                 SIZE=(24,80)
*
          DFHMDF POS=(01,01),                                     X
                 ATTRB=ASKIP,                                     X
                 LENGTH=05,                                       X
                 INITIAL='DATE:'
*
MDDATE    DFHMDF POS=(01,07),                                     X
                 ATTRB=ASKIP,                                     X
                 LENGTH=08
*
          DFHMDF POS=(01,27),                                     X
                 ATTRB=ASKIP,                                     X
                 LENGTH=25,                                       X
                 INITIAL='ABC MANUFACTURING COMPANY'
*
          DFHMDF POS=(01,72),                                     X
                 ATTRB=ASKIP,                                     X
                 LENGTH=07,                                       X
                 INITIAL='POVMAD2'
*
          DFHMDF POS=(02,01),                                     X
                 ATTRB=ASKIP,                                     X
                 LENGTH=05,                                       X
                 INITIAL='TIME:'
*
MDTIME    DFHMDF POS=(02,07),                                     X
                 ATTRB=ASKIP,                                     X
                 LENGTH=08
*
          DFHMDF POS=(02,30),                                     X
                 ATTRB=ASKIP,                                     X
                 LENGTH=20,                                       X
                 INITIAL='VENDOR FILE ADDITION'
*
          DFHMDF POS=(04,01),                                     X
                 ATTRB=ASKIP,                                     X
                 LENGTH=12,                                       X
                 INITIAL='VENDOR CODE:'
*
MDVNDCD   DFHMDF POS=(04,14),                                     X
                 ATTRB=ASKIP,                                     X
                 LENGTH=08
*
MDCVMNM   DFHMDF POS=(05,08),                                     X
                 ATTRB=ASKIP,                                     X
                 LENGTH=05,                                       X
                 INITIAL='NAME:'
*
MDVNDNM   DFHMDF POS=(05,14),                                     X
                 ATTRB=UNPROT,                                    X
                 LENGTH=25
*
          DFHMDF POS=(05,40),                                     X
                 ATTRB=ASKIP,                                     X
                 LENGTH=01
*
MDCPHON   DFHMDF POS=(05,45),                                     X
                 ATTRB=ASKIP,                                     X
                 LENGTH=06,                                       X
                 INITIAL='PHONE:'
*
          DFHMDF POS=(05,54),                                     X
                 ATTRB=ASKIP,                                     X
                 LENGTH=01,                                       X
                 INITIAL='('
*
MDAREAC   DFHMDF POS=(05,56),                                     X
                 ATTRB=UNPROT,                                    X
                 LENGTH=03
```

Figure 13-3 *(Continued)*

```
*
          DFHMDF POS=(05,60),                                    X
                 ATTRB=ASKIP,                                    X
                 LENGTH=01,                                      X
                 INITIAL=')'
*
MDPHON1   DFHMDF POS=(05,62),                                    X
                 ATTRB=UNPROT,                                   X
                 LENGTH=03
*
          DFHMDF POS=(05,66),                                    X
                 ATTRB=ASKIP,                                    X
                 LENGTH=01,                                      X
                 INITIAL='-'
*
MDPHON2   DFHMDF POS=(05,68),                                    X
                 ATTRB=UNPROT,                                   X
                 LENGTH=04
*
          DFHMDF POS=(05,73),                                    X
                 ATTRB=ASKIP,                                    X
                 LENGTH=01
*
          DFHMDF POS=(06,45),                                    X
                 ATTRB=ASKIP,                                    X
                 LENGTH=08,                                      X
                 INITIAL='CONTACT:'
*
MDCONTA   DFHMDF POS=(06,54),                                    X
                 ATTRB=UNPROT,                                   X
                 LENGTH=25
*
          DFHMDF POS=(06,80),                                    X
                 ATTRB=ASKIP,                                    X
                 LENGTH=01
*
MDCSTRT   DFHMDF POS=(08,01),                                    X
                 ATTRB=ASKIP,                                    X
                 LENGTH=17,                                      X
                 INITIAL='ADDRESS - STREET:'
*
MDSTRET   DFHMDF POS=(08,19),                                    X
                 ATTRB=UNPROT,                                   X
                 LENGTH=20
*
          DFHMDF POS=(08,40),                                    X
                 ATTRB=ASKIP,                                    X
                 LENGTH=01
*
MDCCITY   DFHMDF POS=(09,13),                                    X
                 ATTRB=ASKIP,                                    X
                 LENGTH=05,                                      X
                 INITIAL='CITY:'
*
MDCITY    DFHMDF POS=(09,19),                                    X
                 ATTRB=UNPROT,                                   X
                 LENGTH=18
*
          DFHMDF POS=(09,38),                                    X
                 ATTRB=ASKIP,                                    X
                 LENGTH=01
*
MDCSTAT   DFHMDF POS=(10,12),                                    X
                 ATTRB=ASKIP,                                    X
                 LENGTH=06,                                      X
                 INITIAL='STATE:'
*
MDSTATE   DFHMDF POS=(10,19),                                    X
                 ATTRB=UNPROT,                                   X
                 LENGTH=02
*
MDSTANM   DFHMDF POS=(10,22),                                    X
                 ATTRB=ASKIP,                                    X
                 LENGTH=14
*
```

Figure 13-3 *(Continued)*

```
MDCZIP     DFHMDF POS=(11,14),                                        X
           ATTRB=ASKIP,                                              X
           LENGTH=04,                                                X
           INITIAL='ZIP:'
*
MDZIP      DFHMDF POS(11,19),                                        X
           ATTRB=UNPROT,                                             X
           LENGTH=05
*
           DFHMDF POS=(11,25),                                       X
           ATTRB=ASKIP,                                              X
           LENGTH=01
*
           DFHMDF POS=(13,02),                                       X
           ATTRB=ASKIP,                                              X
           LENGTH=16,                                                X
           INITIAL='TO ATTENTION OF:'
*
MDATTOF    DFHMDF POS=(13,19),                                       X
           ATTRB=UNPROT,                                             X
           LENGTH=20
*
           DFHMDF POS=(13,40),                                       X
           ATTRB=ASKIP,                                              X
           LENGTH=01
*
           DFHMDF POS=(18,10),                                       X
           ATTRB=ASKIP,                                              X
           LENGTH=56,                                                X
           INITIAL='1. ADDITIONS, KEY IN REQUIRED DATA       - PRX
           ESS ENTER'
*
           DFHMDF POS=(19,10),                                       X
           ATTRB=ASKIP,                                              X
           LENGTH=54,                                                X
           INITIAL='2. RETURN TO ADDITION CONTROL SCREEN     - PRX
           ESS PF3'
*
           DFHMDF POS=(20,10),                                       X
           ATTRB=ASKIP,                                              X
           LENGTH=54,                                                X
           INITIAL='3. RETURN TO MENU                        - PRX
           ESS PF5'
*
           DFHMDF POS=(21,10),                                       X
           ATTRB=ASKIP,                                              X
           LENGTH=56,                                                X
           INITIAL='4. END OF SESSION                        - PRX
           ESS CLEAR'
*
MDMESSG    DFHMDF POS=(24,01),                                       X
           ATTRB=ASKIP,                                              X
           LENGTH=79
*
           DFHMSD TYPE=FINAL
           END
```

the file, it is read into the working-storage area VENDOR-MASTER-RECORD and a G is moved to STATUS-OF-READ. A vendor record should not be found for a record which is being added, and a record-found condition will be treated as an error in the invoking section (C400-VERIFY-VENDOR-FILE-STATUS).

C500-SEND-DETAIL-MAP-AND-DATA. This section is similar to that of the Inquiry program in Chap. 12. The differences are

1. Perform C520-SET-MAP-ATTRIBUTES.

Figure 13-4 Vendor File Addition Program Source Code.

```
0001 IDENTIFICATION DIVISION.
0002 PROGRAM-ID. POVMADDN.
0003 REMARKS.
0004****************************************************************************
0005*          PURCHASING SYSTEM - VENDOR FILE ADDITIONS          *
0006*     - STARTED BY PURCHASING SYSTEM SUB-MENU PROGRAM 'POVMAINT'  *
0007*          COULD ALSO BE STARTED BY TRANSID 'POVA'            *
0008****************************************************************************
0009 ENVIRONMENT DIVISION.
0010 DATA DIVISION.
0011*
0012 WORKING-STORAGE  SECTION.
0013*
0014 01  WS-PROGRAM-FIELDS.
0015     05  FILLER            PIC X(8)      VALUE 'POVMADDN'.
0016     05  WS-CRT-MESSAGE    PIC X(17)     VALUE 'SESSION COMPLETED'.
0017*
0018 01  VENDOR-MASTER-RECORD          COPY    VENDMAST.
0019 01  JOURNAL-RECORD               COPY    JRNLRECD.
0020 01  WS-COMMAREA                  COPY    POWSVMCA.
0021 01  WS-STATUS-FIELDS             COPY    STWSSTAT.
0022 01  VM-CONTROL-MAP               COPY    MAPVMCTL.
0023 01  VM-DETAIL-MAP                COPY    MAPVDTL2.
0024 01  WS-DATE-AND-TIME             COPY    STWSDTTM.
0025 01  WS-STATE-CODE-SEARCH-ENTRIES COPY    STWST037.
0026 01  ATTRIBUTE-LIST               COPY    STWSATTR.
0027 01  DFHAID                       COPY    DFHAID.
0028*
0029 01  END-OF-WORKING-STORAGE  PIC X(15)   VALUE 'END WS POVMADDN'.
0030*
0031 LINKAGE SECTION.
0032*
0033 01  DFHCOMMAREA                    PIC X(8).
0034*
0035 01  BLL-CELLS.
0036     05  FILLER                     PIC S9(8)    COMP.
0037     05  BLL-CWA-ADDRESS            PIC S9(8)    COMP.
0038     05  BLL-T037-STATE-TABLE-ADDRESS  PIC S9(8) COMP.
0039*
0040 01  CWA DATA           COPY    STLNKCWA.
0041 01  T037-STATE-TABLE   COPY    T037STAT.
0042 PROCEDURE DIVISION.
0043****************************************************************************
0044*     PROGRAM STRUCTURE IS:                                    *
0045*          AA00-MAINLINE                                       *
0046*               B000-INITIAL-ENTRY                             *
0047*                    B100-SEND-CONTROL-MAP-AND-DATA            *
0048*                         B110-GET-DATE-AND-TIME               *
0049*                                                             *
0050*               C000-PROCESS-CONTROL-MAP                       *
0051*                    C100-RECEIVE-CONTROL-MAP                  *
0052*                         C110-END-SESSION                     *
0053*                         C120-TRANSFER-XCTL-TO-MENU           *
0054*                         C130-TRANSFER-XCTL-TO-BROWSE         *
0055*                    C200-VERIFY-VENDOR-FORMAT                 *
0056*                    C400-VERIFY-VENDOR-FILE-STATUS            *
0057*                         C410-READ-VENDOR-FILE                *
0058*                    C500-SEND-DETAIL-MAP-AND-DATA             *
0059*                         B110-GET-DATE-AND-TIME               *
0060*                         C520-SET-MAP-ATTRIBUTES              *
0061*                         C530-FORMAT-DETAIL-MAP               *
0062*                              C531-GET-STATE-NAME             *
0063*                    C600-SEND-CONTROL-MAP-DATAONLY            *
0064*                                                             *
0065*               E000-ADDITION-PROCESSING                       *
0066*                    D100-RECEIVE-DETAIL-MAP                   *
0067*                         C110-END-SESSION                     *
0068*                         C120-TRANSFER-XCTL-TO-MENU           *
0069*                    E100-ADD-VENDOR-RECORD                    *
0070*                         E110-EDIT-MAP-FORMAT-VM-RECORD       *
0071*                              C531-GET-STATE-NAME             *
0072*                         E120-WRITE-VENDOR-RECORD             *
0073*                              E121-POST-JOURNAL-RECORD        *
0074*                    B100-SEND-CONTROL-MAP-AND-DATA            *
0075*                    D200-SEND-DETAIL-MAP-DATAONLY             *
0076*                         C520-SET-MAP-ATTRIBUTES              *
0077****************************************************************************
```

Figure 13-4 *(Continued)*

```
0078*
0079 AA00-MAINLINE  SECTION.
0080*
0081*    SERVICE RELOAD BLL-CELLS.
0082*
0083     IF EIBCALEN  =  0
0084          PERFORM B000-INITIAL-ENTRY
0085     ELSE
0086          MOVE DFHCOMMAREA  TO  WS-COMMAREA
0087          IF CA-RECEIVE-CTL-MAP
0088               PERFORM C000-PROCESS-CONTROL-MAP
0089          ELSE
0090               PERFORM E000-ADDITION-PROCESSING.
0091*
0092     EXEC CICS RETURN
0093               TRANSID  ('POVA')
0094               COMMAREA (WS-COMMAREA)
0095               LENGTH   (8)
0096     END-EXEC.
0097*
0098 B000-INITIAL-ENTRY  SECTION.
0099*****************************************************************
0100*             PERFORMED FROM:  AA00-MAINLINE               *
0101*****************************************************************
0102*
0103     MOVE LOW-VALUES  TO  VM-CONTROL-MAP.
0104     PERFORM B100-SEND-CONTROL-MAP-AND-DATA.
0105*
0106 B000-EXIT.
0107     EXIT.
0108*
0109 B100-SEND-CONTROL-MAP-AND-DATA  SECTION.
0110*****************************************************************
0111*         PERFORMED FROM:  B000-INITIAL-ENTRY             *
0112*                          E000-ADDITION-PROCESSING        *
0113*****************************************************************
0114*
0115     PERFORM B110-GET-DATE-AND-TIME.
0116     MOVE WS-CURRENT-DATE  TO  MVC-D-DATE.
0117     MOVE WS-MAP-TIME      TO  MVC-D-TIME.
0118*
0119     MOVE -1  TO  MVC-L-VEND-CD-1.
0120     MOVE '1'  TO  CA-MAP-CONTROL.
0121*
0122     EXEC CICS SEND
0123               MAP     ('MAPPOVC')
0124               MAPSET ('POVMAD1')
0125               FROM    (VM-CONTROL-MAP)
0126               ERASE
0127               CURSOR
0128     END-EXEC.
0129*
0130 B100-EXIT.
0131     EXIT.
0132*
0133 B110-GET-DATE-AND-TIME  SECTION   COPY   STPDDTTM.
0134*****************************************************************
0135*      STPDDTTM - OBTAIN DATE FROM CWA AND FORMAT TIME    *
0136*          PERFORMED FROM:  B100-SEND-CONTROL-MAP-AND-DATA *
0137*                           C500-SEND-DETAIL-MAP-AND-DATA  *
0138*****************************************************************
0139*
0140 B110-EXIT.
0141     EXIT.
0142*
0143 C000-PROCESS-CONTROL-MAP  SECTION.
0144*****************************************************************
0145*             PERFORMED FROM:  AA00-MAINLINE               *
0146*      PROCESS CONTROL MAP - IF VALID SEND DETAIL MAP      *
0147*         ELSE SEND CONTROL MAP WITH INVALID MESSAGE:      *
0148*  1) STATUS-OF-RECEIVE  =  'I'   INVALID KEY PRESSED      *
0149*  2) STATUS-OF-RECEIVE  =  'M'   MAPFAIL - NO DATA ENTERED*
0150*  3) STATUS-OF-FORMAT   =  'E'   INVALID VENDOR KEYED FORMAT*
0151*  4) STATUS-OF-VERIFY   =  'E'   VENDOR FILE STATUS ERROR *
0152*****************************************************************
```

Figure 13-4 *(Continued)*

```
0153*
0154      PERFORM C100-RECEIVE-CONTROL-MAP.
0155      IF GOOD-RECEIVE
0156          PERFORM C200-VERIFY-VENDOR-FORMAT
0157          IF VALID-FORMAT
0158              PERFORM C400-VERIFY-VENDOR-FILE-STATUS
0159              IF GOOD-VERIFY
0160                  PERFORM C500-SEND-DETAIL-MAP-AND-DATA
0161              ELSE
0162                  PERFORM C600-SEND-CONTROL-MAP-DATAONLY
0163          ELSE
0164              PERFORM C600-SEND-CONTROL-MAP-DATAONLY
0165      ELSE
0166          IF MAPFAIL-ON-RECEIVE
0167              MOVE 'VENDOR CODE MUST BE ENTERED - PLEASE KEY-IN'
0168                          TO MVC-D-MESSAGE
0169              MOVE ASKIP-BRT  TO MVC-A-MESSAGE
0170              PERFORM C600-SEND-CONTROL-MAP-DATAONLY
0171          ELSE
0172              PERFORM C600-SEND-CONTROL-MAP-DATAONLY.
0173*
0174 C000-EXIT.
0175      EXIT.
0176*
0177 C100-RECEIVE-CONTROL-MAP  SECTION.
0178**************************************************************************
0179*          PERFORMED FROM:  C000-PROCESS-CONTROL-MAP                    *
0180*              ENTER IS ONLY VALID DATA ENTRY KEY                       *
0181* CLEAR KEY - ENDS TERMINAL SESSION       PF5 - RETURNS TO MENU        *
0182*                                         PF4 - XCTL TO BROWSE         *
0183*          ALL OTHER AID KEYS ARE INVALID                              *
0184*      STATUS-OF-RECEIVE  =  'G'  =  GOOD RECEIVE                       *
0185*                            'M'  =  MAPFAIL                            *
0186*                            'I'  =  INVALID KEY PRESSED                *
0187**************************************************************************
0188*
0189      MOVE LOW-VALUES  TO  VM-CONTROL-MAP.
0190*
0191      IF EIBAID  =  DFHENTER
0192          MOVE 'M'  TO  STATUS-OF-RECEIVE
0193*
0194          EXEC CICS HANDLE CONDITION
0195                    MAPFAIL (C100-EXIT)
0196          END-EXEC
0197*
0198          EXEC CICS RECEIVE
0199                    MAP     ('MAPPOVC')
0200                    MAPSET  ('POVMAD1')
0201                    INTO    (VM-CONTROL-MAP)
0202          END-EXEC
0203*
0204          MOVE 'G'  TO  STATUS-OF-RECEIVE
0205      ELSE
0206          IF EIBAID  =  DFHCLEAR
0207              PERFORM C110-END-SESSION
0208          ELSE
0209          IF EIBAID  =  DFHPF5
0210              PERFORM C120-TRANSFER-XCTL-TO-MENU
0211          ELSE
0212          IF EIBAID  =  DFHPF4
0213              PERFORM C130-TRANSFER-XCTL-TO-BROWSE
0214          ELSE
0215              MOVE 'I'      TO  STATUS-OF-RECEIVE
0216              MOVE 'INVALID KEY PRESSED - PLEASE TRY AGAIN'
0217                          TO  MVC-D-MESSAGE
0218              MOVE ASKIP-BRT  TO  MVC-A-MESSAGE.
0219*
0220 C100-EXIT.
0221      EXIT.
0222*
0223 C110-END-SESSION  SECTION.
0224**************************************************************************
0225*   CRT OPERATOR PRESSED CLEAR KEY TO END TERMINAL SESSION             *
0226*          PERFORMED FROM:  C100-RECEIVE-CONTROL-MAP                    *
0227*                           D100-RECEIVE-DETAIL-MAP                     *
0228**************************************************************************
```

Figure 13-4 *(Continued)*

```
0229*
0230     EXEC CICS SEND
0231              FROM     (WS-CRT-MESSAGE)
0232              LENGTH  (17)
0233              ERASE
0234     END-EXEC.
0235*
0236     EXEC CICS RETURN
0237     END-EXEC.
0238*
0239 C110-EXIT.
0240     EXIT.
0241*
0242 C120-TRANSFER-XCTL-TO-MENU  SECTION.
0243*****************************************************************
0244*         OPERATOR PRESSED PF5 TO RETURN TO MENU PROGRAM      *
0245*             PERFORMED FROM:  C100-RECEIVE-CONTROL-MAP        *
0246*                             D100-RECEIVE-DETAIL-MAP          *
0247*****************************************************************
0248*
0249     EXEC CICS XCTL
0250                 PROGRAM ('POVMAINT')
0251     END-EXEC.
0252*
0253 C120-EXIT.
0254     EXIT.
0255*
0256 C130-TRANSFER-XCTL-TO-BROWSE  SECTION.
0257*****************************************************************
0258*         OPERATOR PRESSED PF4 TO TRANSFER CONTROL TO BROWSE  *
0259*             PERFORMED FROM:  C100-RECEIVE-CONTROL-MAP        *
0260*                             D100-RECEIVE-DETAIL-MAP          *
0261*****************************************************************
0262*
0263     MOVE LOW-VALUES   TO  WS-COMMAREA.
0264     MOVE 'A'          TO  CA-FUNCTION-CODE.
0265*
0266     EXEC CICS XCTL
0267                 PROGRAM ('POVMBROW')
0268                 COMMAREA (WS-COMMAREA)
0269                 LENGTH   (8)
0270     END-EXEC.
0271*
0272 C130-EXIT.
0273     EXIT.
0274*
0275 C200-VERIFY-VENDOR-FORMAT  SECTION.
0276*****************************************************************
0277*         VERIFY FORMAT OF VENDOR CODE KEYED-IN = A-9999-9     *
0278*             PERFORMED FROM:  C000-PROCESS-CONTROL-MAP        *
0279*     IF VALID FORMAT - MOVE CODE TO WS-COMMAREA FIELDS (CA- ) *
0280*****************************************************************
0281*
0282     IF (MVC-D-VENDOR-CD-1  IS  ALPHABETIC
0283              AND
0284       MVC-D-VENDOR-CD-1  IS NOT =  SPACE)
0285     AND
0286       MVC-D-VENDOR-CD-2  IS  NUMERIC
0287     AND
0288       MVC-D-VENDOR-CD-3  IS  NUMERIC
0289          MOVE MVC-D-VEND-CD-1  TO  CA-VEND-1
0290          MOVE MVC-D-VEND-CD-2  TO  CA-VEND-2
0291          MOVE MVC-D-VEND-CD-3  TO  CA-VEND-3
0292          MOVE 'G'              TO  STATUS-OF-FORMAT
0293     ELSE
0294          MOVE 'E'          TO  STATUS-OF-FORMAT
0295          MOVE 'VENDOR CODE FORMAT MUST BE: A-9999-9 - PLEASE RE-EN
0296-             'TER'      TO  MVC-D-MESSAGE
0297          MOVE ASKIP-BRT  TO  MVC-A-MESSAGE.
0298*
0299 C200-EXIT.
0300     EXIT.
0301*
0302 C400-VERIFY-VENDOR-FILE-STATUS  SECTION.
0303*****************************************************************
0304*             PERFORMED FROM:  C000-PROCESS-CONTROL-MAP        *
0305*             MUST NOT BE A VENDOR RECORD FOR ADDITIONS        *
0306*****************************************************************
```

Figure 13-4 *(Continued)*

```
0307*
0308      MOVE 'G'  TO  STATUS-OF-VERIFY.
0309*
0310      PERFORM C410-READ-VENDOR-FILE.
0311*
0312      IF RECORD-NOT-FOUND
0313          NEXT SENTENCE
0314      ELSE
0315          MOVE 'E'         TO  STATUS-OF-VERIFY
0316          MOVE 'VENDOR TO BE ADDED IS ALREADY ON THE FILE'
0317                           TO  MVC-D-MESSAGE
0318          MOVE ASKIP-BRT   TO  MVC-A-MESSAGE.
0319*
0320 C400-EXIT.
0321      EXIT.
0322*
0323 C410-READ-VENDOR-FILE  SECTION.
0324************************************************************
0325*         PERFORMED FROM:  C400-VERIFY-VENDOR-FILE-STATUS       *
0326************************************************************
0327*
0328      MOVE 'E' TO  STATUS-OF-READ.
0329*
0330      EXEC CICS HANDLE CONDITION
0331               NOTFND  (C410-EXIT)
0332      END-EXEC.
0333*
0334      EXEC CICS READ
0335               DATASET ('VENDMAST')
0336               INTO    (VENDOR-MASTER-RECORD)
0337               RIDFLD  (CA-VENDOR-CODE)
0338      END-EXEC.
0339*
0340      MOVE 'G'  TO  STATUS-OF-READ.
0341*
0342 C410-EXIT.
0343      EXIT.
0344*
0345 C500-SEND-DETAIL-MAP-AND-DATA  SECTION.
0346************************************************************
0347*         SEND DETAIL MAP - PHYSICAL AND SYMBOLIC MAPS       *
0348*             PERFORMED FROM:  C000-PROCESS-CONTROL-MAP       *
0349*    SENT WHEN ALL VALIDATION AND EDIT CONDITIONS HAVE BEEN MET   *
0350************************************************************
0351*
0352      MOVE LOW-VALUES  TO  VM-DETAIL-MAP.
0353*
0354      PERFORM B110-GET-DATE-AND-TIME.
0355      MOVE WS-CURRENT-DATE  TO  MVD-D-DATE.
0356      MOVE WS-MAP-TIME      TO  MVD-D-TIME.
0357*
0358      PERFORM C520-SET-MAP-ATTRIBUTES.
0359      PERFORM C530-FORMAT-DETAIL-MAP.
0360*
0361      MOVE -1  TO  MVD-L-VENDOR-NAME.
0362      MOVE '2' TO  CA-MAP-CONTROL.
0363*
0364      EXEC CICS SEND
0365               MAP     ('MAPPOVD')
0366               MAPSET  ('POVMAD2')
0367               FROM    (VM-DETAIL-MAP)
0368               ERASE
0369               CURSOR
0370      END-EXEC.
0371*
0372 C500-EXIT.
0373      EXIT.
0374*
0375 C520-SET-MAP-ATTRIBUTES  SECTION.
0376************************************************************
0377*         PERFORMED FROM:  C500-SEND-DETAIL-MAP-AND-DATA     *
0378*                          D200-SEND-DETAIL-MAP-DATAONLY      *
0379************************************************************
0380*
0381      MOVE UNPROT-FSET  TO  MVD-A-PHONE-AREA-CD
0382                            MVD-A-PHONE-1
0383                            MVD-A-PHONE-2
0384                            MVD-A-VENDOR-NAME
0385                            MVD-A-CONTACT
```

Figure 13-4 *(Continued)*

```
0386                                MVD-A-STREET
0387                                MVD-A-CITY
0388                                MVD-A-STATE-CODE
0389                                MVD-A-ZIP-CODE
0390                                MVD-A-ATTENTION-OF.
0391*
0392 C520-EXIT.
0393     EXIT.
0394*
0395 C530-FORMAT-DETAIL-MAP  SECTION.
0396*******************************************************************
0397*            FORMAT DETAIL MAP FOR INITIAL SEND               *
0398*        PERFORMED FROM:  C500-SEND-DETAIL-MAP-AND-DATA        *
0399*******************************************************************
0400*
0401* FORMAT VENDOR CODE: A-9999-9   WS- FIELDS ARE AT END OF VENDMAST
0402     MOVE CA-VEND-1      TO  WS-VENDOR-CD-1.
0403     MOVE CA-VEND-2      TO  WS-VENDOR-CD-2.
0404     MOVE CA-VEND-3      TO  WS-VENDOR-CD-3.
0405     MOVE WS-VENDOR-CODE TO  MVD-D-VENDOR-CODE.
0406*
0407 C530-EXIT.
0408     EXIT.
0409*
0410 C531-GET-STATE-NAME  SECTION   COPY   STPDT037.
0411*******************************************************************
0412*             LOAD AND SEARCH STATE CODE TABLE               *
0413*         PERFORMED FROM: E110-EDIT-MAP-FORMAT-VM-RECORD      *
0414*******************************************************************
0415*
0416 C531-EXIT.
0417     EXIT.
0418*
0419 C600-SEND-CONTROL-MAP-DATAONLY  SECTION.
0420*******************************************************************
0421*         SEND CONTROL MAP DATAONLY - SYMBOLIC MAP           *
0422*         PERFORMED FROM:  C000-PROCESS-CONTROL-MAP          *
0423*              SENT FOR INVALID CONDITIONS                   *
0424*******************************************************************
0425*
0426     MOVE '1'  TO  CA-MAP-CONTROL.
0427     MOVE -1   TO  MVC-L-VEND-CD-1.
0428*
0429     MOVE UNPROT-FSET  TO  MVC-A-VEND-CD-1
0430                           MVC-A-VEND-CD-2
0431                           MVC-A-VEND-CD-3.
0432*
0433     EXEC CICS SEND
0434               MAP      ('MAPPOVC')
0435               MAPSET   ('POVMAD1')
0436               FROM     (VM-CONTROL-MAP)
0437               DATAONLY
0438               CURSOR
0439     END-EXEC.
0440*
0441 C600-EXIT.
0442     EXIT.
0443*
0444 D100-RECEIVE-DETAIL-MAP  SECTION.
0445*******************************************************************
0446*         PERFORMED FROM:  E000-ADDITION-PROCESSING          *
0447* ENTER - PROCESSES TRANSACTION       CLEAR - ENDS SESSION   *
0448* PF3   - SETS DISPLAY OF CTL MAP    PF5   - RETURNS TO MENU *
0449*              ALL OTHER KEYS ARE INVALID                    *
0450*     STATUS-OF-RECEIVE  =  'G'  =  GOOD RECEIVE            *
0451*                           'C'  =  RETURN TO CTL-MAP        *
0452*                           'I'  =  INVALID KEY PRESSED      *
0453*******************************************************************
0454*
0455     MOVE LOW-VALUES  TO  VM-DETAIL-MAP.
0456*
0457     IF EIBAID  =  DFHENTER
0458*
0459         EXEC CICS IGNORE CONDITION
0460                   MAPFAIL
0461         END-EXEC
```

Figure 13-4 *(Continued)*

```
0462*
0463         EXEC CICS RECEIVE
0464                     MAP       ('MAPPOVD')
0465                     MAPSET    ('POVMAD2')
0466                     INTO      (VM-DETAIL-MAP)
0467         END-EXEC
0468*
0469         MOVE 'G'  TO  STATUS-OF-RECEIVE
0470     ELSE
0471         IF EIBAID  =  DFHCLEAR
0472             PERFORM C110-END-SESSION
0473         ELSE
0474         IF EIBAID  =  DFHPF3
0475             MOVE 'C'  TO  STATUS-OF-RECEIVE
0476*        ELSE
0477         IF EIBAID  =  DFHPF5
0478             PERFORM C120-TRANSFER-XCTL-TO-MENU
0479         ELSE
0480             MOVE 'I'       TO  STATUS-OF-RECEIVE
0481             MOVE 'INVALID KEY PRESSED - PLEASE TRY AGAIN'
0482                            TO  MVD-D-MESSAGE
0483             MOVE ASKIP-BRT TO  MVD-A-MESSAGE.
0484*
0485 D100-EXIT.
0486     EXIT.
0487*
0488 D200-SEND-DETAIL-MAP-DATAONLY  SECTION.
0489*****************************************************************
0490*         SEND DETAIL MAP DATA ONLY - SYMBOLIC MAP           *
0491*             PERFORMED FROM:  E000-ADDITION-PROCESSING       *
0492* SENT IF INVALID KEY IS PRESSED ON A RECEIVE OF THE DETAIL MAP *
0493*****************************************************************
0494*
0495     MOVE '2'  TO  CA-MAP-CONTROL.
0496*
0497     PERFORM C520-SET-MAP-ATTRIBUTES.
0498*
0499     EXEC CICS SEND
0500                 MAP       ('MAPPOVD')
0501                 MAPSET    ('POVMAD2')
0502                 FROM      (VM-DETAIL-MAP)
0503                 DATAONLY
0504                 CURSOR
0505     END-EXEC.
0506*
0507 D200-EXIT.
0508     EXIT.
0509*
0510 E000-ADDITION-PROCESSING  SECTION.
0511*****************************************************************
0512*             PERFORMED FROM:  AA00-MAINLINE                  *
0513*     DETAIL MAP IS SENT IF AN INVALID KEY WAS PRESSED        *
0514*             OR IF ADD WAS UNSUCCESSFUL                      *
0515*****************************************************************
0516*
0517     PERFORM D100-RECEIVE-DETAIL-MAP.
0518*
0519     IF GOOD-RECEIVE
0520         PERFORM E100-ADD-VENDOR-RECORD
0521         IF GOOD-ADD
0522             PERFORM B100-SEND-CONTROL-MAP-AND-DATA
0523         ELSE
0524             PERFORM D200-SEND-DETAIL-MAP-DATAONLY
0525     ELSE
0526         IF RETURN-TO-CTL-MAP
0527             PERFORM B100-SEND-CONTROL-MAP-AND-DATA
0528         ELSE
0529             PERFORM D200-SEND-DETAIL-MAP-DATAONLY.
0530*
0531 E000-EXIT.
0532     EXIT.
0533*
0534 E100-ADD-VENDOR-RECORD SECTION.
0535*****************************************************************
0536*             PERFORMED FROM:  E000-ADDITION-PROCESSING       *
0537*         PERFORMS EDITS AND FORMATS VENDOR-MASTER-RECORD     *
0538*             IF GOOD EDIT - ADDS RECORD TO THE FILE          *
0539* RECORD ALREADY ON FILE MESSAGE COULD ONLY OCCUR IF RECORD WAS *
0540* ADDED BY ANOTHER TERMINAL SINCE KEYED-IN ON CONTROL SCREEN   *
0541*****************************************************************
```

Figure 13-4 *(Continued)*

```
0542*
0543      MOVE SPACES              TO   VENDOR-MASTER-RECORD.
0544      MOVE CA-VENDOR-CODE   TO   VM-VENDOR-CODE.
0545*
0546      MOVE 'E'  TO  STATUS-OF-ADD.
0547*
0548      PERFORM E110-EDIT-MAP-FORMAT-VM-RECORD.
0549*
0550      IF GOOD-EDIT
0551          PERFORM E120-WRITE-VENDOR-RECORD
0552          IF GOOD-WRITE
0553              MOVE 'RECORD SUCCESSFULLY ADDED'
0554                             TO   MVC-D-MESSAGE
0555              MOVE ASKIP-BRT   TO   MVC-A-MESSAGE
0556              MOVE 'G'  TO  STATUS-OF-ADD
0557          ELSE
0558              MOVE 'RECORD TO BE ADDED -ALREADY ON VENDOR FILE'
0559                             TO   MVD-D-MESSAGE
0560              MOVE ASKIP-BRT   TO   MVD-A-MESSAGE.
0561*
0562 E100-EXIT.
0563      EXIT.
0564*
0565 E110-EDIT-MAP-FORMAT-VM-RECORD  SECTION.
0566****************************************************************
0567*        EDIT DETAIL MAP DATA - FORMAT VENDOR MASTER RECORD    *
0568*        PERFORMED FROM:  E100-ADD-VENDOR-RECORD               *
0569*           HIGHLIGHT FIELDS WHICH CONTAIN INCORRECT DATA      *
0570*                OR WHICH ARE MISSING REQUIRED ENTRIES         *
0571****************************************************************
0572*
0573      MOVE 'G'  TO  STATUS-OF-EDIT.
0574*
0575* ASSUME ALL PHONE DIGITS SHOULD BE NUMERIC
0576*
0577      IF MVD-D-PHONE-AREA-CD  IS  NUMERIC
0578        AND
0579        MVD-D-PHONE-1        IS  NUMERIC
0580        AND
0581        MVD-D-PHONE-2        IS  NUMERIC
0582          MOVE MVD-D-PHONE-AREA-CD   TO  VM-AREA-CD
0583          MOVE MVD-D-PHONE-1         TO  VM-PHONE-1-3
0584          MOVE MVD-D-PHONE-2         TO  VM-PHONE-4-7
0585          MOVE ASKIP-NORM            TO  MVD-C-A-PHONE
0586      ELSE
0587          MOVE -1          TO  MVD-L-PHONE-AREA-CD
0588          MOVE ASKIP-BRT   TO  MVD-C-A-PHONE
0589          MOVE 'E'         TO  STATUS-OF-EDIT.
0590*
0591      IF MVD-D-VENDOR-NAME  =  LOW-VALUES  OR  SPACES
0592          MOVE -1          TO  MVD-L-VENDOR-NAME
0593          MOVE ASKIP-BRT   TO  MVD-C-A-VENDOR-NAME
0594          MOVE 'E'         TO  STATUS-OF-EDIT
0595      ELSE
0596          MOVE MVD-D-VENDOR-NAME   TO  VM-VENDOR-NAME
0597          MOVE ASKIP-NORM          TO  MVD-C-A-VENDOR-NAME.
0598*
0599* 'CONTACT' AND 'TO ATTENTION OF' ARE OPTIONAL FIELDS
0600*
0601      IF MVD-L-CONTACT  =  ZERO
0602          MOVE SPACES         TO  VM-CONTACT
0603      ELSE
0604          MOVE MVD-D-CONTACT  TO  VM-CONTACT.
0605*
0606      IF MVD-L-STREET  =  0     OR
0607        MVD-D-STREET  =  SPACES
0608          MOVE -1          TO  MVD-L-STREET
0609          MOVE ASKIP-BRT   TO  MVD-C-A-STREET
0610          MOVE 'E'         TO  STATUS-OF-EDIT
0611      ELSE
0612          MOVE MVD-D-STREET   TO  VM-STREET-ADDRESS
0613          MOVE ASKIP-NORM     TO  MVD-C-A-STREET.
0614*
0615      MOVE ZEROES  TO  VM-DOLLARS-COMMITTED.
0616*
0617      IF MVD-D-CITY  =  LOW-VALUES  OR  SPACES
0618          MOVE -1          TO  MVD-L-CITY
0619          MOVE ASKIP-BRT   TO  MVD-C-A-CITY
0620          MOVE 'E'         TO  STATUS-OF-EDIT
```

Figure 13-4   *(Continued)*

```
0621        ELSE
0622            MOVE MVD-D-CITY   TO   VM-CITY
0623            MOVE ASKIP-NORM   TO   MVD-C-A-CITY.
0624*
0625        MOVE MVD-D-STATE-CODE   TO   WS-STATE-CODE.
0626        PERFORM C531-GET-STATE-NAME.
0627        IF STATE-FOUND
0628            MOVE MVD-D-STATE-CODE   TO   VM-STATE
0629            MOVE WS-STATE-NAME       TO   MVD-D-STATE-NAME
0630            MOVE ASKIP-NORM          TO   MVD-C-A-STATE
0631        ELSE
0632            MOVE ALL '*'    TO   MVD-D-STATE-NAME
0633            MOVE -1         TO   MVD-L-STATE-CODE
0634            MOVE ASKIP-BRT  TO   MVD-C-A-STATE
0635            MOVE 'E'        TO   STATUS-OF-EDIT.
0636*
0637        IF MVD-D-ZIP-CODE   IS   NUMERIC
0638            MOVE MVD-D-ZIP-CODE   TO   VM-ZIP-CODE
0639            MOVE ASKIP-NORM       TO   MVD-C-A-ZIP-CODE
0640        ELSE
0641            MOVE -1              TO   MVD-L-ZIP-CODE
0642            MOVE ASKIP-BRT       TO   MVD-C-A-ZIP-CODE
0643            MOVE 'E'             TO   STATUS-OF-EDIT.
0644*
0645        IF MVD-L-ATTENTION-OF   =   ZERO
0646            MOVE SPACES                  TO   VM-TO-ATTN-OF
0647        ELSE
0648            MOVE MVD-D-ATTENTION-OF   TO   VM-TO-ATTN-OF.
0649*
0650        IF STATUS-OF-EDIT   =   'E'
0651            MOVE 'PLEASE CORRECT HIGHLIGHTED FIELDS'
0652                            TO   MVD-D-MESSAGE
0653            MOVE ASKIP-BRT  TO   MVD-A-MESSAGE.
0654*
0655    E110-EXIT.
0656        EXIT.
0657*
0658    E120-WRITE-VENDOR-RECORD   SECTION.
0659****************************************************************
0660*         WRITE VENDOR RECORD - PERFORM JOURNAL POSTING       *
0661*             PERFORMED FROM:  E100-ADD-VENDOR-RECORD          *
0662****************************************************************
0663        MOVE 'E'   TO   STATUS-OF-WRITE.
0664*
0665        EXEC CICS HANDLE CONDITION
0666                DUPREC   (E120-EXIT)
0667        END-EXEC.
0668*
0669        EXEC CICS WRITE
0670                DATASET   ('VENDMAST')
0671                FROM      (VENDOR-MASTER-RECORD)
0672                RIDFLD    (CA-VENDOR-CODE)
0673        END-EXEC.
0674*
0675        MOVE 'G'   TO   STATUS-OF-WRITE.
0676*
0677        MOVE 'A'   TO   JR-TYPE.
0678        PERFORM E121-POST-JOURNAL-RECORD.
0679*
0680    E120-EXIT.
0681        EXIT.
0682*
0683    E121-POST-JOURNAL-RECORD   SECTION.
0684****************************************************************
0685*     POST JOURNAL ENTRY - LINK TO JOURNAL PROGRAM 'JRNLPOST' *
0686*        PERFORMED FROM:  E120-WRITE-VENDOR-RECORD            *
0687****************************************************************
0688*
0689        MOVE 'VM'                    TO   JR-PREFIX.
0690        MOVE VENDOR-MASTER-RECORD    TO   JR-RECORD-DATA.
0691        MOVE SPACES                  TO   JR-PASSWORD.
0692*
0693        EXEC CICS LINK
0694                PROGRAM   ('JRNLPOST')
0695                COMMAREA  (JOURNAL-RECORD)
0696                LENGTH    (524)
0697        END-EXEC.
0698*
0699    E121-EXIT.
0700        EXIT.
```

2. MOVE -1 TO MVD-L-VENDOR-NAME. Moving a -1 to the symbolic map length field sets the cursor initially at this item.

C520-SET-MAP-ATTRIBUTES. This section turns on the MDT for all data entry fields by moving the UNPROT,FSET attribute to each field prior to the SEND MAP command. The MDT is turned on any time data is keyed into a field. A map could be received after data had been keyed into its fields in order to edit and process the fields. The editing might detect errors in some of the fields and send the map DATAONLY with the field identifiers of the incorrectly entered fields highlighted. The map would be sent with a brightened error message. When FRSET is specified on the BMS map DFHMSD macro, a SEND MAP command turns off all MDTs. This section ensures that all data-entry fields on the map are returned on subsequent receives of the map. There are more sophisticated ways to handle this situation, but this is one of the easier methods. Vendor code is not a data-entry field on the detail map; its BMS map attribute is ASKIP.

C530-FORMAT-DETAIL-MAP. Moves vendor code fields obtained from WS-COMMAREA subfields to the appropriate map locations prior to the send of the detail map. There are no vendor record fields to display since no record exists.

E100-ADD-VENDOR-RECORD. Performs an edit of map data and a format of the vendor record. If the edit and format are successful, a write of the vendor record is performed. The message RECORD SUCCESSFULLY ADDED is normally returned and displayed on the control screen. The message RECORD TO BE ADDED—ALREADY ON VENDOR FILE could only be displayed if an operator at another terminal added the same record you are attempting to add, after you had entered vendor code on the control screen. This program would have previously read the vendor file for the entered vendor code (in section C410-READ-VENDOR-FILE) and determined that it was not online, in order to reach this point. Do not be overly concerned with the possibility of this happening, because it is not a common occurrence. There are techniques, beyond the scope of this book, to control this situation.

E110-EDIT-MAP-FORMAT-VM-RECORD. This section expects that all fields which were entered will be available each time the detail map is received. This will be the case because section C520-SET-MAP-ATTRIBUTES resets the MDTs each time the detail map is sent. There are many different acceptable ways to validate input data received from a screen. This section employs several different methods.

1. A field can be checked for data expected to be numeric such as area code, phone number, and zip code.

2. Fields which contain low-values or spaces may be considered invalid. Using the techniques chosen for the maintenance programs, a field would contain

low-values only if nothing was keyed into the field or if the EOF key was pressed. Spaces would be present in a field only if the operator keyed in at least one space, or if the program moved spaces to a map field prior to a send.

3. Field length could be tested in order to determine if data had been keyed into a field. The field's length would be greater than zero if at least one character had been entered. Be careful how you use the length field because it is sometimes different on the initial receive of a map than it is on subsequent receives of the same map. When an operator enters data, the initial receive of the map returns the actual length keyed in. Subsequent receives of the same map, if the program sets the attribute to FSET and if a field was not rekeyed, will return the full length of the field regardless of how many characters were originally entered.

I have chosen the technique of highlighting (ASKIP,BRT) the field identifiers of items which have been entered incorrectly or for which data has been omitted. I move an error indicator to STATUS-OF-EDIT for invalid fields. On subsequent receives of the same map, the ASKIP,NORM attribute is moved to the field identifier of correctly entered fields. At the end of this section, I check if STATUS-OF-EDIT equals E, and, if so, move the message PLEASE CORRECT HIGHLIGHTED FIELDS to the detail map message field. The detail map is sent DATAONLY in section E000-ADDITION-PROCESSING.

E120-WRITE-VENDOR-RECORD.   Write the addition record to the vendor master file. If the record is already on the file, the DUPREC handle condition will be invoked and an E will be returned in STATUS-OF-WRITE. A good write will return a G in STATUS-OF-WRITE. An after (A) journal record posting will be performed; there is no before-record for an add. The DUPREC indicator will be invoked only if an operator at another terminal has already added the same record you are attempting to add.

SUMMARY

This chapter presented an addition program which can be used as a model for most addition programs you will have to write. Several of the commands discussed in preceding chapters were used. The use of attributes was expanded upon, and different techniques for editing data received from the map were discussed. The READ and WRITE file commands were used, and the DUPREC handle condition was coded before the WRITE command was issued.

14

THE CHANGE PROGRAM

After a file has been created, records added to the file, and an inquiry program written to check the status of various fields, it is often necessary to change records in the file. This chapter discusses the change program.

Control and detail maps are used for the change program. The control map shown in Fig. 14-1 requires the terminal operator to key in a vendor code and to press ENTER in order to display the change detail screen. The operator also has the option of transferring control to the vendor file browse, returning to the vendor file maintenance submenu (see Fig. 6-3), or ending the session. The vendor file change program detail map shown in Fig. 2-8 is displayed when the operator keys in an existing vendor code on the control screen and then presses ENTER. The detail map shows all vendor file fields which can be changed on the vendor's record. The detail change screen permits the operator to key in the vendor's new data and then press ENTER in order to update the record. The program will then return to the control screen to allow entry of another vendor's code. The detail screen also permits the operator to return to the change control screen without changing the record, return to the submenu, or to end the session.

BMS Maps

Figures 14-2 and 14-3 show the BMS maps for the control and detail screens, respectively.

BMS Control Map

Only the differences between this map and the BMS control map for the inquiry program (see Fig. 12-1) are shown in Fig. 14-2.

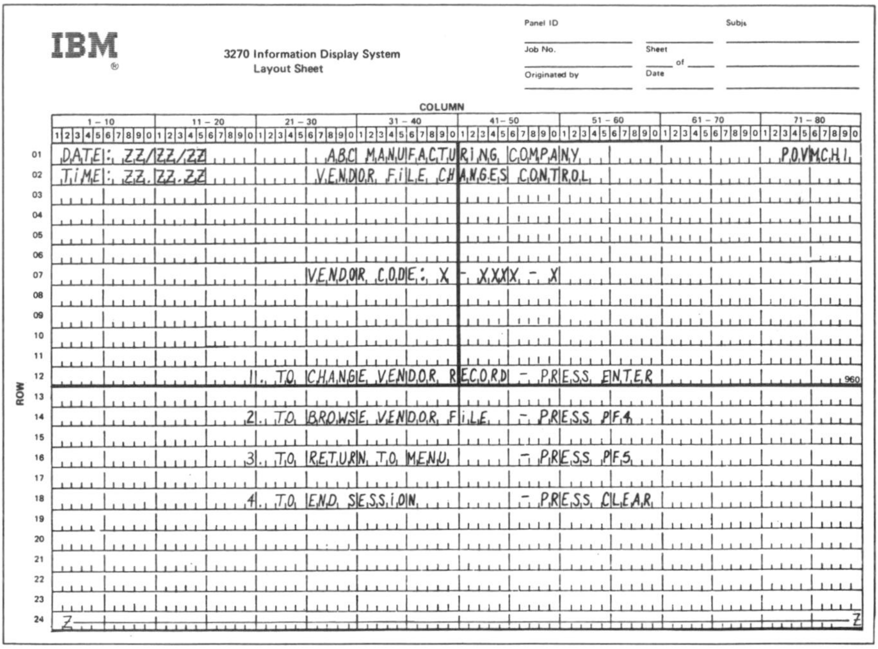

Figure 14-1 Vendor File Changes Control Map.

BMS Detail Map

This map is similar to the addition detail map shown in Fig. 13-3. Only the differences are shown in Fig. 14-3. Keep map fields in similar columns; for related maps, it makes map creation easy.

User-Friendly Symbolic Maps

The user-friendly symbolic maps created to correspond to the generated BMS maps are shown in the copy library (App. B, members MAPVMCTL and MAPVDTL2).

Change Program Source Code

The change program source code, shown in Fig. 14-4, follows the format used in previous examples. I will only discuss the sections which differ from previous examples.

Procedure Division

AA00-MAINLINE. This section is similar to that of the inquiry program in

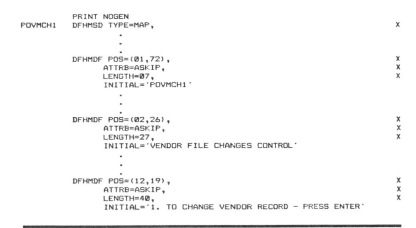

```
        PRINT NOGEN
POVMCH1 DFHMSD TYPE=MAP,                                          X
            .
            .
            .
        DFHMDF POS=(01,72),                                       X
              ATTRB=ASKIP,                                        X
              LENGTH=07,                                          X
              INITIAL='POVMCH1'
              .
              .
              .
        DFHMDF POS=(02,26),                                       X
              ATTRB=ASKIP,                                        X
              LENGTH=27,                                          X
              INITIAL='VENDOR FILE CHANGES CONTROL'
              .
              .
              .
        DFHMDF POS=(12,19),                                       X
              ATTRB=ASKIP,                                        X
              LENGTH=40,                                          X
              INITIAL='1. TO CHANGE VENDOR RECORD - PRESS ENTER'
```

Figure 14-2 Vendor File Changes BMS Control Map.

Chap. 12, except that perform F000-CHANGE-PROCESSING replaces D000-INQUIRY-PROCESSING and TRANSID POVC replaces POVI.

C400-VERIFY-VENDOR-FILE-STATUS.   This section performs a read of the vendor file in order to make sure the vendor record exists. If the vendor is not on the file, an error indicator is set and an error message is returned.

C410-READ-VENDOR-FILE.   An E is moved immediately to STATUS-OF-READ prior to executing the READ command for the vendor file. If the record is on the file, it is read into the working-storage area VENDOR-MASTER-RECORD, and a G is moved to STATUS-OF-READ. A vendor record should be on the file for a record which is being changed. A record-not-found condition will be treated as an error in the invoking section.

F100-CHANGE-VENDOR-RECORD.   This section reads the change record for update. If the record is not found, an indicative message will be displayed on the detail map. If the record is found, the map's data is edited and the vendor's record is formatted. If the edit and format are successful, a rewrite of the vendor record is performed. The message CHANGE COMPLETED SUCCESSFULLY is normally displayed on the control screen. The message UPDATE VENDOR RECORD—NOT FOUND would only be displayed if an operator at another terminal had deleted the same record you are attempting to read for update, after you had entered the vendor code on the control screen. This program would have previously read the vendor file for the entered vendor code (in section C410-READ-VENDOR-FILE) and determined that it was online in order to reach this point.

```
              PRINT NOGEN
POVMCH2       DFHMSD TYPE=MAP,                                             X
                    .
                    .
              DFHMDF POS=(01,72),                                          X
                    ATTRB=ASKIP,                                          X
                    LENGTH=07,                                           X
                    INITIAL='POVMCH2'
                    .
                    .
              DFHMDF POS=(02,30),                                          X
                    ATTRB=ASKIP,                                          X
                    LENGTH=19,                                           X
                    INITIAL='VENDOR FILE CHANGES'
                    .
                    .
              DFHMDF POS=(18,10),                                          X
                    ATTRB=ASKIP,                                          X
                    LENGTH=56,                                           X
                    INITIAL='1. CHANGES, KEY IN NEW DATA         - PRX
                    ESS ENTER'
   *
              DFHMDF POS=(19,10),                                          X
                    ATTRB=ASKIP,                                          X
                    LENGTH=54,                                           X
                    INITIAL='2. RETURN TO CHANGES CONTROL SCREEN  - PRX
                    ESS PF3'
   *
              DFHMDF POS=(20,10),                                          X
                    ATTRB=ASKIP,                                          X
                    LENGTH=54,                                           X
                    INITIAL='3. RETURN TO MENU                    - PRX
                    ESS PF5'
   *
              DFHMDF POS=(21,10),                                          X
                    ATTRB=ASKIP,                                          X
                    LENGTH=56,                                           X
                    INITIAL='4. END OF SESSION                    - PRX
                    ESS CLEAR'
                    .
                    .
                    .
```

Figure 14-3   Vendor File Changes BMS Detail Map.

F110-READ-VENDOR-FOR-UPDATE. This section reads the change vendor record for update. If the record is not on the file, the NOTFND handle condition will be turned on and an E will be returned in STATUS-OF-READ. A good read will return a G in STATUS-OF-READ. A before (B) journal record posting is performed. The after-record will be posted after the rewrite in section F120-REWRITE-VENDOR-RECORD. The NOTFND indicator will only be invoked if an operator at another terminal has deleted the same record you are attempting to change, after you had keyed in vendor code on the control screen.

F120-REWRITE-VENDOR-RECORD. Rewrite the changed vendor record. An after (A) journal record posting will be performed. When the program reaches this point, it has read the vendor record for update and has established exclusive control of the record to be changed.

Figure 14-4 Vendor File Changes Program Source Code.

```
0001 IDENTIFICATION DIVISION.
0002 PROGRAM-ID. POVMCHGE.
0003 REMARKS.
0004*******************************************************************
0005*         PURCHASING SYSTEM - VENDOR FILE CHANGES              *
0006*     - STARTED BY PURCHASING SYSTEM SUB-MENU PROGRAM 'POVMAINT' *
0007*         COULD ALSO BE STARTED BY TRANSID 'POVC'              *
0008*******************************************************************
0009 ENVIRONMENT DIVISION.
0010 DATA DIVISION.
0011*
0012 WORKING-STORAGE  SECTION.
0013*
0014 01  WS-PROGRAM-FIELDS.
0015     05  FILLER              PIC X(8)     VALUE 'POVMCHGE'.
0016     05  WS-CRT-MESSAGE      PIC X(17)    VALUE 'SESSION COMPLETED'.
0017*
0018 01  VENDOR-MASTER-RECORD          COPY   VENDMAST.
0019 01  JOURNAL-RECORD               COPY   JRNLRECD.
0020 01  WS-COMMAREA                  COPY   POWSVMCA.
0021 01  WS-STATUS-FIELDS             COPY   STWSSTAT.
0022 01  VM-CONTROL-MAP               COPY   MAPVMCTL.
0023 01  VM-DETAIL-MAP                COPY   MAPVDTL2.
0024 01  WS-DATE-AND-TIME             COPY   STWSDTTM.
0025 01  WS-STATE-CODE-SEARCH-ENTRIES COPY   STWST037.
0026 01  ATTRIBUTE-LIST               COPY   STWSATTR.
0027 01  DFHAID                       COPY   DFHAID.
0028*
0029 01  END-OF-WORKING-STORAGE  PIC X(15)   VALUE 'END WS POVMCHGE'.
0030*
0031 LINKAGE SECTION.
0032*
0033 01  DFHCOMMAREA                       PIC X(8).
0034*
0035 01  BLL-CELLS.
0036     05  FILLER                    PIC S9(8)   COMP.
0037     05  BLL-CWA-ADDRESS           PIC S9(8)   COMP.
0038     05  BLL-T037-STATE-TABLE-ADDRESS PIC S9(8) COMP.
0039*
0040 01  CWA-DATA          COPY   STLNKCWA.
0041 01  T037-STATE-TABLE  COPY   T037STAT.
0042 PROCEDURE DIVISION.
0043*******************************************************************
0044*     PROGRAM STRUCTURE IS:                                     *
0045*         AA00-MAINLINE                                         *
0046*           B000-INITIAL-ENTRY                                  *
0047*             B100-SEND-CONTROL-MAP-AND-DATA                    *
0048*               B110-GET-DATE-AND-TIME                          *
0049*                                                               *
0050*           C000-PROCESS-CONTROL-MAP                            *
0051*             C100-RECEIVE-CONTROL-MAP                          *
0052*               C110-END-SESSION                                *
0053*               C120 TRANSFER-XCTL-TO-MENU                      *
0054*               C130-TRANSFER-XCTL-TO-BROWSE                    *
0055*             C200-VERIFY-VENDOR-FORMAT                         *
0056*             C400-VERIFY-VENDOR-FILE-STATUS                    *
0057*               C410-READ-VENDOR-FILE                           *
0058*             C500-SEND-DETAIL-MAP-AND-DATA                     *
0059*               B110-GET-DATE-AND-TIME                          *
0060*               C520-SET-MAP-ATTRIBUTES                         *
0061*               C530-FORMAT-DETAIL-MAP                          *
0062*                 C531-GET-STATE-NAME                           *
0063*             C600-SEND-CONTROL-MAP-DATAONLY                    *
0064*                                                               *
0065*           F000-CHANGE-PROCESSING                              *
0066*             D100-RECEIVE-DETAIL-MAP                           *
0067*               C110-END-SESSION                                *
0068*               C120-TRANSFER-XCTL-TO-MENU                      *
0069*             F100-CHANGE-VENDOR-RECORD                         *
0070*               F110-READ-VENDOR-FOR-UPDATE                     *
0071*                 E121-POST-JOURNAL-RECORD                      *
0072*               E110-EDIT-MAP-FORMAT-VM-RECORD                  *
0073*                 C531-GET-STATE-NAME                           *
0074*               F120-REWRITE-VENDOR-RECORD                      *
0075*                 E121-POST-JOURNAL-RECORD                      *
0076*             B100-SEND-CONTROL-MAP-AND-DATA                    *
0077*             D200-SEND-DETAIL-MAP-DATAONLY                     *
0078*               C520-SET-MAP-ATTRIBUTES                         *
0079*******************************************************************
```

Figure 14-4 *(Continued)*

```
0080*
0081 AA00-MAINLINE  SECTION.
0082*
0083*     SERVICE RELOAD BLL-CELLS.
0084*
0085     IF EIBCALEN = 0
0086         PERFORM B000-INITIAL-ENTRY
0087     ELSE
0088         MOVE DFHCOMMAREA  TO  WS-COMMAREA
0089         IF CA-RECEIVE-CTL-MAP
0090             PERFORM C000-PROCESS-CONTROL-MAP
0091         ELSE
0092             PERFORM F000-CHANGE-PROCESSING.
0093*
0094     EXEC CICS RETURN
0095             TRANSID  ('POVC')
0096             COMMAREA (WS-COMMAREA)
0097             LENGTH   (8)
0098     END-EXEC.
0099*
0100 B000-INITIAL-ENTRY  SECTION.
0101******************************************************************
0102*             PERFORMED FROM:  AA00-MAINLINE            *
0103******************************************************************
0104*
0105     MOVE LOW-VALUES  TO  VM-CONTROL-MAP.
0106     PERFORM B100-SEND-CONTROL-MAP-AND-DATA.
0107*
0108 B000-EXIT.
0109     EXIT.
0110*
0111 B100-SEND-CONTROL-MAP-AND-DATA  SECTION.
0112******************************************************************
0113*         SEND CONTROL MAP - SYMBOLIC AND PHYSICAL MAPS      *
0114*             PERFORMED FROM:  B000-INITIAL-ENTRY            *
0115*                              F000-CHANGE-PROCESSING        *
0116******************************************************************
0117*
0118     PERFORM B110-GET-DATE-AND-TIME.
0119     MOVE WS-CURRENT-DATE  TO  MVC-D-DATE.
0120     MOVE WS-MAP-TIME      TO  MVC-D-TIME.
0121*
0122     MOVE -1   TO  MVC-L-VEND-CD-1.
0123     MOVE '1'  TO  CA-MAP-CONTROL.
0124*
0125     EXEC CICS SEND
0126             MAP     ('MAPPOVC')
0127             MAPSET  ('POVMCH1')
0128             FROM    (VM-CONTROL-MAP)
0129             ERASE
0130             CURSOR
0131     END-EXEC.
0132*
0133 B100-EXIT.
0134     EXIT.
0135*
0136 B110-GET-DATE-AND-TIME  SECTION   COPY   STPDDTTM.
0137******************************************************************
0138*     STPDDTTM - OBTAIN DATE FROM CWA AND FORMAT TIME       *
0139*         PERFORMED FROM:  B100-SEND-CONTROL-MAP-AND-DATA   *
0140*                          C500-SEND-DETAIL-MAP-AND-DATA    *
0141******************************************************************
0142*
0143 B110-EXIT.
0144     EXIT.
0145*
0146 C000-PROCESS-CONTROL-MAP  SECTION.
0147******************************************************************
0148*             PERFORMED FROM:  AA00-MAINLINE               *
0149*         PROCESS CONTROL MAP - IF VALID SEND DETAIL MAP    *
0150*         ELSE SEND CONTROL MAP WITH INVALID MESSAGE:       *
0151*     1) STATUS-OF-RECEIVE  =  'I'   INVALID KEY PRESSED    *
0152*     2) STATUS-OF-RECEIVE  =  'M'   MAPFAIL - NO DATA ENTERED *
0153*     3) STATUS-OF-FORMAT   =  'E'   INVALID VENDOR KEYED FORMAT *
0154*     4) STATUS-OF-VERIFY   =  'E'   VENDOR FILE STATUS ERROR *
0155******************************************************************
```

Figure 14-4 *(Continued)*

```
0156*
0157      PERFORM C100-RECEIVE-CONTROL-MAP.
0158      IF GOOD-RECEIVE
0159          PERFORM C200-VERIFY-VENDOR-FORMAT
0160          IF VALID-FORMAT
0161              PERFORM C400-VERIFY-VENDOR-FILE-STATUS
0162              IF GOOD-VERIFY
0163                  PERFORM C500-SEND-DETAIL-MAP-AND-DATA
0164              ELSE
0165                  PERFORM C600-SEND-CONTROL-MAP-DATAONLY
0166          ELSE
0167              PERFORM C600-SEND-CONTROL-MAP-DATAONLY
0168      ELSE
0169          IF MAPFAIL-ON-RECEIVE
0170              MOVE 'VENDOR CODE MUST BE ENTERED - PLEASE KEY-IN'
0171                  TO MVC-D-MESSAGE
0172              MOVE ASKIP-BRT  TO MVC-A-MESSAGE
0173              PERFORM C600-SEND-CONTROL-MAP-DATAONLY
0174          ELSE
0175              PERFORM C600-SEND-CONTROL-MAP-DATAONLY.
0176*
0177  C000-EXIT.
0178      EXIT.
0179*
0180  C100-RECEIVE-CONTROL-MAP  SECTION.
0181*******************************************************************
0182*             PERFORMED FROM:  C000-PROCESS-CONTROL-MAP          *
0183*             ENTER IS ONLY VALID DATA ENTRY KEY                 *
0184*  CLEAR KEY - ENDS TERMINAL SESSION      PF5 - RETURNS TO MENU  *
0185*                                          PF4 - XCTL TO BROWSE   *
0186*             ALL OTHER AID KEYS ARE INVALID                     *
0187*      STATUS-OF-RECEIVE = 'G' =  GOOD RECEIVE                   *
0188*                          'M' =  MAPFAIL                        *
0189*                          'I' =  INVALID KEY PRESSED            *
0190*******************************************************************
0191*
0192      MOVE LOW-VALUES  TO  VM-CONTROL-MAP.
0193*
0194      IF EIBAID  =  DFHENTER
0195          MOVE 'M'  TO  STATUS-OF-RECEIVE
0196*
0197          EXEC CICS HANDLE CONDITION
0198              MAPFAIL (C100-EXIT)
0199          END-EXEC
0200*
0201          EXEC CICS RECEIVE
0202              MAP     ('MAPPOVC')
0203              MAPSET  ('POVMCH1')
0204              INTO    (VM-CONTROL-MAP)
0205          END-EXEC
0206*
0207          MOVE 'G'  TO  STATUS-OF-RECEIVE
0208      ELSE
0209          IF EIBAID  =  DFHCLEAR
0210              PERFORM C110-END-SESSION
0211          ELSE
0212          IF EIBAID  =  DFHPF5
0213              PERFORM C120-TRANSFER-XCTL-TO-MENU
0214          ELSE
0215          IF EIBAID  =  DFHPF4
0216              PERFORM C130-TRANSFER-XCTL-TO-BROWSE
0217          ELSE
0218              MOVE 'I'         TO  STATUS-OF-RECEIVE
0219              MOVE 'INVALID KEY PRESSED - PLEASE TRY AGAIN'
0220                  TO  MVC-D-MESSAGE
0221              MOVE ASKIP-BRT  TO  MVC-A-MESSAGE.
0222*
0223  C100-EXIT.
0224      EXIT.
0225*
0226  C110-END-SESSION  SECTION.
0227*******************************************************************
0228*  CRT OPERATOR PRESSED CLEAR KEY TO END TERMINAL SESSION        *
0229*      PERFORMED FROM:  C100-RECEIVE-CONTROL-MAP                 *
0230*                       D100-RECEIVE-DETAIL-MAP                  *
0231*******************************************************************
```

Figure 14-4 (*Continued*)

```
0232*
0233      EXEC CICS SEND
0234                FROM     (WS-CRT-MESSAGE)
0235                LENGTH   (17)
0236                ERASE
0237      END-EXEC.
0238*
0239      EXEC CICS RETURN
0240      END-EXEC.
0241*
0242 C110-EXIT.
0243      EXIT.
0244*
0245 C120-TRANSFER-XCTL-TO-MENU  SECTION.
0246*****************************************************************
0247*      OPERATOR PRESSED PF5 TO RETURN TO MENU PROGRAM         *
0248*          PERFORMED FROM:  C100-RECEIVE-CONTROL-MAP           *
0249*                           D100-RECEIVE-DETAIL-MAP            *
0250*****************************************************************
0251*
0252      EXEC CICS XCTL
0253                PROGRAM ('POVMAINT')
0254      END-EXEC.
0255*
0256 C120-EXIT.
0257      EXIT.
0258*
0259 C130-TRANSFER-XCTL-TO-BROWSE  SECTION.
0260*****************************************************************
0261*      OPERATOR PRESSED PF4 TO TRANSFER CONTROL TO BROWSE     *
0262*          PERFORMED FROM:  C100-RECEIVE-CONTROL-MAP           *
0263*****************************************************************
0264*
0265      MOVE LOW-VALUES  TO  WS-COMMAREA.
0266      MOVE 'C'         TO  CA-FUNCTION-CODE.
0267*
0268      EXEC CICS XCTL
0269                PROGRAM   ('POVMBROW')
0270                COMMAREA  (WS-COMMAREA)
0271                LENGTH    (8)
0272      END-EXEC.
0273*
0274 C130-EXIT.
0275      EXIT.
0276*
0277 C200-VERIFY-VENDOR-FORMAT  SECTION.
0278*****************************************************************
0279*      VERIFY FORMAT OF VENDOR CODE KEYED-IN = A-9999-9       *
0280*          PERFORMED FROM:  C000-PROCESS-CONTROL-MAP           *
0281*   IF VALID FORMAT - MOVE CODE TO WS-COMMAREA FIELDS (CA- )   *
0282*****************************************************************
0283*
0284      IF (MVC-D-VENDOR-CD-1  IS  ALPHABETIC
0285                AND
0286        MVC-D-VENDOR-CD-1  IS NOT =  SPACE)
0287      AND
0288        MVC-D-VENDOR-CD-2  IS  NUMERIC
0289      AND
0290        MVC-D-VENDOR-CD-3  IS  NUMERIC
0291          MOVE MVC-D-VEND-CD-1  TO  CA-VEND-1
0292          MOVE MVC-D-VEND-CD-2  TO  CA-VEND-2
0293          MOVE MVC-D-VEND-CD-3  TO  CA-VEND-3
0294          MOVE 'G'              TO  STATUS-OF-FORMAT
0295      ELSE
0296          MOVE 'E'          TO  STATUS-OF-FORMAT
0297          MOVE 'VENDOR CODE FORMAT MUST BE: A-9999-9 - PLEASE RE-EN
0298-             'TER'         TO  MVC-D-MESSAGE
0299          MOVE ASKIP-BRT   TO  MVC-A-MESSAGE.
0300*
0301 C200-EXIT.
0302      EXIT.
0303*
0304 C400-VERIFY-VENDOR-FILE-STATUS  SECTION.
0305*****************************************************************
0306*          PERFORMED FROM:  C000-PROCESS-CONTROL-MAP           *
0307*             MUST BE A VENDOR RECORD FOR CHANGES              *
0308*****************************************************************
```

Figure 14-4 *(Continued)*

```
0309*
0310      MOVE 'G'  TO  STATUS-OF-VERIFY.
0311*
0312      PERFORM C410-READ-VENDOR-FILE.
0313*
0314      IF RECORD-NOT-FOUND
0315          MOVE 'E'         TO   STATUS-OF-VERIFY
0316          MOVE 'VENDOR RECORD NOT ON FILE'
0317                           TO   MVC-D-MESSAGE
0318          MOVE ASKIP-BRT   TO   MVC-A-MESSAGE.
0319*
0320 C400-EXIT.
0321      EXIT.
0322*
0323 C410-READ-VENDOR-FILE  SECTION.
0324***********************************************************
0325*        PERFORMED FROM:  C400-VERIFY-VENDOR-FILE-STATUS       *
0326***********************************************************
0327*
0328      MOVE 'E' TO  STATUS-OF-READ.
0329*
0330      EXEC CICS HANDLE CONDITION
0331              NOTFND  (C410-EXIT)
0332      END-EXEC.
0333*
0334      EXEC CICS READ
0335              DATASET ('VENDMAST')
0336              INTO    (VENDOR-MASTER-RECORD)
0337              RIDFLD  (CA-VENDOR-CODE)
0338      END-EXEC.
0339*
0340      MOVE 'G'  TO  STATUS-OF-READ.
0341*
0342 C410-EXIT.
0343      EXIT.
0344*
0345 C500-SEND-DETAIL-MAP-AND-DATA  SECTION.
0346***********************************************************
0347*          SEND DETAIL MAP - PHYSICAL AND SYMBOLIC MAPS      *
0348*            PERFORMED FROM:  C000-PROCESS-CONTROL-MAP        *
0349*   SENT WHEN ALL VALIDATION AND EDIT CONDITIONS HAVE BEEN MET *
0350***********************************************************
0351*
0352      MOVE LOW-VALUES  TO  VM-DETAIL-MAP.
0353*
0354      PERFORM B110-GET-DATE-AND-TIME.
0355      MOVE WS-CURRENT-DATE  TO  MVD-D-DATE.
0356      MOVE WS-MAP-TIME      TO  MVD-D-TIME.
0357*
0358      PERFORM C520-SET-MAP-ATTRIBUTES.
0359*
0360      PERFORM C530-FORMAT-DETAIL-MAP.
0361*
0362      MOVE -1   TO  MVD-L-VENDOR-NAME.
0363      MOVE '2'  TO  CA-MAP-CONTROL.
0364*
0365      EXEC CICS SEND
0366              MAP     ('MAPPOVD')
0367              MAPSET  ('POVMCH2')
0368              FROM    (VM-DETAIL-MAP)
0369              ERASE
0370              CURSOR
0371      END-EXEC.
0372*
0373 C500-EXIT.
0374      EXIT.
0375*
0376 C520-SET-MAP-ATTRIBUTES  SECTION.
0377***********************************************************
0378*        PERFORMED FROM:  C500-SEND-DETAIL-MAP-AND-DATA        *
0379*                         D200-SEND-DETAIL-MAP-DATAONLY        *
0380***********************************************************
```

Figure 14-4 *(Continued)*

```
0381*
0382      MOVE UNPROT-FSET   TO   MVD-A-PHONE-AREA-CD
0383                              MVD-A-PHONE-1
0384                              MVD-A-PHONE-2
0385                              MVD-A-VENDOR-NAME
0386                              MVD-A-CONTACT
0387                              MVD-A-STREET
0388                              MVD-A-CITY
0389                              MVD-A-STATE-CODE
0390                              MVD-A-ZIP-CODE
0391                              MVD-A-ATTENTION-OF.
0392      MOVE ASKIP-DRK     TO   MVD-C-A-DLRS-COMMITTED.
0393*
0394 C520-EXIT.
0395      EXIT.
0396*
0397 C530-FORMAT-DETAIL-MAP . SECTION.
0398***************************************************************
0399*         PERFORMED FROM:  C500-SEND-DETAIL-MAP-AND-DATA      *
0400***************************************************************
0401*
0402* FORMAT VENDOR CODE: A-9999-9    WS- FIELDS ARE AT END OF VENDMAST
0403      MOVE CA-VEND-1          TO   WS-VENDOR-CD-1.
0404      MOVE CA-VEND-2          TO   WS-VENDOR-CD-2.
0405      MOVE CA-VEND-3          TO   WS-VENDOR-CD-3.
0406      MOVE WS-VENDOR-CODE     TO   MVD-D-VENDOR-CODE.
0407*
0408      MOVE VM-AREA-CD         TO   MVD-D-PHONE-AREA-CODE.
0409      MOVE VM-PHONE-1-3       TO   MVD-D-PHONE-1.
0410      MOVE VM-PHONE-4-7       TO   MVD-D-PHONE-2.
0411      MOVE VM-VENDOR-NAME     TO   MVD-D-VENDOR-NAME.
0412      MOVE VM-CONTACT         TO   MVD-D-CONTACT.
0413      MOVE VM-STREET-ADDRESS  TO   MVD-D-STREET.
0414      MOVE VM-CITY            TO   MVD-D-CITY.
0415      MOVE VM-STATE           TO   MVD-D-STATE-CODE.
0416*
0417      MOVE VM-STATE           TO   WS-STATE-CODE.
0418      PERFORM C531-GET-STATE-NAME.
0419      MOVE WS-STATE-NAME      TO   MVD-D-STATE-NAME.
0420*
0421      MOVE VM-ZIP-CODE        TO   MVD-D-ZIP-CODE.
0422      MOVE VM-TO-ATTN-OF      TO   MVD-D-ATTENTION-OF.
0423*
0424 C530-EXIT.
0425      EXIT.
0426*
0427 C531-GET-STATE-NAME  SECTION   COPY   STPDT037.
0428***************************************************************
0429*            LOAD AND SEARCH STATE CODE TABLE                *
0430*         PERFORMED FROM:  C530-SEND-DETAIL-MAP-AND-DATA      *
0431*                          E110-EDIT-MAP-FORMAT-VM-RECORD     *
0432***************************************************************
0433*
0434 C531-EXIT.
0435      EXIT.
0436*
0437 C600-SEND-CONTROL-MAP-DATAONLY  SECTION.
0438***************************************************************
0439*         SEND CONTROL MAP DATAONLY - SYMBOLIC MAP           *
0440*         PERFORMED FROM:  C000-PROCESS-CONTROL-MAP          *
0441*              SENT FOR INVALID CONDITIONS                   *
0442***************************************************************
0443*
0444      MOVE UNPROT-FSET   TO   MVC-A-VEND-CD-1
0445                              MVC-A-VEND-CD-2
0446                              MVC-A-VEND-CD-3.
0447*
0448      MOVE -1   TO   MVC-L-VEND-CD-1.
0449      MOVE '1'  TO   CA-MAP-CONTROL.
0450*
0451      EXEC CICS SEND
0452                MAP       ('MAPPOVC')
0453                MAPSET    ('POVMCH1')
0454                FROM      (VM-CONTROL-MAP)
0455                DATAONLY
0456                CURSOR
0457      END-EXEC.
0458*
0459 C600-EXIT.
0460      EXIT.
0461*
```

Figure 14-4 *(Continued)*

```
0462 D100-RECEIVE-DETAIL-MAP  SECTION.
0463********************************************************************
0464*         PERFORMED FROM:  F000-CHANGE-PROCESSING              *
0465*  ENTER - PROCESSES TRANSACTION          CLEAR - ENDS SESSION *
0466*  PF3   - SET DISPLAY OF CTL MAP         PF5   - RETURNS TO MENU *
0467*              ALL OTHER KEYS ARE INVALID                       *
0468*     STATUS-OF-RECEIVE  =  'G'  =   GOOD RECEIVE               *
0469*                           'C'  =   RETURN TO CTL-MAP          *
0470*                           'I'  =   INVALID KEY PRESSED        *
0471********************************************************************
0472*
0473      MOVE LOW-VALUES  TO  VM-DETAIL-MAP.
0474*
0475      IF EIBAID  =  DFHENTER
0476*
0477          EXEC CICS IGNORE CONDITION
0478                    MAPFAIL
0479          END-EXEC
0480*
0481          EXEC CICS RECEIVE
0482                    MAP      ('MAPPOVD')
0483                    MAPSET   ('POVMCH2')
0484                    INTO     (VM-DETAIL-MAP)
0485          END-EXEC
0486*
0487          MOVE 'G'  TO  STATUS-OF-RECEIVE
0488      ELSE
0489          IF EIBAID  =  DFHCLEAR
0490              PERFORM C110-END-SESSION
0491          ELSE
0492          IF EIBAID  =  DFHPF3
0493              MOVE 'C'  TO  STATUS-OF-RECEIVE
0494*         ELSE
0495          IF EIBAID  =  DFHPF5
0496              PERFORM C120-TRANSFER-XCTL-TO-MENU
0497          ELSE
0498                  MOVE 'I'       TO  STATUS-OF-RECEIVE
0499                  MOVE 'INVALID KEY PRESSED - PLEASE TRY AGAIN'
0500                                 TO  MVD-D-MESSAGE
0501                  MOVE ASKIP-BRT  TO  MVD-A-MESSAGE.
0502*
0503 D100-EXIT.
0504      EXIT.
0505*
0506 D200-SEND-DETAIL-MAP-DATAONLY  SECTION.
0507********************************************************************
0508*         SEND DETAIL MAP DATA ONLY - SYMBOLIC MAP             *
0509*      PERFORMED FROM:  F000-CHANGE-PROCESSING                 *
0510*  SENT IF INVALID KEY IS PRESSED ON A RECEIVE OF THE DETAIL MAP *
0511********************************************************************
0512*
0513      MOVE '2'  TO  CA-MAP-CONTROL.
0514*
0515      PERFORM C520-SET-MAP-ATTRIBUTES.
0516*
0517      EXEC CICS SEND
0518                MAP      ('MAPPOVD')
0519                MAPSET   ('POVMCH2')
0520                FROM     (VM-DETAIL-MAP)
0521                DATAONLY
0522                CURSOR
0523      END-EXEC.
0524*
0525 D200-EXIT.
0526      EXIT.
0527*
0528 E110-EDIT-MAP-FORMAT-VM-RECORD  SECTION.
0529********************************************************************
0530*      EDIT DETAIL MAP DATA - FORMAT VENDOR MASTER RECORD      *
0531*          PERFORMED FROM:  F100-CHANGE-VENDOR-RECORD          *
0532*      HIGHLIGHT FIELDS WHICH CONTAIN INCORRECT DATA           *
0533*          OR WHICH ARE MISSING REQUIRED ENTRIES               *
0534********************************************************************
0535*
0536*     IDENTICAL TO SAME SECTION IN FIGURE 13-4
0537*
0538 E110-EXIT.
0539      EXIT.
```

Figure 14-4 *(Continued)*

```
0540*
0541 E121-POST-JOURNAL-RECORD  SECTION.
0542************************************************************************
0543*     POST JOURNAL ENTRY - LINK TO JOURNAL PROGRAM 'JRNLPOST'    *
0544*        PERFORMED FROM:  F110-READ-VENDOR-FOR-UPDATE            *
0545*                         F120-REWRITE-VENDOR-RECORD             *
0546************************************************************************
0547*
0548     MOVE 'VM'                    TO  JR-PREFIX.
0549     MOVE VENDOR-MASTER-RECORD    TO  JR-RECORD-DATA.
0550     MOVE SPACES                  TO  JR-PASSWORD.
0551*
0552     EXEC CICS LINK
0553             PROGRAM  ('JRNLPOST')
0554             COMMAREA (JOURNAL-RECORD)
0555             LENGTH   (524)
0556     END-EXEC.
0557*
0558 E121-EXIT.
0559     EXIT.
0560*
0561 F000-CHANGE-PROCESSING  SECTION.
0562************************************************************************
0563*                 PERFORMED FROM:  AA00-MAINLINE                 *
0564*      DETAIL MAP IS SENT IF INVALID KEY WAS PRESSED             *
0565*            OR IF CHANGE WAS UNSUCCESSFUL                       *
0566************************************************************************
0567*
0568     PERFORM D100-RECEIVE-DETAIL-MAP.
0569*
0570     IF GOOD-RECEIVE
0571         PERFORM F100-CHANGE-VENDOR-RECORD
0572         IF GOOD-CHANGE
0573             PERFORM B100-SEND-CONTROL-MAP-AND-DATA
0574         ELSE
0575             PERFORM D200-SEND-DETAIL-MAP-DATAONLY
0576     ELSE
0577         IF RETURN-TO-CTL-MAP
0578             PERFORM B100-SEND-CONTROL-MAP-AND-DATA
0579         ELSE
0580             PERFORM D200-SEND-DETAIL-MAP-DATAONLY.
0581*
0582 F000-EXIT.
0583     EXIT.
0584*
0585 F100-CHANGE-VENDOR-RECORD  SECTION.
0586************************************************************************
0587*             PERFORMED FROM:  F000-CHANGE PROCESSING            *
0588*     READ RECORD FOR UPDATE, EDIT MAP DATA AND REWRITE RECORD   *
0589*     RECORD NOT FOUND COULD NOT OCCUR UNLESS RECORD WAS DELETED  *
0590*     BY ANOTHER TERMINAL SINCE BEING KEYED-IN ON CONTROL SCREEN *
0591************************************************************************
0592*
0593     MOVE 'E' TO STATUS-OF-CHANGE.
0594*
0595     PERFORM F110-READ-VENDOR-FOR-UPDATE.
0596*
0597     IF RECORD-NOT-FOUND
0598         MOVE 'UPDATE VENDOR RECORD - NOT FOUND'
0599                         TO  MVD-D-MESSAGE
0600         MOVE ASKIP-BRT  TO  MVD-A-MESSAGE
0601         MOVE ASKIP-BRT  TO  MVD-C-A-VENDOR-CODE
0602     ELSE
0603         PERFORM E110-EDIT-MAP-FORMAT-VM-RECORD
0604         IF GOOD-EDIT
0605             PERFORM F120-REWRITE-VENDOR-RECORD
0606             MOVE 'CHANGE COMPLETED SUCCESSFULLY'
0607                         TO  MVC-D-MESSAGE
0608             MOVE ASKIP-BRT  TO  MVC-A-MESSAGE
0609             MOVE 'G'        TO  STATUS-OF-CHANGE.
0610*
0611 F100-EXIT.
0612     EXIT.
0613*
0614 F110-READ-VENDOR-FOR-UPDATE  SECTION.
0615************************************************************************
0616*    READ VENDOR RECORD FOR UPDATE - POST BEFORE JOURNAL RECORD  *
0617*            PERFORMED FROM:  F100-CHANGE-VENDOR-RECORD          *
0618************************************************************************
```

Figure 14-4 *(Continued)*

```
0619*
0620       MOVE 'E'  TO  STATUS-OF-READ.
0621*
0622       EXEC CICS HANDLE CONDITION
0623                 NOTFND  (F110-EXIT)
0624       END-EXEC.
0625*
0626       EXEC CICS READ
0627                 DATASET ('VENDMAST')
0628                 INTO    (VENDOR-MASTER-RECORD)
0629                 RIDFLD  (CA-VENDOR-CODE)
0630                 UPDATE
0631       END-EXEC.
0632*
0633       MOVE 'S'  TO  STATUS-OF-READ.
0634*
0635       MOVE 'B'  TO  JR-TYPE.
0636       PERFORM E121-POST-JOURNAL-RECORD.
0637*
0638 F110-EXIT.
0639       EXIT.
0640*
0641 F120-REWRITE VENDOR-RECORD  SECTION.
0642************************************************************************
0643*      REWRITE VENDOR RECORD - POST 'AFTER' JOURNAL RECORD          *
0644*             PERFORMED FROM:  F100-CHANGE-VENDOR-RECORD            *
0645************************************************************************
0646*
0647       EXEC CICS REWRITE
0648                 DATASET ('VENDMAST')
0649                 FROM    (VENDOR-MASTER-RECORD)
0650       END-EXEC.
0651*
0652       MOVE 'A'  TO  JR-TYPE.
0653       PERFORM E121-POST-JOURNAL-RECORD.
0654*
0655 F120-EXIT.
0656       EXIT.
```

SUMMARY

This chapter presented the change program. It can be used as a model for most change programs you will have to write. Several of the commands discussed in preceding chapters were used. The READ FOR UPDATE and REWRITE file commands were used in the change program.

15

THE DELETE PROGRAM

After a record has been on a file for a period of time, circumstances sometimes require the record to be deleted from the file. This chapter discusses the delete program.

Control and detail maps are used for the delete program. The control map shown in Fig. 15-1 requires the terminal operator to key in a vendor code and to press ENTER in order to display the delete detail screen. The operator also has the option of transferring control to the vendor file browse, returning to the vendor file maintenance submenu (see Fig. 8-3), or ending the session. The vendor file delete program detail map shown in Fig. 2-9 is displayed when the operator enters an existing vendor code on the control screen (Fig. 15-1). The delete detail screen permits the operator to verify the vendor's data in order to make sure the correct record is being deleted. The operator then presses ENTER in order to delete the record. The detail screen also permits the operator to return to the delete control screen without deleting the record, return to the submenu, or to end the session.

BMS Maps

Figures 15-2 and 15-3 show the BMS maps for the control and detail screens, respectively.

BMS Control Map

Only the differences between this map and the BMS control map for the inquiry program (see Fig. 12-1) are shown in Fig. 15-2.

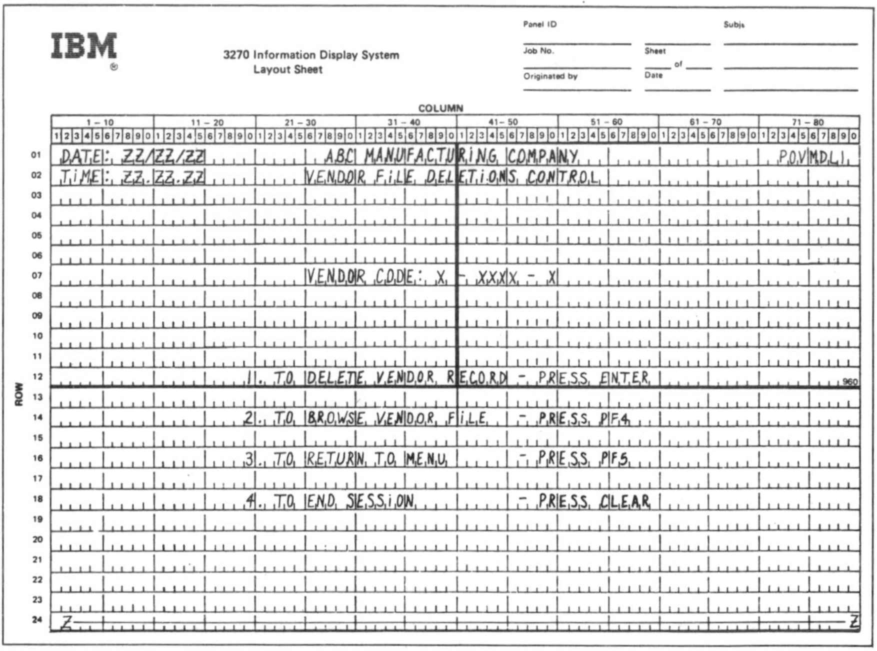

Figure 15-1 Vendor File Deletions Control Map.

BMS Detail Map

This map is similar to the inquiry detail map shown in Fig. 12-2. Only the differences are shown in Fig. 15-3.

User-Friendly Symbolic Maps

The user-friendly symbolic maps which correspond to BMS-generated maps are shown in the copy library (App. B, members MAPVMCTL and MAPVDTL1).

Delete Program Source Code

The delete program source code shown in Fig. 15-4 follows the format used in previous examples. I will only discuss sections which differ from previous examples.

Procedure Division

AA00-MAINLINE. This section is similar to that of the inquiry program in Chap. 12 except that perform G000-DELETE-PROCESSING replaces D000-INQUIRY-PROCESSING and TRANSID POVD replaces POVI.

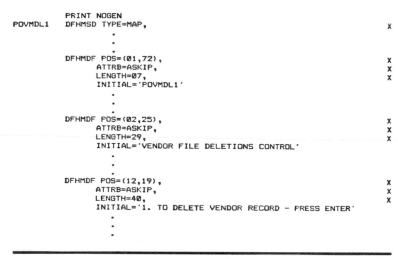

```
          PRINT NOGEN
POVMDL1   DFHMSD TYPE=MAP,                                                X
                  .
                  .
                  .
          DFHMDF POS=(01,72),                                             X
                  ATTRB=ASKIP,                                            X
                  LENGTH=07,                                              X
                  INITIAL='POVMDL1'
                  .
                  .
                  .
          DFHMDF POS=(02,25),                                             X
                  ATTRB=ASKIP,                                            X
                  LENGTH=29,                                              X
                  INITIAL='VENDOR FILE DELETIONS CONTROL'
                  .
                  .
                  .
          DFHMDF POS=(12,19),                                             X
                  ATTRB=ASKIP,                                            X
                  LENGTH=40,                                              X
                  INITIAL='1. TO DELETE VENDOR RECORD - PRESS ENTER'
                  .
                  .
                  .
```

Figure 15-2 Vendor File Deletions BMS Control Map.

C400-VERIFY-VENDOR-FILE-STATUS. This section performs a read of the vendor file to make sure the vendor to be deleted is on the file. If the vendor is not on the file, an error indicator is set and an error message returned.

C410-READ-VENDOR-FILE. A record should be on the file for a vendor which is being deleted. A NOTFND condition will be treated as an error in the invoking section.

F110-READ-VENDOR-FOR-UPDATE. A before (B) journal record posting is performed. There is no after-record on a delete function.

G100-DELETE-VENDOR-RECORD. This section reads the delete record for update. If the record is not found, an indicative message will be displayed on the detail map. It would not be necessary to read the record for update prior to deleting if no journal record was being posted. In that case the DELETE command would have to contain the RIDFLD option. A successfully read record is deleted and the message RECORD DELETED SUCCESSFULLY is displayed on the control screen. The message RECORD TO BE DELETED—NOT FOUND would only be displayed if an operator at another terminal deleted the same record you are attempting to delete, after you had entered vendor code on the control screen. The program would have previously read the vendor file for the entered vendor code (in section C410-READ-VENDOR-FILE) and determined that it was online in order to reach this point.

G110-DELETE-VM-RECORD. Delete the vendor record which was read for update. A before (B) journal record could be posted in this section instead of

```
        PRINT NOGEN
POVMDL2 DFHMSD TYPE=MAP,                                             X
          .
          .
          .
        DFHMDF POS=(01,72),                                         X
             ATTRB=ASKIP,                                           X
             LENGTH=07,                                             X
             INITIAL='POVMDL2'
             .
             .
             .
        DFHMDF POS=(02,30),                                         X
             ATTRB=ASKIP,                                           X
             LENGTH=20,                                             X
             INITIAL='VENDOR FILE DELETION'
             .
             .
             .
        DFHMDF POS=(18,10),                                         X
             ATTRB=ASKIP,                                           X
             LENGTH=56,                                             X
             INITIAL='1. DELETIONS, VERIFY DATA BEFORE DELETING   - PRX
             ESS ENTER'
*
        DFHMDF POS=(19,10),                                         X
             ATTRB=ASKIP,                                           X
             LENGTH=54,                                             X
             INITIAL='2. RETURN TO DELETION CONTROL SCREEN        - PRX
             ESS PF3'
*
        DFHMDF POS=(20,10),                                         X
             ATTRB=ASKIP,                                           X
             LENGTH=54,                                             X
             INITIAL='3. RETURN TO MENU                           - PRX
             ESS PF5'
*
        DFHMDF POS=(21,10),                                         X
             ATTRB=ASKIP,                                           X
             LENGTH=56,                                             X
             INITIAL='4. END OF SESSION                           - PRX
             ESS CLEAR'
             .
             .
             .
```

Figure 15-3   Vendor File Deletions BMS Detail Map.

in section F110-READ-VENDOR-FOR-UPDATE, in which the logic was performed. When the program reaches this point, it has read the vendor record for update and has established exclusive control of the record to be deleted.

SUMMARY

This chapter presented the delete program. The program given here can be used as a model for most delete programs you will have to write. Several of the commands which were discussed in preceding chapters were used. The READ FOR UPDATE and DELETE file commands were used in the delete program.

Figure 15-4 Vendor File Deletions Program Source Code.

```
0001 IDENTIFICATION DIVISION.
0002 PROGRAM-ID. POVMDLET.
0003 REMARKS.
0004*****************************************************************
0005*            PURCHASING SYSTEM - VENDOR FILE DELETIONS         *
0006*     - STARTED BY PURCHASING SYSTEM SUB-MENU PROGRAM 'POVMAINT'   *
0007*            COULD ALSO BE STARTED BY TRANSID 'POVD'           *
0008*****************************************************************
0009 ENVIRONMENT DIVISION.
0010 DATA DIVISION.
0011*
0012 WORKING-STORAGE  SECTION.
0013*
0014 01  WS-PROGRAM-FIELDS.
0015     05  FILLER            PIC X(8)     VALUE 'POVMDLET'.
0016     05  WS-CRT-MESSAGE    PIC X(17)    VALUE 'SESSION COMPLETED'.
0017*
0018 01  VENDOR-MASTER-RECORD             COPY   VENDMAST.
0019 01  JOURNAL-RECORD                   COPY   JRNLRECD.
0020 01  WS-COMMAREA                      COPY   POWSVMCA.
0021 01  WS-STATUS-FIELDS                 COPY   STWSSTAT.
0022 01  VM-CONTROL-MAP                   COPY   MAPVMCTL.
0023 01  VM-DETAIL-MAP                    COPY   MAPVDTL1.
0024 01  WS-DATE-AND-TIME                 COPY   STWSDTTM.
0025 01  WS-STATE-CODE-SEARCH-ENTRIES     COPY   STWST037.
0026 01  ATTRIBUTE-LIST                   COPY   STWSATTR.
0027 01  DFHAID                           COPY   DFHAID.
0028*
0029 01  END-OF-WORKING-STORAGE  PIC X(15)   VALUE 'END WS POVMDLET'.
0030*
0031 LINKAGE SECTION.
0032*
0033 01  DFHCOMMAREA                      PIC X(8).
0034*
0035 01  BLL-CELLS.
0036     05  FILLER                       PIC S9(8)    COMP.
0037     05  BLL-CWA-ADDRESS              PIC S9(8)    COMP.
0038     05  BLL-T037-STATE-TABLE-ADDRESS PIC S9(8)    COMP.
0039*
0040 01  CWA-DATA           COPY   STLNKCWA.
0041 01  T037-STATE-TABLE   COPY   T037STAT.
0042 PROCEDURE DIVISION.
0043*****************************************************************
0044*    PROGRAM STRUCTURE IS:                                     *
0045*        AA00-MAINLINE                                         *
0046*          B000-INITIAL-ENTRY                                  *
0047*            B100-SEND-CONTROL-MAP-AND-DATA                    *
0048*              B110-GET-DATE-AND-TIME                          *
0049*                                                              *
0050*          C000-PROCESS-CONTROL-MAP                            *
0051*            C100-RECEIVE-CONTROL-MAP                          *
0052*              C110-END-SESSION                                *
0053*              C120-TRANSFER-XCTL-TO-MENU                      *
0054*              C130-TRANSFER-XCTL-TO-BROWSE                    *
0055*            C200-VERIFY-VENDOR-FORMAT                         *
0056*            C400-VERIFY-VENDOR-FILE-STATUS                    *
0057*              C410-READ-VENDOR-FILE                           *
0058*            C500-SEND-DETAIL-MAP-AND-DATA                     *
0059*              B110-GET-DATE-AND-TIME                          *
0060*              C530-FORMAT-DETAIL-MAP                          *
0061*                C531-GET-STATE-NAME                           *
0062*            C600-SEND-CONTROL-MAP-DATAONLY                    *
0063*                                                              *
0064*          G000-DELETE-PROCESSING                              *
0065*            D100-RECEIVE-DETAIL-MAP                           *
0066*              C110-END-SESSION                                *
0067*              C120-TRANSFER-XCTL-TO-MENU                      *
0068*            G100-DELETE-VENDOR-RECORD                         *
0069*              F110-READ-VENDOR-FOR-UPDATE                     *
0070*                E121-POST-JOURNAL-RECORD                      *
0071*              G110-DELETE-VM-RECORD                           *
0072*            B100-SEND-CONTROL-MAP-AND-DATA                    *
0073*            D200-SEND-DETAIL-MAP-DATAONLY                     *
0074*****************************************************************
0075*
0076 AA00-MAINLINE  SECTION.
0077*
0078*    SERVICE RELOAD BLL-CELLS.
```

Figure 15-4 *(Continued)*

```
0079*
0080     IF EIBCALEN = 0
0081         PERFORM B000-INITIAL-ENTRY
0082     ELSE
0083         MOVE DFHCOMMAREA TO WS-COMMAREA
0084         IF CA-RECEIVE-CTL-MAP
0085             PERFORM C000-PROCESS-CONTROL-MAP
0086         ELSE
0087             PERFORM G000-DELETE-PROCESSING.
0088*
0089     EXEC CICS RETURN
0090             TRANSID  ('POVD')
0091             COMMAREA (WS-COMMAREA)
0092             LENGTH   (8)
0093     END-EXEC.
0094*
0095 B000-INITIAL-ENTRY  SECTION.
0096*****************************************************************
0097*              PERFORMED FROM:  AA00-MAINLINE                   *
0098*****************************************************************
0099*
0100     MOVE LOW-VALUES  TO  VM-CONTROL-MAP.
0101     PERFORM B100-SEND-CONTROL-MAP-AND-DATA.
0102*
0103 B000-EXIT.
0104     EXIT.
0105*
0106 B100-SEND-CONTROL-MAP-AND-DATA  SECTION.
0107*****************************************************************
0108*        SEND CONTROL MAP - SYMBOLIC AND PHYSICAL MAPS         *
0109*             PERFORMED FROM:  B000-INITIAL-ENTRY               *
0110*                              G000-DELETE-PROCESSING           *
0111*****************************************************************
0112*
0113     PERFORM B110-GET-DATE-AND-TIME.
0114     MOVE WS-CURRENT-DATE  TO  MVC-D-DATE.
0115     MOVE WS-MAP-TIME      TO  MVC-D-TIME.
0116*
0117     MOVE -1  TO  MVC-L-VEND-CD-1.
0118     MOVE '1' TO  CA-MAP-CONTROL.
0119*
0120     EXEC CICS SEND
0121             MAP    ('MAPPOVC')
0122             MAPSET ('POVMDL1')
0123             FROM   (VM-CONTROL-MAP)
0124             ERASE
0125             CURSOR
0126     END-EXEC.
0127*
0128 B100-EXIT.
0129     EXIT.
0130*
0131 B110-GET-DATE-AND-TIME  SECTION   COPY   STPDDTTM.
0132*****************************************************************
0133*        STPDDTTM - OBTAIN DATE FROM CWA AND FORMAT TIME       *
0134*           PERFORMED FROM:  B100-SEND-CONTROL-MAP-AND-DATA     *
0135*                            C500-SEND-DETAIL-MAP-AND-DATA      *
0136*****************************************************************
0137*
0138 B110-EXIT.
0139     EXIT.
0140*
0141 C000-PROCESS-CONTROL-MAP  SECTION.
0142*****************************************************************
0143*              PERFORMED FROM:  AA00-MAINLINE                   *
0144*        PROCESS CONTROL MAP - IF VALID SEND DETAIL MAP         *
0145*           ELSE SEND CONTROL MAP WITH INVALID MESSAGE:         *
0146*  1) STATUS-OF-RECEIVE = 'I'   INVALID KEY PRESSED            *
0147*  2) STATUS-OF-RECEIVE = 'M'   MAPFAIL - NO DATA ENTERED      *
0148*  3) STATUS-OF-FORMAT  = 'E'   INVALID VENDOR KEYED FORMAT    *
0149*  4) STATUS-OF-VERIFY  = 'E'   VENDOR FILE STATUS ERROR       *
0150*****************************************************************
0151*
0152     PERFORM C100-RECEIVE-CONTROL-MAP.
0153     IF GOOD-RECEIVE
0154         PERFORM C200-VERIFY-VENDOR-FORMAT
0155         IF VALID-FORMAT
0156             PERFORM C400-VERIFY-VENDOR-FILE-STATUS
0157             IF GOOD-VERIFY
0158                 PERFORM C500-SEND-DETAIL-MAP-AND-DATA
0159             ELSE
0160                 PERFORM C600-SEND-CONTROL-MAP-DATAONLY
```

Figure 15-4 *(Continued)*

```
0161            ELSE
0162                 PERFORM C600-SEND-CONTROL-MAP-DATAONLY
0163        ELSE
0164            IF MAPFAIL-ON-RECEIVE
0165                MOVE 'VENDOR CODE MUST BE ENTERED - PLEASE KEY-IN'
0166                                TO MVC-D-MESSAGE
0167                MOVE ASKIP-BRT  TO MVC-A-MESSAGE
0168                PERFORM C600-SEND-CONTROL-MAP-DATAONLY
0169            ELSE
0170                PERFORM C600-SEND-CONTROL-MAP-DATAONLY.
0171*
0172 C000-EXIT.
0173     EXIT.
0174*
0175 C100-RECEIVE-CONTROL-MAP  SECTION.
0176*****************************************************************
0177*          PERFORMED FROM:  C000-PROCESS-CONTROL-MAP           *
0178*              ENTER IS ONLY VALID DATA ENTRY KEY              *
0179* CLEAR KEY - ENDS TERMINAL SESSION      PF5 - RETURNS TO MENU *
0180*                                        PF4 - XCTL TO BROWSE  *
0181*            ALL OTHER AID KEYS ARE INVALID                    *
0182*      STATUS-OF-RECEIVE  =  'G'  =  GOOD RECEIVE              *
0183*                            'M'  =  MAPFAIL                   *
0184*                            'I'  =  INVALID KEY PRESSED       *
0185*****************************************************************
0186*
0187     MOVE LOW-VALUES  TO  VM-CONTROL-MAP.
0188*
0189     IF EIBAID  =  DFHENTER
0190         MOVE 'M'  TO  STATUS-OF-RECEIVE
0191*
0192         EXEC CICS HANDLE CONDITION
0193                 MAPFAIL (C100-EXIT)
0194         END-EXEC
0195*
0196         EXEC CICS RECEIVE
0197                 MAP    ('MAPPOVC')
0198                 MAPSET ('POVMDL1')
0199                 INTO   (VM-CONTROL-MAP)
0200         END-EXEC
0201*
0202         MOVE 'G'  TO  STATUS-OF-RECEIVE
0203     ELSE
0204         IF EIBAID  =  DFHCLEAR
0205             PERFORM C110-END-SESSION
0206         ELSE
0207         IF EIBAID  =  DFHPF5
0208             PERFORM C120-TRANSFER-XCTL-TO-MENU
0209         ELSE
0210         IF EIBAID  =  DFHPF4
0211             PERFORM C130-TRANSFER-XCTL-TO-BROWSE
0212         ELSE
0213             MOVE 'I'        TO  STATUS-OF-RECEIVE
0214             MOVE 'INVALID KEY PRESSED - PLEASE TRY AGAIN'
0215                             TO  MVC-D-MESSAGE
0216             MOVE ASKIP-BRT  TO  MVC-A-MESSAGE.
0217*
0218 C100-EXIT.
0219     EXIT.
0220*
0221 C110-END-SESSION  SECTION.
0222*****************************************************************
0223*    CRT OPERATOR PRESSED CLEAR KEY TO END TERMINAL SESSION    *
0224*        PERFORMED FROM:  C100-RECEIVE-CONTROL-MAP            *
0225*                         D100-RECEIVE-DETAIL-MAP             *
0226*****************************************************************
0227*
0228     EXEC CICS SEND
0229             FROM    (WS-CRT-MESSAGE)
0230             LENGTH (17)
0231             ERASE
0232     END-EXEC.
0233*
0234     EXEC CICS RETURN
0235     END-EXEC.
0236*
0237 C110-EXIT.
0238     EXIT.
```

Figure 15-4 *(Continued)*

```
0239*
0240 C120-TRANSFER-XCTL-TO-MENU  SECTION.
0241**********************************************************************
0242*         OPERATOR PRESSED PF5  TO RETURN TO MENU PROGRAM       *
0243*             PERFORMED FROM:  C100-RECEIVE-CONTROL-MAP         *
0244*                             D100-RECEIVE-DETAIL-MAP           *
0245**********************************************************************
0246*
0247    EXEC CICS XCTL
0248            PROGRAM ('POVMAINT')
0249    END-EXEC.
0250*
0251 C120-EXIT.
0252    EXIT.
0253*
0254 C130-TRANSFER-XCTL-TO-BROWSE  SECTION.
0255**********************************************************************
0256*         OPERATOR PRESSED PF4 TO TRANSFER CONTROL TO BROWSE    *
0257*             PERFORMED FROM:  C100-RECEIVE-CONTROL-MAP         *
0258**********************************************************************
0259*
0260    MOVE LOW-VALUES  TO  WS-COMMAREA.
0261    MOVE 'D'  TO  CA-FUNCTION-CODE.
0262*
0263    EXEC CICS XCTL
0264            PROGRAM  ('POVMBROW')
0265            COMMAREA (WS-COMMAREA)
0266            LENGTH   (8)
0267    END-EXEC.
0268*
0269 C130-EXIT.
0270    EXIT.
0271*
0272 C200-VERIFY-VENDOR-FORMAT  SECTION.
0273**********************************************************************
0274*         VERIFY FORMAT OF VENDOR CODE KEYED-IN = A-9999-9       *
0275*             PERFORMED FROM:  C000-PROCESS-CONTROL-MAP          *
0276*    IF VALID FORMAT - MOVE CODE TO WS-COMMAREA FIELDS (CA- )    *
0277**********************************************************************
0278*
0279    IF (MVC-D-VENDOR-CD-1  IS  ALPHABETIC
0280              AND
0281      MVC-D-VENDOR-CD-1  IS NOT =  SPACE)
0282    AND
0283      MVC-D-VENDOR-CD-2  IS  NUMERIC
0284    AND
0285      MVC-D-VENDOR-CD-3  IS  NUMERIC
0286      MOVE MVC-D-VEND-CD-1  TO  CA-VEND-1
0287      MOVE MVC-D-VEND-CD-2  TO  CA-VEND-2
0288      MOVE MVC-D-VEND-CD-3  TO  CA-VEND-3
0289      MOVE 'G'              TO  STATUS-OF-FORMAT
0290    ELSE
0291      MOVE 'E'         TO  STATUS-OF-FORMAT
0292      MOVE 'VENDOR CODE FORMAT MUST BE: A-9999-9 - PLEASE RE-EN
0293-          'TER'    TO  MVC-D-MESSAGE
0294      MOVE ASKIP-BRT  TO  MVC-A-MESSAGE.
0295*
0296 C200-EXIT.
0297    EXIT.
0298*
0299 C400-VERIFY-VENDOR-FILE-STATUS  SECTION.
0300**********************************************************************
0301*             PERFORMED FROM:  C000-PROCESS-CONTROL-MAP          *
0302*             MUST BE A VENDOR RECORD FOR DELETIONS              *
0303**********************************************************************
0304*
0305    MOVE 'G'  TO  STATUS-OF-VERIFY.
0306*
0307    PERFORM C410-READ-VENDOR-FILE.
0308*
0309    IF RECORD-NOT-FOUND
0310      MOVE 'E'         TO  STATUS-OF-VERIFY
0311      MOVE 'VENDOR RECORD NOT ON FILE'
0312                       TO  MVC-D-MESSAGE
0313      MOVE ASKIP-BRT  TO  MVC-A-MESSAGE
```

Figure 15-4 *(Continued)*

```
0314        ELSE
0315            IF VM-DOLLARS-COMMITTED  GREATER THAN  ZERO
0316                MOVE 'E'         TO  STATUS-OF-VERIFY
0317                MOVE 'DOLLARS COMMITTED ARE SIGNIFICANT - CAN
0318-                    ' NOT DELETE' TO  MVC-D-MESSAGE
0319                MOVE ASKIP-BRT  TO  MVC-A-MESSAGE.
0320*
0321 C400-EXIT.
0322     EXIT.
0323*
0324 C410-READ-VENDOR-FILE  SECTION.
0325***************************************************************
0326*         PERFORMED FROM:  C400-VERIFY-VENDOR-FILE-STATUS      *
0327***************************************************************
0328*
0329     MOVE 'E' TO  STATUS-OF-READ.
0330*
0331     EXEC CICS HANDLE CONDITION
0332              NOTFND  (C410-EXIT)
0333     END-EXEC.
0334*
0335     EXEC CICS READ
0336              DATASET ('VENDMAST')
0337              INTO    (VENDOR-MASTER-RECORD)
0338              RIDFLD  (CA-VENDOR-CODE)
0339     END-EXEC.
0340*
0341     MOVE '8' TO  STATUS-OF-READ.
0342*
0343 C410-EXIT.
0344     EXIT.
0345*
0346 C500-SEND-DETAIL-MAP-AND-DATA  SECTION.
0347***************************************************************
0348*         SEND DETAIL MAP - PHYSICAL AND SYMBOLIC MAPS        *
0349*             PERFORMED FROM:  C000-PROCESS-CONTROL-MAP        *
0350*    SENT WHEN ALL VALIDATION AND EDIT CONDITIONS HAVE BEEN MET *
0351***************************************************************
0352*
0353     MOVE LOW-VALUES  TO  VM-DETAIL-MAP.
0354*
0355     PERFORM B110-GET-DATE-AND-TIME.
0356     MOVE WS-CURRENT-DATE  TO  MVD-D-DATE.
0357     MOVE WS-MAP-TIME      TO  MVD-D-TIME.
0358*
0359     PERFORM C530-FORMAT-DETAIL-MAP.
0360*
0361     MOVE '2' TO  CA-MAP-CONTROL.
0362*
0363     EXEC CICS SEND
0364              MAP     ('MAPPOVD')
0365              MAPSET  ('POVMDL2')
0366              FROM    (VM-DETAIL-MAP)
0367              ERASE
0368     END-EXEC.
0369*
0370 C500-EXIT.
0371     EXIT.
0372*
0373 C530-FORMAT-DETAIL-MAP  SECTION.
0374***************************************************************
0375*         PERFORMED FROM:  C500-SEND-DETAIL-MAP-AND-DATA       *
0376***************************************************************
0377*
0378* FORMAT VENDOR CODE: A-9999-9   WS- FIELDS ARE AT END OF VENDMAST
0379     MOVE CA-VEND-1          TO  WS-VENDOR-CD-1.
0380     MOVE CA-VEND-2          TO  WS-VENDOR-CD-2.
0381     MOVE CA-VEND-3          TO  WS-VENDOR-CD-3.
0382     MOVE WS-VENDOR-CODE     TO  MVD-D-VENDOR-CODE.
0383*
0384     MOVE VM-AREA-CD         TO  MVD-D-PHONE-AREA-CODE.
0385     MOVE VM-PHONE-1-3       TO  MVD-D-PHONE-1.
0386     MOVE VM-PHONE-4-7       TO  MVD-D-PHONE-2.
0387     MOVE VM-VENDOR-NAME     TO  MVD-D-VENDOR-NAME.
0388     MOVE VM-CONTACT         TO  MVD-D-CONTACT.
0389     MOVE VM-STREET-ADDRESS  TO  MVD-D-STREET.
0390     MOVE VM-CITY            TO  MVD-D-CITY.
0391     MOVE VM-STATE           TO  MVD-D-STATE-CODE.
```

Figure 15-4 *(Continued)*

```
0392*
0393    MOVE VM-STATE               TO  WS-STATE-CODE.
0394    PERFORM C531-GET-STATE-NAME.
0395    MOVE WS-STATE-NAME          TO  MVD-D-STATE-NAME.
0396*
0397    MOVE VM-ZIP-CODE            TO  MVD-D-ZIP-CODE.
0398    MOVE VM-TO-ATTN-OF          TO  MVD-D-ATTENTION-OF.
0399    MOVE VM-DOLLARS-COMMITTED   TO  MVD-D-DLRS-COMMITTED.
0400*
0401 C530-EXIT.
0402    EXIT.
0403*
0404 C531-GET-STATE-NAME  SECTION  COPY  STPDT037.
0405************************************************************************
0406*             LOAD AND SEARCH STATE CODE TABLE               *
0407*        PERFORMED FROM:  C530-SEND-DETAIL-MAP-AND-DATA       *
0408************************************************************************
0409*
0410 C531-EXIT.
0411    EXIT.
0412*
0413 C600-SEND-CONTROL-MAP-DATAONLY  SECTION.
0414************************************************************************
0415*         SEND CONTROL MAP DATAONLY - SYMBOLIC MAP           *
0416*         PERFORMED FROM: C000-PROCESS-CONTROL-MAP           *
0417*                SENT FOR INVALID CONDITIONS                 *
0418************************************************************************
0419*
0420    MOVE UNPROT-FSET TO  MVC-A-VEND-CD-1
0421                         MVC-A-VEND-CD-2
0422                         MVC-A-VEND-CD-3.
0423*
0424    MOVE -1  TO  MVC-L-VEND-CD-1.
0425    MOVE '1' TO  CA-MAP-CONTROL.
0426*
0427    EXEC CICS SEND
0428              MAP     ('MAPPOVC')
0429              MAPSET  ('POVMDL1')
0430              FROM    (VM-CONTROL-MAP)
0431              DATAONLY
0432              CURSOR
0433    END-EXEC.
0434*
0435 C600-EXIT.
0436    EXIT.
0437*
0438 D100-RECEIVE-DETAIL-MAP  SECTION.
0439************************************************************************
0440*        PERFORMED FROM:  G000-DELETE-PROCESSING            *
0441* ENTER - PROCESSES TRANSACTION        CLEAR - ENDS SESSION  *
0442* PF3   - SETS DISPLAY OF CTL MAP      PF5   - RETURNS TO MENU *
0443*               ALL OTHER KEYS ARE INVALID                    *
0444*        STATUS-OF-RECEIVE  =  'G'  =  GOOD RECEIVE           *
0445*                              'C'  =  RETURN TO CTL-MAP      *
0446*                              'I'  =  INVALID KEY PRESSED    *
0447************************************************************************
0448*
0449    MOVE LOW-VALUES  TO  VM-DETAIL-MAP.
0450*
0451    IF EIBAID  =  DFHENTER
0452*
0453         EXEC CICS IGNORE CONDITION
0454                   MAPFAIL
0455         END-EXEC
0456*
0457         EXEC CICS RECEIVE
0458                   MAP     ('MAPPOVD')
0459                   MAPSET  ('POVMDL2')
0460                   INTO    (VM-DETAIL-MAP)
0461         END-EXEC
0462*
0463         MOVE 'G'  TO  STATUS-OF-RECEIVE
0464    ELSE
0465       IF EIBAID  =  DFHCLEAR
0466          PERFORM C110-END-SESSION
0467       ELSE
0468          IF EIBAID  =  DFHPF3
0469             MOVE 'C'  TO  STATUS-OF-RECEIVE
```

Figure 15-4 *(Continued)*

```
0470*          ELSE
0471           IF EIBAID  =  DFHPF5
0472               PERFORM C120-TRANSFER-XCTL-TO-MENU
0473           ELSE
0474               MOVE 'I'         TO  STATUS-OF-RECEIVE
0475               MOVE 'INVALID KEY PRESSED - PLEASE TRY AGAIN'
0476                                TO  MVD-D-MESSAGE
0477               MOVE ASKIP-BRT   TO  MVD-A-MESSAGE.
0478*
0479 D100-EXIT.
0480     EXIT.
0481*
0482 D200-SEND-DETAIL-MAP-DATAONLY  SECTION.
0483******************************************************************
0484*        SEND DETAIL MAP DATA ONLY - SYMBOLIC MAP             *
0485*     PERFORMED FROM:  G000-DELETE-PROCESSING                 *
0486*  SENT IF INVALID KEY IS PRESSED ON A RECEIVE OF THE DETAIL MAP *
0487******************************************************************
0488*
0489     MOVE '2'  TO  CA-MAP-CONTROL.
0490*
0491     EXEC CICS SEND
0492               MAP       ('MAPPOVD')
0493               MAPSET    ('POVMDL2')
0494               FROM      (VM-DETAIL-MAP)
0495               DATAONLY
0496     END-EXEC.
0497*
0498 D200-EXIT.
0499     EXIT.
0500*
0501 E121-POST-JOURNAL-RECORD  SECTION.
0502******************************************************************
0503*    POST JOURNAL ENTRY - LINK TO JOURNAL PROGRAM 'JRNLPOST'  *
0504*      PERFORMED FROM:  G110-DELETE-VM-RECORD                 *
0505******************************************************************
0506*
0507     MOVE 'VM'                    TO  JR-PREFIX.
0508     MOVE VENDOR-MASTER-RECORD    TO  JR-RECORD-DATA.
0509     MOVE SPACES                  TO  JR-PASSWORD.
0510*
0511     EXEC CICS LINK
0512               PROGRAM  ('JRNLPOST')
0513               COMMAREA (JOURNAL-RECORD)
0514               LENGTH   (524)
0515     END-EXEC.
0516*
0517 E121-EXIT.
0518     EXIT.
0519*
0520 F110-READ-VENDOR-FOR-UPDATE  SECTION.
0521******************************************************************
0522*  READ VENDOR RECORD FOR UPDATE - POST BEFORE JOURNAL RECORD  *
0523*            PERFORMED FROM:  G100-DELETE-VENDOR-RECORD        *
0524******************************************************************
0525*
0526     MOVE 'E'  TO  STATUS-OF-READ.
0527*
0528     EXEC CICS HANDLE CONDITION
0529               NOTFND  (F110-EXIT)
0530     END-EXEC.
0531*
0532     EXEC CICS READ
0533               DATASET ('VENDMAST')
0534               INTO    (VENDOR-MASTER-RECORD)
0535               RIDFLD  (CA-VENDOR-CODE)
0536               UPDATE
0537     END-EXEC.
0538*
0539     MOVE 'G'  TO  STATUS-OF-READ.
0540*
0541     MOVE 'B'  TO  JR-TYPE.
0542     PERFORM E121-POST-JOURNAL-RECORD.
0543*
0544 F110-EXIT.
0545     EXIT.
```

Figure 15-4 *(Continued)*

```
0546*
0547 G000-DELETE-PROCESSING  SECTION.
0548******************************************************************
0549*                   PERFORMED FROM:  AA00-MAINLINE            *
0550*        DETAIL MAP IS SENT IF AN INVALID KEY WAS PRESSED     *
0551*                OR DELETE RECORD WAS NOT FOUND               *
0552******************************************************************
0553*
0554     PERFORM D100-RECEIVE-DETAIL-MAP.
0555*
0556     IF GOOD-RECEIVE
0557         PERFORM G100-DELETE-VENDOR-RECORD
0558         IF GOOD-DELETE
0559             PERFORM B100-SEND-CONTROL-MAP-AND-DATA
0560         ELSE
0561             PERFORM D200-SEND-DETAIL-MAP-DATAONLY
0562     ELSE
0563         IF RETURN-TO-CTL-MAP
0564             PERFORM B100-SEND-CONTROL-MAP-AND-DATA
0565         ELSE
0566             PERFORM D200-SEND-DETAIL-MAP-DATAONLY.
0567*
0568 G000-EXIT.
0569     EXIT.
0570*
0571 G100-DELETE-VENDOR-RECORD  SECTION.
0572******************************************************************
0573*             PERFORMED FROM:  G000-DELETE-PROCESSING         *
0574*    RECORD NOT FOUND COULD NOT OCCUR UNLESS RECORD WAS DELETED *
0575*    BY ANOTHER TERMINAL SINCE BEING KEYED-IN ON CONTROL SCREEN *
0576******************************************************************
0577*
0578     MOVE 'E'  TO  STATUS-OF-DELETE.
0579*
0580     PERFORM F110-READ-VENDOR-FOR-UPDATE.
0581*
0582     IF RECORD-NOT-FOUND
0583         MOVE 'RECORD TO BE DELETED - NOT FOUND'
0584                            TO  MVD-D-MESSAGE
0585         MOVE ASKIP-BRT  TO  MVD-A-MESSAGE
0586                             MVD-C-A-VENDOR-CODE
0587     ELSE
0588         PERFORM G110-DELETE-VM-RECORD
0589         MOVE 'RECORD DELETED SUCCESSFULLY'  TO  MVC-D-MESSAGE
0590         MOVE ASKIP-BRT                      TO  MVC-A-MESSAGE
0591         MOVE 'G'                            TO  STATUS-OF-DELETE.
0592*
0593 G100-EXIT.
0594     EXIT.
0595*
0596 G110-DELETE-VM-RECORD  SECTION.
0597******************************************************************
0598*      DELETE VENDOR RECORD - POST 'BEFORE' JOURNAL RECORD     *
0599*         PERFORMED FROM:  G100-DELETE-VENDOR-RECORD           *
0600******************************************************************
0601*
0602     EXEC CICS DELETE
0603              DATASET ('VENDMAST')
0604     END-EXEC.
0605*
0606 G110-EXIT.
0607     EXIT.
```

16

TEMPORARY-STORAGE CONTROL

Temporary-storage control, like the use of field attributes, seems to cause application programmers some difficulty. The use of a single temporary storage record does not seem to pose any special problems, but the employment of multiple queue records in a browse program's paging logic often causes much difficulty. I will first discuss temporary-storage control commands and then the use of single queue records in this chapter. I will then cover several techniques used for paging logic which employ multiple temporary-storage (TS) queue records. Chapter 17 will present a complete browse program detailing one of the paging methods presented in this chapter.

A TS queue created by one program or task can be used in the same or different program or task. TS queues may be created in either main storage or auxiliary storage. Main-storage queues are not used very often, and the browse program in the next chapter will use auxiliary storage. COMMAREA can be used to supplement or replace TS queues in many situations. These queues are available from the time they are created until they are deleted by a program or by the startup of the CICS system. They do not require that any predefined CICS table entries be made.

Relating TS Queues to VSAM Files

TS auxiliary queues can be likened to VSAM files. The key to a queue consists of up to eight characters which are defined in the creating and using programs. It is common practice to use an eight-character queue name. These queues can be used by many different programs which are executing at different terminals. It is advisable to make a TS queue unique to the terminal at which the task is being executed; otherwise, a program running at another terminal could unknowingly delete your queue. This is generally accomplished by using the EIB field EIBTRMID as the first four positions of the queue name. The next four positions should be characters which are meaningful to the program or system such as MAP1, BROW, or PAGE. If only one queue is being used in a program, EIBTRNID may be used for the second four characters of the queue name. It is the responsibility of the application programmer to delete TS queues when they are no longer needed. TS is a finite resource and could become full if queues which were no longer needed were not deleted. In addition to the eight-position key, these queues have an item number attached to the queue record. It is easier to understand TS queues if you consider the item number as part of the queue's key. For instance, if EIBTRMID is TERM and the transaction code is POVB, a queue of three records can be visualized as having keys of TERMPOVB/1, TERMPOVB/2, and TERMPOVB/3.

TS control commands include:

1. WRITEQ TS—Writes a new or additional TS queue record.

2. WRITEQ TS REWRITE—Updates a TS queue record.

3. READQ TS—Reads a TS queue record which has been previously created.

4. DELETEQ TS—Deletes a TS queue which is no longer needed.

Required Working-Storage Fields

Prior to using TS queues, it is necessary to define several fields in working storage: the queue name, the data portion of the queue, the length of the queue, and an item number. Length and item can be hard-coded if they are not variable. The names used in the command descriptions are

```
01  TS-QUEUE.
    05  TS-TERMID          PIC X(4).
    05  TS-QUEUE-NAME      PIC X(4).

01  TS-DATA.
    05  TS-FIELD-1          . . .
    05  TS-FIELD-2          . . .
        .
        .
        .
01  TS-LENGTH             PIC S9999   COMP   VALUE ZEROES.
01  TS-ITEM               PIC S9999   COMP   VALUE ZEROES.
```

The terminal identifier EIBTRMID will be moved into TS-TERMID, and the transaction code EIBTRNID, or a programmer-defined suffix, will be moved into TS-QUEUE-NAME. Queue length, TS-LENGTH, can be defined as a constant or can have length moved to it prior to executing a TS command. Item number, TS-ITEM, can be a constant or can have a value moved to it, added to it, or subtracted from it. Both TS-LENGTH and TS-ITEM must be defined as halfword binary values. For example,

```
MOVE EIBTRMID   TO   TS-TERMID.
MOVE EIBTRNID   TO   TS-QUEUE-NAME.
MOVE 1          TO   TS-ITEM.
MOVE 100        TO   TS-LENGTH.
```

Write a TS Queue

It is necessary to create or write a TS queue before it can be accessed. TS queue WRITE command format is

```
EXEC CICS WRITEQ TS
          QUEUE   (TS-QUEUE)
          FROM    (TS-DATA)
          LENGTH (TS-LENGTH)
          ITEM    (TS-ITEM)
END-EXEC.
```

The letters TS following the WRITEQ command are optional but are customarily included. The queue name is TS-QUEUE, and the data written is in the working-storage field TS-DATA. Working-storage fields TS-LENGTH and TS-ITEM, defined as binary halfwords, are set prior to the write. The system will assign a sequential item number starting from 1 when a queue is written. I have found that fewer problems occur when the item is set by the program prior to the write. All examples will move a value to the working-storage field used to hold the value of ITEM, prior to issuing a write.

• Handle Conditions—It is normally not necessary to check for any handle conditions prior to writing a TS queue.

Rewrite a TS Queue

TS queues are updated by including a REWRITE option. The format of the TS queue REWRITE option is similar to that of the WRITEQ TS command with the REWRITE option added as follows:

```
EXEC CICS WRITEQ   TS
            QUEUE      (TS-QUEUE)
            FROM       (TS-DATA)
            LENGTH     (TS-LENGTH)
            ITEM       (TS-ITEM)
            REWRITE
      END-EXEC.
```

The queue name is TS-QUEUE, and the data rewritten is located in the working-storage field TS-DATA. Working-storage fields TS-LENGTH and TS-ITEM, defined in working storage as binary halfwords, are set prior to the write. A TS record which is to be changed must be read prior to issuing a REWRITE.

- Handle Conditions—It is normally not necessary to check for any handle conditions prior to rewriting a queue. Conditions which might occur during testing include: QIDERR (queue not found) and ITEMERR (the queue exists but the item specified was not found).

Read a TS Queue

The READQ TS command format is similar to that of the write queue. READQ TS and INTO (TS-DATA) replace WRITEQ TS and the FROM option. A previously written queue is read by setting the item number to the proper value before reading the queue INTO (TS-DATA). READQ TS command format is

```
EXEC CICS READQ   TS
           QUEUE      (TS-QUEUE)
           INTO       (TS-DATA)
           LENGTH     (TS-LENGTH)
           ITEM       (TS-ITEM)
      END-EXEC.
```

ITEM could be omitted, in which case the next TS queue record would be retrieved. Always include ITEM on all applicable TS commands because there is less chance of errors occurring when a program directly controls item number. TS queue records can be read either sequentially or randomly by specifying the appropriate ITEM number. They can be read in reverse sequence by decreasing ITEM.

- Handle Conditions—It is normally not necessary to check for any handle conditions prior to reading a TS queue. Conditions which could occur during testing include QIDERR and ITEMERR.

Delete a TS Queue

The TS delete queue command format requires only the queue name. The entire queue must be deleted; it is not possible to delete individual items. DELETEQ TS command format is

```
EXEC CICS DELETEQ TS
              QUEUE   (TS-QUEUE)
END-EXEC.
```

- Handle Conditions—It is normally advisable to check for the QIDERR handle condition before deleting a queue. QIDERR occurs because programs using queues often delete the queue, if it exists, at the beginning of a program and should delete it prior to exiting the program, if it is no longer required.

- Ignore Condition—QIDERR is often handled by ignoring the condition if it occurs. If the program attempts to delete the queue and it does not exist, no ABEND will occur.

Using Single Queue Records

The use of single queue records is rather simple. One program writes a TS queue record and that record will be read and rewritten in other programs. The queue would probably be deleted only in the program which creates the queue. A single queue might be used to hold keys of records which are passed from program to program. When many programs in a system are interrelated, it sometimes simplifies a system if a TS queue is used. Passing record keys from program to program or from task to task in the COMMAREA in a multiprogram system can sometimes become complicated if different-size COMMAREAs are used.

TS Paging Logic Techniques

You may be wondering how you would send previously displayed screens when using the file control browse commands described in Chap. 11. TS queues are often employed for paging logic (scrolling) in browse programs. Paging refers to the sequential scrolling forward or backward through a list of sequential records, such as a vendor code and name list. A selection is often made from this list and passed to another program. Chapter 17 will detail one technique for performing this logic.

Paging done using temporary storage is usually controlled *in* a program by item number and *externally* by the use of PF keys. It is customary to use PF1 for forward scrolling and PF2 for backward paging. Program logic could be included to start a browse at the first or last map written to the queue. Logic must be included in all paging routines to prevent scrolling beyond the limits of the item numbers which have been created.

Your data processing installation may have standard scrolling routines already defined which you can incorporate into your programs. Many different approaches may be taken to paging logic depending on the situation and file being accessed. Most of the techniques employing temporary storage and used to write paging logic routines fall into one of the following categories:

1. Write the entire symbolic map out to temporary storage and retrieve records as necessary.

2. Write only significant map data to temporary storage. The items can be retrieved as needed and the symbolic map formatted with significant data which was saved.

3. Write only record keys to temporary storage. This method requires rereading records when paging backward.

4. Read all records before displaying any maps.

Write the Entire Symbolic Map to Temporary Storage

As each map is displayed during a browse function, the symbolic map is written out to a TS queue and the item number is incremented by one. Displaying the prior map requires decreasing the item number by 1 and reading the queue which contains the last symbolic map displayed. The queue record is read into the symbolic map's working-storage area, and the map is displayed. Each time the item number is incremented, its highest value must be saved. This is done so that when backward paging is performed, followed by forward paging, the program will know when to stop paging forward or to start creating additional TS records. Logic would have to be employed to prevent decrementing the item number below 1 when paging backward.

Write Only Significant Map Data to Temporary Storage

This technique is similar to writing the entire symbolic map to temporary storage, but only significant map data is saved in working storage and written to a queue. When a program pages backward or forward, it reconstructs the symbolic map from the data which was saved in the queue record. This method has the advantage of creating smaller queues, but it requires more program code. You should develop your techniques in accordance with company standards or, if none exist, establish standards for your installation.

Write Only Record Keys to Temporary Storage

The key of the first or last record displayed on each map can be saved in a TS queue. As the terminal operator scrolls backward or forward, the program can reread records starting with keys which are equal to or greater than the saved keys. Each map can be reformatted as it was the first time the map was displayed. This method requires the least amount of temporary storage and is the technique used for the browse program in Chap. 17. A disadvantage of this method is that records will have to be reread when paging takes place in order to format the map.

Read All Records Before Displaying Any Maps

This is perhaps the simplest scrolling method to work with. All maps to be displayed as part of a browse are written to temporary storage before any map is displayed. When all the maps for a given browse have been written to the queue, the program starts the display from the first map written. Forward and backward scrolling is permitted. This method differs from the first scrolling method discussed in that the latter writes maps to temporary storage only when they are initially displayed, whereas this method writes all maps to temporary storage before any map is displayed. The drawback to using this method for long browses is that many more records would have to be read and their maps saved even if they did not need to be displayed.

Paging Logic Techniques Without Using Temporary Storage

Paging logic can be accomplished without using TS queues. Two methods which are sometimes employed are

1. Save the first and last key displayed on a map in the COMMAREA. Then, depending on the AID key pressed, issue a READNEXT or READPREV command. This logic can get complicated. For instance, when paging backward, the READPREV command is executed and a map is formatted from bottom to top. If 15 items are displayed per page and you page backward and only 10 records are read, the first five lines of the screen's multiple data would contain spaces and have to be adjusted.

2. The COMMAREA could be used to store the code of the first or last item on each page. These codes could be indexed through and records reread in order to affect paging logic. This is a good method if key size is small and you can limit the number of pages to be browsed.

TS Random Access Methods

As mentioned previously, your understanding of TS queues will be enhanced if you can relate queues to VSAM files. If the terminal at which a program was being executed had an ID of TERM and the TRANSID was POVB, symbolic map data saved could be conceptualized as follows:

KEY		First or		
Queue Name	Item	Last Key	or	Symbolic Map Data
TERMPOVB	1	Map 1 key		Map 1 data
"	2	" 2 "		" 2 "
"	3	" 3 "		" 3 "

When a program sends the first map, it writes out a TS queue with a key of TEMPPOVB/1. The program increments item number as the program pages forward by adding one to the working-storage item field. It creates queue records with keys of TEMPPOVB/2, TEMPPOVB/3, etc. An alternate approach would be to save the first or last record key displayed on the map. The map could be reconstructed as paging takes place, instead of saving the entire map in temporary storage.

Backward scrolling is accomplished by subtracting 1 from item number each time the program scrolls backward. Item number must be defined in the working-storage COMMAREA when scrolling, since it changes with forward or backward paging. You would also save the item number of the last map which was displayed in COMMAREA. Routines can be written to skip to the first or last record which was displayed, after scrolling forward or backward several pages.

SUMMARY

I found the use of a TS queue valuable in a case where a database file was loaded in ascending date sequence and the user wanted a display in descending date order. This database did not permit backward reading through the use of a command such as READPREV. I was able to simulate the use of STARTBR and READPREV commands by employing a TS queue. The technique required reading each of the required records which were in ascending date sequence and writing a TS queue ITEM for each record. The records were then accessed in descending date sequence by reading the TS queue items in reverse order by subtracting 1 from ITEM number as each queue item was retrieved. The TS queue was read in reverse order until ITEM was decremented to zero. This use of a TS queue worked well because the number of date records was small and the transaction was not used frequently. The technique employed would be inefficient if there were numerous date records and the display was a high-use transaction. It is inefficient to read, write, and then reread each record. You are, in effect, sorting a segment of the file into a different sequence. The use of a SORT is not permitted in an online system. It is important when online files are created that their records be loaded in the sequence which corresponds to the order in which records will most commonly be read.

TS queues can aid a designer/programmer in many situations, and their use is limited only by the creativity of the programmer in accordance with good design principles. Since there are inefficiencies involved when TS queues are used, you should consider the use of the COMMAREA in their place whenever practical.

The intent of this chapter was to familiarize you with TS queues. TS commands are easy to understand but sometimes difficult to use for paging logic. The commands discussed were WRITEQ TS, WRITEQ TS REWRITE, READQ TS, and DELETEQ TS. Single-record TS queues were discussed, as were multiple queue records which are used for paging logic. Some practical applications of TS queues were discussed. Creative application programmers will find many uses for TS queues. Some installations have developed standards for paging techniques. Chapter 17 will illustrate the use of some TS commands in the browse program.

This chapter attempted to convey ideas for the use of TS queues. Once you understand the concept and the commands, you will be able to implement design ideas which may, at first, have seemed difficult to perform. Consider alternate approaches to the solution of a problem before deciding on the method to be employed. For instance, the use of the COMMAREA may be more efficient than is the use of a TS queue. An understanding of various techniques for solving a problem will make you more effective in your design and programming.

17

THE BROWSE PROGRAM

Several paging techniques were discussed in Chap. 16. The technique of writing only a record's key to temporary storage, as a map is displayed, is employed for the browse program in this chapter. This example covers most of the functions you will be required to perform in a browse program.

Only one map (see Fig. 2-10) is used for the browse program. The terminal operator can key in the TRANSID POVB and press ENTER in order to display the browse map. The browse can also be invoked by a transfer of control from another program. The operator has the option of returning to the vendor file maintenance submenu (see Fig. 6-3) or ending the session. The screen displays up to 15 vendor file records from which the terminal operator can make a selection and pass the selected vendor code to an invoking program. The operator can page forward if the required vendor is not displayed and can page backward in order to view a previously displayed screen. This example does not permit backward paging beyond the vendor used as a starting point for the browse.

The operator can reset the browse starting point during any point of the display by entering a new code on the screen and pressing a designated PF key. When the browse starting point is reset, the operator can scroll forward and then backward from that point. You would reset the browse after displaying a map and finding that the desired record was far from the record shown on the screen. The RESET BROWSE option encourages an operator to limit the scope of a browse.

BMS Browse Map

Figure 17-1 contains the BMS map corresponding to the browse map shown in Fig. 2-10. All browse map field attributes are defined as ASKIP, except for the SELECTION and RESET VENDOR CODE fields. The SELECTION field

Figure 17-1 Vendor File Browse BMS Map.

```
             PRINT NOGEN
POVMBR1      DFHMSD TYPE=MAP,                                       X
                    CTRL=(FREEKB,FRSET),                            X
                    LANG=COBOL,                                     X
                    MODE=INOUT,                                     X
                    TERM=3270,                                      X
                    TIOAPFX=YES
*
MAPPOVC      DFHMDI LINE=01,                                        X
                    COLUMN=01,                                      X
                    SIZE=(24,80)
*
             DFHMDF POS=(01,01),                                    X
                    ATTRB=ASKIP,                                    X
                    LENGTH=05,                                      X
                    INITIAL='DATE:'
*
MCDATE       DFHMDF POS=(01,07),                                    X
                    ATTRB=ASKIP,                                    X
                    LENGTH=08
*
             DFHMDF POS=(01,27),                                    X
                    ATTRB=ASKIP,                                    X
                    LENGTH=25,                                      X
                    INITIAL='ABC MANUFACTURING COMPANY'
*
             DFHMDF POS=(01,72),                                    X
                    ATTRB=ASKIP,                                    X
                    LENGTH=07,                                      X
                    INITIAL='POVMBR1'
*
             DFHMDF POS=(02,01),                                    X
                    ATTRB=ASKIP,                                    X
                    LENGTH=05,                                      X
                    INITIAL='TIME:'
*
MCTIME       DFHMDF POS=(02,07),                                    X
                    ATTRB=ASKIP,                                    X
                    LENGTH=08
*
             DFHMDF POS=(02,30),                                    X
                    ATTRB=ASKIP,                                    X
                    LENGTH=18,                                      X
                    INITIAL='VENDOR FILE BROWSE'
*
             DFHMDF POS=(03,03),                                    X
                    ATTRB=ASKIP,                                    X
                    LENGTH=21,                                      X
                    INITIAL='VENDOR CD VENDOR NAME'
*
             DFHMDF POS=(03,39),                                    X
                    ATTRB=ASKIP,                                    X
                    LENGTH=06,                                      X
                    INITIAL='STREET'
*
```

attribute is defined as IC,NUM, which makes the field UNPROT and inserts the cursor at this field when the map is sent. The RESET VENDOR CODE field attribute is set to UNPROT. The DFHMDF macro labeled MCOCCUR shows how the OCCURS clause can be used to generate 15 lines of map data, each of which contains 79 characters plus an attribute.

User-Friendly Symbolic Maps

The user-friendly symbolic map is unique to the vendor browse and is hard-coded in the program.

Figure 17-1 *(Continued)*

```
              DFHMDF POS=(03,60),                                    X
                     ATTRB=ASKIP,                                    X
                     LENGTH=12,                                      X
                     INITIAL='CITY / STATE'
*
MCOCCUR       DFHMDF POS=(04,01),                                    X
                     ATTRB=ASKIP,                                    X
                     LENGTH=79,                                      X
                     OCCURS=15
*
MCSELEC       DFHMDF POS=(19,01),                                    X
                     ATTRB=(IC,NUM),                                 X
                     LENGTH=02
*
              DFHMDF POS=(19,04),                                    X
                     ATTRB=ASKIP,                                    X
                     LENGTH=11,                                      X
                     INITIAL=': SELECTION'
*
              DFHMDF POS=(20,06),                                    X
                     ATTRB=ASKIP,                                    X
                     LENGTH=18,                                      X
                     INITIAL='RESET VENDOR CODE: '
*
MCRVCOD       DFHMDF POS=(20,25),                                    X
                     ATTRB=(UNPROT),                                 X
                     LENGTH=06
*
              DFHMDF POS=(20,32),                                    X
                     ATTRB=ASKIP,                                    X
                     LENGTH=01
*
              DFHMDF POS=(21,01),                                    X
                     ATTRB=ASKIP,                                    Y
                     LENGTH=51,                                      X
                     INITIAL='1. FWD  - PF1        4. KEY IN SELECTION    -X
                     PF6'
*
              DFHMDF POS=(22,01),                                    X
                     ATTRB=ASKIP,                                    X
                     LENGTH=51,                                      X
                     INITIAL='2. BWD  - PF2        5. KEY IN RESET VENDOR -X
                     PF7'
*
              DFHMDF POS=(23,01),                                    X
                     ATTRB=ASKIP,                                    X
                     LENGTH=53,                                      X
                     INITIAL='3. MENU - PF5        6. END OF SESSION      -X
                     CLEAR'
*
MCMESSG       DFHMDF POS=(24,01),                                    X
                     ATTRB=ASKIP,                                    X
                     LENGTH=79
*
              DFHMSD TYPE=FINAL
              END
```

Browse Program Source Code

The browse program's source code is shown in Fig. 17-2. The program's initial entry logic is shown following the main processing logic which is executed much more frequently than is initial entry in a browse program. This technique is often employed in online programming in order to minimize paging requirements.

Procedure Division

AA00-MAINLINE.   If this program was started by a TRANSID, the program will move low-values to WS-COMMAREA and will start its browse at the beginning

Figure 17-2 Vendor File Browse Program Source Code.

```
0001 IDENTIFICATION DIVISION.
0002 PROGRAM-ID. POVMBROW.
0003 REMARKS.
0004*****************************************************************
0005*            PURCHASING SYSTEM - VENDOR FILE BROWSE           *
0006*      - STARTED BY PURCHASING SYSTEM MAINTENANCE PROGRAMS    *
0007*          OR DIRECTLY BY ENTERING  TRANSID 'POVB'            *
0008*      PF1 - PAGE FORWARD          PF6 - RETURN WITH SELECTION *
0009*      PF2 - PAGE BACKWARD         PF7 - RESET BROWSE KEY      *
0010*****************************************************************
0011 ENVIRONMENT DIVISION.
0012 DATA DIVISION.
0013*
0014 WORKING-STORAGE  SECTION.
0015*
0016 01  WS-PROGRAM-FIELDS.
0017     05  FILLER            PIC X(8)      VALUE 'POVMBROW'.
0018     05  WS-CRT-MESSAGE    PIC X(17)     VALUE 'SESSION COMPLETED'.
0019     05  SUB               PIC S9999   COMP  VALUE ZEROES.
0020     05  WS-SELECTION      PIC 99              VALUE ZEROES.
0021     05  WS-XCTL-PROGRAM   PIC X(8)            VALUE SPACES.
0022*
0023 01  WS-DISPLAY-DATA.
0024     05  WS-SELECT               PIC 99.
0025     05  FILLER                  PIC X.
0026     05  WS-VM-KEY               PIC X(8).
0027     05  FILLER                  PIC X.
0028     05  WS-VENDOR-NAME          PIC X(25).
0029     05  FILLER                  PIC X.
0030     05  WS-STREET-ADDRESS       PIC X(20).
0031     05  FILLER                  PIC X.
0032     05  WS-CITY-STATE           PIC X(20).
0033*
0034 01  TEMPORARY-STORAGE-FIELDS.
0035     05  TS-QUEUE.
0036         10  TS-EIBTRMID         PIC X(4).
0037         10  TS-QUEUE-NAME       PIC X(4).
0038     05  TS-LENGTH               PIC S9999   COMP  VALUE +6.
0039     05  TS-RECORD.
0040         10  TS-VENDOR-CD        PIC X(6).
0041     05  TS-SUB                  PIC S9999   COMP  VALUE ZEROES.
0042*
0043 01  WS-COMMAREA.
0044     05  CA-FUNCTION-CODE        PIC X.
0045         88  CA-INQUIRY                      VALUE 'I'.
0046         88  CA-ADDITION                     VALUE 'A'.
0047         88  CA-CHANGE                       VALUE 'C'.
0048         88  CA-DELETE                       VALUE 'D'.
0049         88  CA-BROWSE                       VALUE 'B'.
0050     05  CA-MAP-CONTROL          PIC X.
0051     05  CA-VENDOR-CODE.
0052         10  CA-VEND-1           PIC X.
0053         10  CA-VEND-2           PIC X(4).
0054         10  CA-VEND-3           PIC X.
0055     05  CA-LAST-KEY             PIC X(6).
0056     05  CA-TS-ITEM              PIC S9999   COMP.
0057     05  CA-TS-MAXIMUM           PIC S9999   COMP.
0058     05  CA-TS-EOF-SWITCH        PIC X.
0059 01  VM-BROWSE-MAP.
0060     05  FILLER                  PIC X(12).
0061*
0062     05  MVC-L-DATE              PIC S9(4)   COMP.
0063     05  MVC-A-DATE              PIC X.
0064     05  MVC-D-DATE              PIC X(8).
0065*
0066     05  MVC-L-TIME              PIC S9(4)   COMP.
0067     05  MVC-A-TIME              PIC X.
0068     05  MVC-D-TIME              PIC X(8).
0069*
0070     05  MVC-OCCURS    OCCURS  15 TIMES.
0071         10  MVC-L-OCCURS        PIC S9(4)   COMP.
0072         10  MVC-A-OCCURS        PIC X.
0073         10  MVC-D-OCCURS        PIC X(79).
0074*
0075     05  MVC-L-SELECTION         PIC S9(4)   COMP.
0076     05  MVC-A-SELECTION         PIC X.
0077     05  MVC-D-SELECTION         PIC XX.
0078*
0079     05  MVC-L-RESET-CODE        PIC S9(4)   COMP.
0080     05  MVC-A-RESET-CODE        PIC X.
0081     05  MVC-D-RESET-CODE        PIC X(6).
```

Figure 17-2 (Continued)

```
0082*
0083     05  MVC-L-MESSAGE              PIC S9(4)    COMP.
0084     05  MVC-A-MESSAGE              PIC X.
0085     05  MVC-D-MESSAGE             PIC X(79).
0086*
0087 01  VENDOR-MASTER-RECORD    COPY   VENDMAST.
0088 01  WS-STATUS-FIELDS        COPY   STWSSTAT.
0089 01  WS-DATE-AND-TIME        COPY   STWSDTTM.
0090 01  ATTRIBUTE-LIST          COPY   STWSATTR.
0091 01  DFHAID                  COPY   DFHAID.
0092*
0093 01  END-OF-WORKING-STORAGE   PIC X(15)    VALUE 'END WS FOVMBROW'.
0094*
0095 LINKAGE SECTION.
0096*
0097 01  DFHCOMMAREA                   PIC X(19).
0098*
0099 01  BLL-CELLS.
0100     05  FILLER                    PIC S9(8)    COMP.
0101     05  BLL-CWA-ADDRESS           PIC S9(8)    COMP.
0102*
0103 01  CWA-DATA    COPY   STLNKCWA.
0104 PROCEDURE DIVISION.
0105***********************************************************************
0106*        PROGRAM STRUCTURE IS:                                      *
0107*             AA00-MAINLINE                                         *
0108*                 B000-PROCESS-MAP                                  *
0109*                     B100-PAGE-FORWARD                             *
0110*                         B110-SEND-MAP-DATAONLY                    *
0111*                             B111-RESET-OCCURS-ATTRIBUTES          *
0112*                         B120-RETURN-TO-CICS                       *
0113*                         B130-READ-TS                             *
0114*                         B140-START-BROWSE                        *
0115*                         B150-BROWSE-PROCESSING                   *
0116*                             B151-FORMAT-OCCURS                    *
0117*                             B152-FORMAT-MAP                       *
0118*                             B153-WRITE-TS-RECORD                  *
0119*                         B110-SEND-MAP-DATAONLY                    *
0120*                             B111-RESET-OCCURS-ATTRIBUTES          *
0121*                     B200-PAGE-BACKWARD                            *
0122*                         B110-SEND-MAP-DATAONLY                    *
0123*                             B111-RESET-OCCURS-ATTRIBUTES          *
0124*                         B120-RETURN-TO-CICS                       *
0125*                         B130-READ-TS                             *
0126*                         B140-START-BROWSE                        *
0127*                         B150-BROWSE-PROCESSING                   *
0128*                             D151-FORMAT-OCCURS                    *
0129*                             B152-FORMAT-MAP                       *
0130*                             B153-WRITE-TS-RECORD                  *
0131*                     B300-TRANSFER-XCTL-TO-MENU                    *
0132*                         B310-INITIALIZE-AND-DELETEQ               *
0133*                     B400-RETURN-WITH-SELECTION                    *
0134*                         B310-INITIALIZE-AND-DELETEQ               *
0135*                         B410-XCTL-TO-INVOKING-PROGRAM             *
0136*                         B110-SEND-MAP-DATAONLY                    *
0137*                             B111-RESET-OCCURS-ATTRIBUTES          *
0138*                         B120-RETURN-TO-CICS                       *
0139*                     B500-RESET-KEY                               *
0140*                         B310-INITIALIZE-AND-DELETEQ               *
0141*                         B140-START-BROWSE                        *
0142*                         B150-BROWSE-PROCESSING                   *
0143*                             B151-FORMAT-OCCURS                    *
0144*                             B152-FORMAT-MAP                       *
0145*                             B153-WRITE-TS-RECORD                  *
0146*                         B110-SEND-MAP-DATAONLY                    *
0147*                             B111-RESET-OCCURS-ATTRIBUTES          *
0148*                         B120-RETURN-TO-CICS                       *
0149*                     B600-END-SESSION                             *
0150*                         B310-INITIALIZE-AND-DELETEQ               *
0151*                                                                  *
0152*                 C000-INITIAL-ENTRY                               *
0153*                     B310-INITIALIZE-AND-DELETEQ                   *
0154*                     B140-START-BROWSE                            *
0155*                     B150-BROWSE-PROCESSING                       *
0156*                         B151-FORMAT-OCCURS                        *
0157*                         B152-FORMAT-MAP                           *
0158*                         B153-WRITE-TS-RECORD                      *
0159*                 C100-SEND-MAP-AND-DATA                           *
0160*                     C110-GET-DATE-AND-TIME                        *
0161*                     B111-RESET-OCCURS-ATTRIBUTES                  *
0162***********************************************************************
```

Figure 17-2 *(Continued)*

```
0163 AA00-MAINLINE  SECTION.
0164
0165*     SERVICE RELOAD BLL-CELLS.
0166
0167     IF EIBCALEN = 0
0168        MOVE LOW-VALUES  TO  WS-COMMAREA
0169        PERFORM C000-INITIAL-ENTRY
0170     ELSE
0171        MOVE DFHCOMMAREA  TO  WS-COMMAREA
0172        IF EIBTRNID = 'POVB'
0173           PERFORM B000-PROCESS-MAP
0174        ELSE
0175           PERFORM C000-INITIAL-ENTRY.
0176*
0177     EXEC CICS RETURN
0178              TRANSID  ('POVB')
0179              COMMAREA (WS-COMMAREA)
0180              LENGTH   (19)
0181     END-EXEC.
0182*
0183*
0184 B000-PROCESS-MAP  SECTION.
0185****************************************************************
0186*             PERFORMED FROM:  AA00-MAINLINE               *
0187****************************************************************
0188*
0189     MOVE LOW-VALUES  TO  VM-BROWSE-MAP.
0190*
0191     EXEC CICS HANDLE AID
0192              PF1    (B100-PAGE-FORWARD)
0193              PF2    (B200-PAGE-BACKWARD)
0194              PF5    (B300-TRANSFER-XCTL-TO MENU)
0195              PF6    (B400-RETURN-WITH-SELECTION)
0196              PF7    (B500-RESET-KEY)
0197              CLEAR  (B600-END-SESSION)
0198              ANYKEY (B000-INVALID-KEY)
0199     END-EXEC.
0200*
0201     EXEC CICS IGNORE CONDITION
0202              MAPFAIL
0203     END-EXEC.
0204*
0205     EXEC CICS RECEIVE
0206              MAP    ('MAPPOVC')
0207              MAPSET ('POVMBR1')
0208              INTO   (VM-BROWSE-MAP)
0209     END-EXEC.
0210*
0211* ENTER IS AN INVALID KEY
0212*
0213 B000-INVALID-KEY.
0214     MOVE 'I'         TO  STATUS-OF-RECEIVE.
0215     MOVE 'INVALID KEY PRESSED - PLEASE TRY AGAIN'
0216                      TO  MVC-D-MESSAGE.
0217     MOVE ASKIP-BRT  TO  MVC-A-MESSAGE.
0218     MOVE -1         TO  MVC-L-SELECTION.
0219     PERFORM B110-SEND-MAP-DATAONLY.
0220*
0221 B000-EXIT.
0222     EXIT.
0223 B100-PAGE-FORWARD  SECTION.
0224****************************************************************
0225*         INVOKED BY HANDLE AID FROM:  B000-PROCESS-MAP      *
0226****************************************************************
0227*
0228     ADD 1  TO  CA-TS-ITEM.
0229*
0230     IF CA-TS-ITEM  IS GREATER THAN  CA-TS-MAXIMUM
0231        IF CA-LAST-KEY = HIGH-VALUES
0232           SUBTRACT 1  FROM  CA-TS-ITEM
0233           MOVE 'CURRENT PAGE IS LAST PAGE'
0234                       TO  MVC-D-MESSAGE
0235           MOVE ASKIP-BRT  TO  MVC-A-MESSAGE
0236           MOVE -1         TO  MVC-L-SELECTION
0237           PERFORM B110-SEND-MAP-DATAONLY
0238           PERFORM B120-RETURN-TO-CICS
0239        ELSE
0240           MOVE CA-LAST-KEY  TO  CA-VENDOR-CODE
```

Figure 17-2   (Continued)

```
0241*
0242****************************************************************
0243* CA-LAST-KEY CONTAINS THE KEY OF THE LAST VENDOR DISPLAYED  *
0244* ON THE PREVIOUS PAGE.   THE START BROWSE WILL, AS THE LOGIC *
0245* IS WRITTEN, DISPLAY THIS ITEM AGAIN AT THE TOP OF THE NEXT *
0246* PAGE.   YOU CAN GET AROUND THIS IN ONE OF TWO WAYS:        *
0247*    1) IF YOUR KEY IS NUMERIC, ADD 1 TO CA-VENDOR-CODE      *
0248*    2) ISSUE AN ADDITIONAL READNEXT AFTER THE STARTBR       *
0249****************************************************************
0250*
0251     ELSE
0252         PERFORM B130-READ-TS
0253         MOVE TS-VENDOR-CD  TO  CA-VENDOR-CODE.
0254*
0255     PERFORM B140-START-BROWSE.
0256     IF GOOD-STARTBR
0257         PERFORM B150-BROWSE-PROCESSING
0258         MOVE -1  TO  MVC-L-SELECTION
0259     ELSE
0260         MOVE 'START BROWSE KEY BEYOND END OF FILE'
0261                          TO  MVC-D-MESSAGE
0262         MOVE ASKIP-BRT   TO  MVC-A-MESSAGE
0263         MOVE -1          TO  MVC-L-RESET-KEY.
0264*
0265     PERFORM B110-SEND-MAP-DATAONLY.
0266     PERFORM B120-RETURN-TO-CICS.
0267*
0268 B100-EXIT.
0269     EXIT.
0270*
0271 B110-SEND-MAP-DATAONLY  SECTION.
0272*
0273****************************************************************
0274*      PERFORMED FROM:   B000-PROCESS-MAP                     *
0275*                        B100-PAGE-FORWARD                    *
0276*                        B200-PAGE-BACKWARD                   *
0277*                        B400-RETURN-WITH-SELECTION           *
0278*                        B500-RESET-KEY                       *
0279****************************************************************
0280*
0281     PERFORM B111-RESET-OCCURS-ATTRIBUTES
0282           VARYING SUB  FROM  1 BY 1  UNTIL  SUB  =  16.
0283*
0284     MOVE UNPROT-FSET  TO  MVC-A-SELECTION
0285                           MVC-A-RESET-CODE.
0286*
0287     EXEC CICS SEND
0288           MAP       ('MAPPOVC')
0289           MAPSET    ('POVMNT1')
0290           FROM      (VM-BROWSE-MAP)
0291           DATAONLY
0292           CURSOR
0293     END-EXEC.
0294*
0295 B110-EXIT.
0296     EXIT.
0297*
0298 B111-RESET-OCCURS-ATTRIBUTES  SECTION.
0299****************************************************************
0300*            PERFORMED FROM:  B110-SEND-MAP-DATAONLY         *
0301****************************************************************
0302*
0303     MOVE ASKIP-NORM-FSET  TO  MVC-A-OCCURS (SUB).
0304*
0305 B111-EXIT.
0306     EXIT.
0307*
0308 B120-RETURN-TO-CICS  SECTION.
0309****************************************************************
0310*            PERFORMED FROM:  B100-PAGE-FORWARD             *
0311*                             B200-PAGE-BACKWARD            *
0312*                             B400-RETURN-WITH-SELECTION    *
0313*                             B500-RESET-KEY                *
0314****************************************************************
0315*
0316     EXEC CICS RETURN
0317           TRANSID   ('POVB')
0318           COMMAREA  (WS-COMMAREA)
0319           LENGTH    (19)
0320     END-EXEC.
```

Figure 17-2 *(Continued)*

```
0321*
0322 B120-EXIT.
0323     EXIT.
0324*
0325 B130-READ-TS  SECTION.
0326**********************************************************************
0327*                PERFORMED FROM:  B100-PAGE-FORWARD                  *
0328*                                 B200-PAGE-BACKWARD                 *
0329**********************************************************************
0330*
0331     MOVE EIBTRMID  TO  TS-EIBTRMID.
0332     MOVE 'POVB'    TO  TS-QUEUE-NAME.
0333*
0334     EXEC CICS READQ TS
0335              QUEUE  (TS-QUEUE)
0336              INTO   (TS-RECORD)
0337              LENGTH (TS-LENGTH)
0338              ITEM   (CA-TS-ITEM)
0339     END-EXEC.
0340*
0341 B130-EXIT.
0342     EXIT.
0343 B140-START-BROWSE  SECTION.
0344**********************************************************************
0345*                PERFORMED FROM:  B100-PAGE-FORWARD                  *
0346*                                 B200-PAGE-BACKWARD                 *
0347*                                 B500-RESET-KEY                     *
0348*                                 C000-INITIAL-ENTRY                 *
0349**********************************************************************
0350*
0351     EXEC CICS HANDLE CONDITION
0352              NOTFND (B140-EXIT)
0353     END-EXEC.
0354*
0355     MOVE 'E'  TO  STATUS-OF-BROWSE.
0356*
0357     EXEC CICS STARTBR
0358              DATASET ('VENDMAST')
0359              RIDFLD  (CA-VENDOR-CODE)
0360              GTEQ
0361     END-EXEC.
0362*
0363     MOVE 'G'  TO  STATUS-OF-BROWSE.
0364*
0365 B140-EXIT.
0366     EXIT.
0367*
0368 B150-BROWSE-PROCESSING  SECTION.
0369**********************************************************************
0370*                PERFORMED FROM:  B100-PAGE-FORWARD                  *
0371*                                 B200-PAGE-BACKWARD                 *
0372*                                 B500-RESET-KEY                     *
0373*                                 C000-INITIAL-ENTRY                 *
0374**********************************************************************
0375*
0376     MOVE LOW-VALUES  TO  VM-BROWSE-MAP.
0377*
0378     PERFORM B151-FORMAT-OCCURS
0379             VARYING SUB FROM 1 BY 1  UNTIL  SUB  GREATER  15.
0380*
0381     MOVE 'F'  TO  STATUS-OF-READ.
0382*
0383     EXEC CICS HANDLE CONDITION
0384              ENDFILE (B150-ENDBR)
0385     END-EXEC.
0386*
0387     PERFORM B152-FORMAT-MAP  UNTIL  TS-SUB  GREATER  14.
0388*
0389     MOVE 'G'  TO  STATUS-OF-READ.
0390*
0391 B150-ENDBR.
0392     EXEC CICS ENDBR
0393              DATASET ('VENDMAST')
0394     END-EXEC.
```

Figure 17-2 (Continued)

```
0395*
0396      IF END-OF-FILE
0397          MOVE HIGH-VALUES   TO   CA-LAST-KEY
0398          MOVE 'CURRENT PAGE IS LAST PAGE'
0399                              TO   MVC-D-MESSAGE
0400          MOVE ASKIP-BRT     TO   MVC-A-MESSAGE
0401      ELSE
0402          MOVE ASKIP-DRK     TO   MVC-A-MESSAGE.
0403      IF CA-TS-EOF-SWITCH  =  'E'
0404          NEXT SENTENCE
0405      ELSE
0406          IF CA-TS-ITEM  IS GREATER THAN  CA-TS-MAXIMUM
0407              PERFORM B153-WRITE-TS-RECORD.
0408*
0409 B150-EXIT.
0410      EXIT.
0411*
0412 B151-FORMAT-OCCURS  SECTION.
0413*
0414***************************************************************
0415*          PERFORMED FROM:   B150 BROWSE-PROCESSING          *
0416***************************************************************
0417*
0418      MOVE SPACES  TO  MVC-D-OCCURS (SUB).
0419*
0420 B151-EXIT.
0421      EXIT.
0422*
0423 B152-FORMAT-MAP  SECTION.
0424***************************************************************
0425*          PERFORMED FROM:   B150-BROWSE-PROCESSING          *
0426***************************************************************
0427*
0428      EXEC CICS READNEXT
0429              DATASET ('VENDMAST')
0430              INTO    (VENDOR-MASTER-RECORD)
0431              RIDFLD  (CA-VENDOR-CODE)
0432      END-EXEC.
0433*
0434      ADD 1  TO  TS-SUB.
0435*
0436      IF TS-SUB  =  1
0437          MOVE CA-VENDOR-CODE  TO  TS-VENDOR-CD..
0438      IF CA-TS-ITEM  IS GREATER THAN  CA-TS-MAXIMUM
0439          MOVE CA-VENDOR-CODE  TO  CA-LAST-KEY.
0440*
0441      MOVE SPACES              TO   WS-DISPLAY-DATA.
0442      MOVE TS-SUB              TO   WS-SELECT.
0443*
0444      MOVE CA-VEND-1           TO   WS-VENDOR-CD-1.
0445      MOVE CA-VEND-2           TO   WS-VENDOR-CD-2.
0446      MOVE CA-VEND-3           TO   WS-VENDOR-CD-3.
0447      MOVE WS-VENDOR-CODE      TO   WS-VM-KEY.
0448*
0449      MOVE VM-VENDOR-NAME      TO   WS-VENDOR-NAME.
0450      MOVE VM-STREET-ADDRESS   TO   WS-STREET-ADDRESS.
0451      MOVE VM-CITY-STATE       TO   WS-CITY-STATE.
0452*
0453      MOVE WS-DISPLAY-DATA     TO   MVC-D-OCCURS (TS-SUB).
0454*
0455 B152-EXIT.
0456      EXIT.
0457*
0458 B153-WRITE-TS-RECORD  SECTION.
0459***************************************************************
0460*          PERFORMED FROM:   B150-BROWSE-PROCESSING          *
0461***************************************************************
0462*
0463      IF END-OF-FILE
0464          MOVE 'E'  TO  CA-TS-EOF-SWITCH.
0465*
0466      ADD 1  TO  CA-TS-MAXIMUM.
0467*
0468      MOVE EIBTRMID  TO  TS-EIBTRMID.
0469      MOVE 'POVB'    TO  TS-QUEUE-NAME.
```

Figure 17-2 *(Continued)*

```
0470*
0471       EXEC CICS WRITEQ TS
0472                 QUEUE  (TS-QUEUE)
0473                 FROM   (TS-RECORD)
0474                 LENGTH (TS-LENGTH)
0475                 ITEM   (CA-TS-ITEM)
0476       END-EXEC.
0477*
0478 B153-EXIT.
0479       EXIT.
0480*
0481 B200-PAGE-BACKWARD  SECTION.
0482****************************************************************
0483*          INVOKED BY HANDLE AID FROM:  B000-PROCESS-MAP      *
0484****************************************************************
0485*
0486       SUBTRACT 1  FROM  CA-TS-ITEM.
0487*
0488       IF CA-TS-ITEM  IS LESS THAN  1
0489            ADD 1  TO  CA-TS-ITEM
0490            MOVE 'CURRENT PAGE IS FIRST PAGE TO BE DISPLAYED'
0491                          TO  MVC-D-MESSAGE
0492            MOVE ASKIP-BRT  TO  MVC-A-MESSAGE
0493            MOVE -1         TO  MVC-L-SELECTION
0494            PERFORM B110-SEND-MAP-DATAONLY
0495            PERFORM B120-RETURN-TO-CICS.
0496
0497       PERFORM B130-READ-TS.
0498       MOVE TS-VENDOR-CD  TO  CA-VENDOR-CODE.
0499       PERFORM B140-START-BROWSE.
0500       IF GOOD-STARTBR
0501            PERFORM B150-BROWSE-PROCESSING
0502            MOVE -1  TO  MVC-L-SELECTION
0503       ELSE
0504            MOVE 'START BROWSE KEY BEYOND END OF FILE'
0505                          TO  MVC-D-MESSAGE
0506            MOVE ASKIP-BRT  TO  MVC-A-MESSAGE
0507            MOVE -1         TO  MVC-L-RESET-KEY.
0508*
0509       PERFORM B110-SEND-MAP-DATAONLY.
0510       PERFORM B120-RETURN-TO-CICS.
0511*
0512 B200-EXIT.
0513       EXIT.
0514*
0515 B300-TRANSFER-XCTL-TO-MENU  SECTION.
0516****************************************************************
0517*          PERFORMED FROM:  B000-PROCESS-MAP                  *
0518****************************************************************
0519*
0520       PERFORM B310-INITIALIZE-AND-DELETEQ.
0521*
0522       EXEC CICS XCTL
0523            PROGRAM ('POVMAINT')
0524       END-EXEC.
0525*
0526 B300-EXIT.
0527       EXIT.
0528*
0529 B310-INITIALIZE-AND-DELETEQ  SECTION.
0530*
0531****************************************************************
0532*          PERFORMED FROM:  B300-TRANSFER-XCTL-TO-MENU        *
0533*                           B400-RETURN-WITH-SELECTION        *
0534*                           B500-RESET-KEY                    *
0535*                           B600-END-SESSION                  *
0536*                           C000-INITIAL-ENTRY                *
0537****************************************************************
0538*
0539       MOVE 1           TO  CA-TS-ITEM.
0540       MOVE ZEROES      TO  CA-TS-MAXIMUM.
0541       MOVE LOW-VALUES  TO  CA-LAST-KEY.
0542       MOVE SPACES      TO  CA-TS-EOF-SWITCH.
0543*
0544       EXEC CICS IGNORE CONDITION
0545            QIDERR
0546       END-EXEC.
```

Figure 17-2 (Continued)

```
0547*
0548      MOVE EIBTRMID  TO  TS-EIBTRMID.
0549      MOVE 'POVB'    TO  TS-QUEUE-NAME.
0550*
0551      EXEC CICS DELETEQ TS
0552              QUEUE (TS-QUEUE)
0553      END-EXEC.
0554*
0555 B310-EXIT.
0556      EXIT.
0557*
0558 B400-RETURN-WITH-SELECTION  SECTION.
0559******************************************************************
0560*         INVOKED BY HANDLE AID FROM:  B000-PROCESS-MAP          *
0561******************************************************************
0562*
0563      IF (MVC-D-SELECTION  IS GREATER THAN   0)   AND
0564         (MVC-D-SELECTION  IS LESS THAN     16)
0565        MOVE MVC-D-SELECTION  TO  WS-SELECTION
0566        MOVE MVC-D-OCCURS (WS-SELECTION)  TO  WS-DISPLAY-DATA
0567        IF WS-SELECT  =  WS-SELECTION
0568          PERFORM B310-INITIALIZE-AND-DELETEQ
0569          MOVE WS-VM-KEY          TO  WS-VENDOR-CODE
0570          MOVE WS-VENDOR-CD-1  TO  CA-VEND-1
0571          MOVE WS-VENDOR-CD-2  TO  CA-VEND-2
0572          MOVE WS-VENDOR-CD-3  TO  CA-VEND-3
0573          PERFORM B410-XCTL-TO-INVOKING-PROGRAM.
0574*
0575      MOVE 'INVALID SELECTION - PLEASE RE-ENTER SELECTION'
0576                     TO  MVC-D-MESSAGE.
0577      MOVE ASKIP-BRT  TO  MVC-A-MESSAGE.
0578*
0579      MOVE -1        TO  MVC-L-SELECTION.
0580*
0581      PERFORM B110-SEND-MAP-DATAONLY.
0582      PERFORM B120-RETURN-TO-CICS.
0583*
0584 B400-EXIT.
0585      EXIT.
0586*
0587 B410-XCTL-TO-INVOKING-PROGRAM  SECTION.
0588******************************************************************
0589*          PERFORMED FROM:  B400-RETURN-WITH-SELECTION           *
0590******************************************************************
0591*
0592      IF CA-ADDITION         MOVE 'POVMADDN'  TO  WS-XCTL-PROGRAM
0593      ELSE  IF CA-CHANGE     MOVE 'POVMCHGE'  TO  WS-XCTL-PROGRAM
0594      ELSE  IF CA-DELETE     MOVE 'POVMDLET'  TO  WS-XCTL-PROGRAM
0595      ELSE                   MOVE 'POVMINQY'  TO  WS-XCTL-PROGRAM.
0596*
0597      MOVE 'B'  TO  CA-FUNCTION-CODE.
0598*
0599      EXEC CICS XCTL
0600              PROGRAM  (WS-XCTL-PROGRAM)
0601              COMMAREA (WS-COMMAREA)
0602              LENGTH   (8)
0603      END-EXEC.
0604*
0605 B410-EXIT.
0606      EXIT.
0607*
0608 B500-RESET-KEY  SECTION.
0609******************************************************************
0610*          INVOKED BY HANDLE AID FROM:  B000-PROCESS-MAP         *
0611******************************************************************
0612*
0613      MOVE MVC-D-RESET-CODE  TO  CA-VENDOR-CODE.
0614      MOVE SPACES            TO  MVC-D-RESET-CODE.
0615*
0616      PERFORM B310-INITIALIZE-AND-DELETEQ.
0617      PERFORM B140-START-BROWSE.
0618      IF GOOD-STARTBR
0619        PERFORM B150-BROWSE-PROCESSING
0620        MOVE -1  TO  MVC-L-SELECTION
```

Figure 17-2 (*Continued*)

```
0621      ELSE
0622          MOVE 'START BROWSE KEY IS BEYOND END OF FILE - PLEASE RE-
0623-             'ENTER KEY'     TO  MVC-D-MESSAGE
0624          MOVE ASKIP-BRT   TO  MVC-A-MESSAGE
0625          MOVE -1          TO  MVC-L-RESET-CODE.
0626*
0627      PERFORM B110-SEND-MAP-DATAONLY.
0628      PERFORM B120-RETURN-TO-CICS.
0629*
0630 B500-EXIT.
0631      EXIT.
0632*
0633 B600-END-SESSION  SECTION.
0634*******************************************************************
0635*                 INVOKED BY :  B000-PROCESS-MAP                 *
0636*******************************************************************
0637*
0638      PERFORM B310-INITIALIZE-AND-DELETEQ.
0639*
0640      EXEC CICS SEND
0641              FROM   (WS-CRT-MESSAGE)
0642              LENGTH (17)
0643              ERASE
0644      END-EXEC.
0645*
0646      EXEC CICS RETURN
0647      END-EXEC.
0648*
0649 B600-EXIT.
0650      EXIT.
0651*
0652 C000-INITIAL-ENTRY  SECTION.
0653*******************************************************************
0654*                 PERFORMED FROM:  AA00-MAINLINE                 *
0655*******************************************************************
0656*
0657      MOVE LOW-VALUES  TO  VM-BROWSE-MAP.
0658      PERFORM B310-INITIALIZE-AND-DELETEQ.
0659      PERFORM B140-START-BROWSE.
0660      IF GOOD-STARTER
0661          PERFORM B150-BROWSE-PROCESSING
0662      ELSE
0663          MOVE 'START BROWSE KEY BEYOND END OF FILE'
0664              TO  MVC-D-MESSAGE
0665          MOVE ASKIP-BRT  TO  MVC-A-MESSAGE.
0666      PERFORM C100-SEND-MAP-AND-DATA.
0667*
0668 C000-EXIT.
0669      EXIT.
0670*
0671 C100-SEND-MAP-AND-DATA  SECTION.
0672*******************************************************************
0673*             PERFORMED FROM:  C000-INITIAL-ENTRY               *
0674*******************************************************************
0675*
0676      PERFORM C110-GET-DATE-AND-TIME.
0677      PERFORM B111-RESET-OCCURS-ATTRIBUTES.
0678*
0679      MOVE WS-CURRENT-DATE  TO  MVC-D-DATE.
0680      MOVE WS-MAP-TIME      TO  MVC-D-TIME.
0681      MOVE -1              TO  MVC-L-SELECTION.
0682*
0683      EXEC CICS SEND
0684              MAP     ('MAPPOVC')
0685              MAPSET  ('POVMBR1')
0686              FROM    (VM-BROWSE-MAP)
0687              ERASE
0688              CURSOR
0689      END-EXEC.
0690*
0691 C100-EXIT.
0692      EXIT.
0693*
0694 C110-GET-DATE-AND-TIME  SECTION  COPY  STPDDTTM.
0695*******************************************************************
0696*             PERFORMED FROM:  C100-SEND-MAP-AND-DATA           *
0697*******************************************************************
0698*
0699 C110-EXIT.
0700      EXIT.
```

of the file. This is done to keep the program as simple as possible. If EIBCALEN is greater than 0, then this program was either started by another program or is returning to itself in the pseudoconversational mode. The EIB field EIBTRNID contains the transaction identifier of the current task. For instance, if this program was started by the inquiry program, EIBTRNID would equal POVI. When this program issues a RETURN command with a TRANSID, a new task will be started and EIBTRNID will equal POVB.

B000-PROCESS-MAP. This section employs the CICS HANDLE AID command. EIBAID could have been tested as done with previous RECEIVE MAP commands, but I want to illustrate how HANDLE AID functions. HANDLE AID is invoked upon an execution of a RECEIVE MAP command. Control would pass to section B100-PAGE-FORWARD if PF1 was pressed. Pressing PF2 would transfer control to section B200-PAGE-BACKWARD, etc. ANYKEY transfers control to B000-INVALID-KEY for any key which is not specified; it does not include the ENTER key. In this example, if ENTER is pressed, control will pass to the statement following the RECEIVE MAP command, paragraph B000-INVALID-KEY.

B100-PAGE-FORWARD. Forward paging is accomplished by adding 1 to the COMMAREA field CA-TS-ITEM and if CA-TS-ITEM is greater than CA-TS-MAXIMUM

1. If CA-LAST-KEY = HIGH-VALUES, this indicates that the end of file had been reached on a previous entry into the program; if so an appropriate message is displayed.

2. If end of file has not been reached, then the CA-LAST-KEY, the last key read during a previous entry into the program, is moved to CA VENDOR-CODE to initialize the browse starting key. As pointed out in the program comments, CA-LAST-KEY contains the key of the last vendor displayed on the previous page. The STARTBR command will start the browse with the last record from the previous page displayed at the top of the new page. This can be prevented by:

    a. Adding 1 to the key, if it is numeric.

    b. If the key is not numeric, issuing an additional READNEXT command after the STARTBR command.

    If CA-TS-ITEM is equal to or less than CA-TS-MAXIMUM, the program has paged backward and is now paging forward. CA-TS-ITEM would be used to read the TS queue. Then the vendor record key obtained, TS-VENDOR-CD, would be moved to CA-VENDOR-CODE to initialize the browse starting point.

B110-SEND-MAP-DATAONLY. Prior to the SEND MAP command, all OCCURS attributes are set by B111-RESET-OCCURS-ATTRIBUTES to ASKIP, NORM,FSET. This results in the data which is displayed in the 15 occurrence fields being returned to the program when the RECEIVE MAP command is executed. This is necessary if a selection is entered on the screen and PF6 is pressed. UNPROT,FSET is moved to attributes in order to make sure fields are returned to the program on a receive. On a subsequent RECEIVE MAP command, only fields which were keyed in immediately prior to the receive will be returned to the program, unless they have been FSET.

B130-READ-TS. This section sets the TS queue name and reads the record which corresponds to the specified item number. All queue names in this program are the same. They contain eight characters and consist of the four-character terminal ID and the four-character transaction code POVB. The EIB field EIBTRNID should not be substituted for the constant POVB because if this program was started by another program, EIBTRNID would not equal POVB upon initial entry. If your program contains more than one TS queue, it will always be necessary to use unique names for the last four positions of queue name.

B140-START-BROWSE. If CA-VENDOR-CODE is greater than the last key on the file then the NOTFND handle condition will be invoked and an E will be returned in STATUS-OF-BROWSE. The STARTBR command will set the starting position in the file at the vendor master file (VENDMAST) vendor code which is greater than or equal to (GTEQ) the code in CA-VENDOR-CODE.

B150-BROWSE-PROCESSING. The OCCURS fields on the symbolic map are initialized to spaces by performing B151-FORMAT-OCCURS. This is necessary when the program is near the end of the file because low-values in a map field are not transmitted on a receive or send of a map. If the last page to be displayed contained only 5 vendors, the data from the last 10 vendors of the previous page would be present at the bottom of the screen. A send which contained low-values in the occurrence fields would not erase the last 10 occurrences. Moving spaces to the occurrence fields prior to the send does erase the unwanted information from the screen because spaces are transmitted.

If the end of file is reached in the routine B152-FORMAT-MAP, control will pass to B150-ENDBR and STATUS-OF-READ will contain an F, which signals END-OF-FILE. A HANDLE CONDITION command can be placed at any point in a program. It is activated when the condition occurs. After a browse is complete, it is good practice to terminate the browse by issuing the ENDBR command. If CA-TS-EOF-SWITCH equals E, this indicates that the end of a file had been reached on a previous entry into the program and the final TS queue has been written. If CA-TS-ITEM is greater than CA-TS-MAXIMUM, the program is paging forward and displaying data for the first time; therefore, a queue record must be written. If CA-TS-ITEM is not greater than CA-TS-MAXIMUM, the program is paging forward after having performed backward paging and the queue record key has already been written to temporary storage.

B120-RETURN-TO-CICS. This section returns control to CICS with a COMM-AREA which contains several fields which are needed for the paging routines. The new fields will be discussed as encountered.

B152-FORMAT-MAP. The READNEXT command is executed 15 times or until the end of file is reached. The first vendor code of each map is saved in the TS field TS-VENDOR-CD. The first time a new screen is formatted, the last key on the screen is saved in CA-LAST-KEY. This key is used in the page-forward routine. The occurrence fields are formatted and moved to the map.

B153-WRITE-TS-RECORD. This section sets the queue name and writes a TS queue which contains the key of the last record displayed on the map. The queue record is written *from* the TS-RECORD in working storage. CA-TS-MAXIMUM is incremented each time a TS queue record is written. It is used as an upper limit when the program pages backward and then forward again. CA-TS-EOF-SWITCH will contain an E when the end of file has been reached. This is a signal that the final TS queue record has been written.

B200-PAGE-BACKWARD. Backward paging is accomplished by subtracting 1 from CA-TS-ITEM. If the result is not less than the first item written to temporary storage, the appropriate queue is retrieved and its data, TS-VENDOR-CD, is used to start the browse.

B300-TRANSFER-XCTL-TO-MENU. This section transfers control back to the submenu program POVMAINT (see map in Fig. 6-3). It is good practice to delete TS queues which are no longer required before exiting a program.

B310-INITIALIZE-AND-DELETEQ. WS-COMMAREA fields which are required for paging logic are initialized and the TS queue is deleted. This program allows the browse starting point to be reset; therefore, it may be necessary to reinitialize certain fields. CA-TS-ITEM is used by paging logic to keep track of the last page displayed. It is added to or subtracted from in forward and backward paging routines. CA-TS-MAXIMUM holds the item number of the last map written to temporary storage. CA-LAST-KEY will hold the key of the last browse record read. CA-TS-EOF-SWITCH signals that the end of file has been reached on a READNEXT command.

Another use for the IGNORE CONDITION command previously discussed is shown. The IGNORE command directs the program to ignore the QIDERR condition if it occurs. The QIDERR condition occurs when a queue to be deleted does not exist. If the program did not provide for this condition, the task would ABEND if the condition occurred. The HANDLE CONDITION command could also be used in this situation:

```
EXEC CICS HANDLE CONDITION
          QIDERR  (B310-EXIT)
END-EXEC.
```

This queue should not normally exist when the program is first entered but might be present if a previous execution of the program had ABENDed. Application programs which use TS queues should always delete the queue when it is no longer required because a queue consumes system resources.

B400-RETURN-WITH-SELECTION. The range of the selected vendor is validated. If the selection is within the allowable range, 1 through 15, the map selection is used as a subscript in order to move the appropriate map occurrence to WS-DISPLAY-DATA. The map received returns only FSET fields. The WS-DISPLAY-DATA field WS-SELECT is compared to WS-SELECTION. The map selection entry could be in the range of 1 through 15, but the last map displayed might have fewer than 15 entries. Once it has been determined that a valid selection has been made, the TS queue is deleted. The vendor code is then moved to WS-COMMAREA subfields and a perform issued to transfer control to the appropriate program.

B410-XCTL-TO-INVOKING-PROGRAM. This section assumes that another program transferred control to this program and passed a COMMAREA function code for the inquiry or maintenance function. The appropriate program name is moved to the field WS-XCTL-PROGRAM; a B is moved to CA-FUNCTION-CODE and control is transferred to the designated program. Section AA00-MAINLINE of the invoking inquiry or maintenance program would have to be modified in order to accept the vendor code which was being transferred. For example,

```
IF EIBCALEN = 0
    PERFORM B000-INITIAL-ENTRY
ELSE
    MOVE DFHCOMMAREA TO WS-COMMAREA
    IF CA-BROWSE
        MOVE LOW-VALUES TO VM-CONTROL-MAP
        PERFORM C400-VERIFY-VENDOR-FILE-STATUS
        IF GOOD-VERIFY
            PERFORM C500-SEND-DETAIL-MAP-AND-DATA
        ELSE
            PERFORM B100-SEND-CONTROL-MAP-AND-DATA
    ELSE
        IF CA-RECEIVE-CTL-MAP
            PERFORM C000-PROCESS-CONTROL-MAP
        ELSE
            PERFORM . . .
```

B500-RESET-KEY. The browse starting key is reset when the terminal operator enters a key into the RESET VENDOR CODE field and presses PF7. A start browse is performed and, if successful, the map is formatted and displayed. If the RESET key is beyond the end of the file, the cursor is positioned at the start of the RESET field and an appropriate message is displayed.

B600-END-SESSION. The TS queue should be deleted before control is returned to CICS.

C000-INITIAL-ENTRY. The TS queue is deleted and related fields are initialized. The STARTBR command will set the starting point at the beginning of the file because CA-VENDOR-CODE will contain low-values. This approach was taken to keep the browse, inquiry, and maintenance programs as simple as possible. B150-BROWSE-PROCESSING will format the screen with the first 15 vendors in the file. If an inquiry or maintenance program had passed a vendor code to this program in COMMAREA, then the first vendor displayed would be equal to or greater than that code.

SUMMARY

DELETEQ, WRITEQ, and READQ TS commands were used in the browse program as were the STARTBR and READNEXT file control commands. The HANDLE AID command was used in place of the EIBAID technique used in previous examples. Routines for forward and backward paging were explained. A method which can be used to return a selected code to an invoking program was covered, and it was shown how a browse starting point could be reset.

Paging logic sometimes presents programming difficulties but is made easier once you understand the basic principles involved. The technique of paging demonstrated is a good way to learn the basics of browse logic. Once you have an understanding of how paging works, you can use this program as a guide to develop more sophisticated browse programs.

18

CICS DEBUGGING AND TESTING

Debugging and testing CICS programs is easier in an online environment than it is for batch systems. Debugging refers to the process of removing obvious errors such as ABENDs from a program, while testing refers to proving that a program functions as specified. Many interactive aids exist which make it easy for the CICS programmer to determine and correct the cause of program errors. Some of the aids available include execution diagnostic facility (EDF), interactive testing tools, CICS ABEND determination aids, and CICS dumps. A programmer familiar with some of these tools can usually diagnose and correct online program problems faster than can be done in a batch environment. Testing may be easier and faster in an online environment, but it must be more thorough than in a batch system. Batch program errors often occur without a user being aware that a problem ever existed. Online program errors may be visible to users at many different locations across the country and can trigger concerned phone calls to data center representatives. It is better to overtest a system and its programs, even if it means a delay in implementation, than to rush a system into production and correct errors as they occur. The best designed and tested systems will contain some oversights and errors, but it is important to minimize their occurrence. The credibility and reputation of a data processing installation is not enhanced when there are numerous ABENDs while a user is working with an on online system in a production environment.

Execution Diagnostic Facility

EDF is often the only tool an online programmer will need in order to debug and test a CICS program. It should only be used for testing command-level CICS programs. The execution of CICS programs is intercepted every time a CICS command is encountered and at other points during the execution of the program. Each command is displayed before execution, and most are displayed after execution is complete. When the commands are displayed, the applications programmer is given the ability to make changes to commands and conditions, display and alter working storage, display the EIB, and bypass the display of undesired CICS commands. During execution of the program, the programmer can force the program to be ABENDed, with or without a CICS dump. EDF can be terminated after the desired point in the program execution has been reached. The last map displayed can be brought back to the screen at each point at which the program stops to display a command. When a program ABEND occurs, the programmer can use EDF to determine and temporarily correct the error condition.

EDF Initiation

EDF is run as a CICS transaction and can be initiated on the terminal being used by entering a TRANSID of CEDF on a cleared screen and pressing ENTER. EDF can be invoked on a different terminal by clearing the screen and entering the ID of the other terminal, after keying in CEDF plus a space (i.e., CEDF T023). When EDF is run on a single terminal, program maps will be displayed interspersed between the display of EDF screens. When two terminals are used to run EDF, one screen will display a program's map while a second terminal will display and monitor EDF screens. EDF is most often run on one terminal, and I will present a typical EDF session as it would be run using this approach. If you run EDF on two adjacent terminals, the technique used will be basically the same.

EDF can be invoked for the browse program discussed in the last chapter as follows:

1. Clear the screen.
2. Key in CEDF and press ENTER.
3. THIS TERMINAL: EDF MODE ON will be displayed.
4. Clear the screen.
5. Key in the TRANSID POVB and press ENTER.
6. The program initiation screen shown in Fig. 18-1 will be displayed.

Program Initiation Screen

The program initiation screen shown in Fig. 18-1 displays the EIB as it exists upon initial entry into the program. Line 1 of the screen is basically the same for all EDF displays and contains:

1. TRANSACTION: POVB—This is the TRANSID associated with the task. For this screen, it is the TRANSID entered to initiate the browse program. If the browse had been invoked from the inquiry program, the TRANSID of

```
TRANSACTION: POVB    PROGRAM: POVMBROW    TASK NUMBER 0000402    DISPLAY:    00
STATUS:   PROGRAM INITIATION

    EIBTIME       = +0112215
    EIBDATE       = +0086023
    EIBTRNID      = 'POVB'
    EIBTASKN      = +0000402
    EIBTRMID      = 'T022'
    EIBCPOSN      = +00004
    EIBCALEN      = +00000
    EIBAID        = X'7D'                              AT X'0014477B'
    EIBFN         = X'0000'                            AT X'0014477C'
    EIBRCODE      = X'000000000000'                    AT X'0014477E'
    EIBDS         = '.........'
    EIBREQID      = '.........'
 +  EIBRSRCE      = '            '


ENTER:   CONTINUE
PF1 : UNDEFINED           PF2 : SWITCH HEX/CHAR     PF3 : END EDF SESSION
PF4 : SUPPRESS DISPLAYS   PF5 : WORKING STORAGE     PF6 : USER DISPLAY
PF7 : SCROLL BACK         PF8 : SCROLL FORWARD      PF9 : STOP CONDITIONS
PF10: PREVIOUS DISPLAY    PF11: UNDEFINED           PF12: UNDEFINED
```

Figure 18-1 EDF Program Initiation Screen.

the inquiry program (POVI) would be displayed on this line until the program executed a return with a TRANSID of POVB. Look at the displayed EIB fields and note that the EIB field EIBTRNID contains the same TRANSID displayed on line 1.

2. PROGRAM: POVMBROW—This is the program name associated with the browse program.

3. TASK NUMBER 0000402—This is a sequential task number assigned by the system. This task number remains the same until the program executes a return. A return terminates the current task, and, if the return contains a TRANSID, a new task is initiated and assigned the next available sequential number. Note that the EIB field EIBTASKN contains this same task number.

4. DISPLAY: 00—This reflects the current screen being displayed. As succeeding screens are displayed, it is possible to view previous displays. The number displayed next to DISPLAY would be decremented by one for each prior screen displayed, i.e., -01, -02, etc.

Line 2 contains the status of the EDF screen being displayed. The status of this first screen is PROGRAM INITIATION. The status will change as different EDF screens are displayed.

Line 3 for this display is blank but would display the COMMAREA, if one existed, as shown in Fig. 18-8.

The remaining EIB fields commonly referenced are

1. EIBTIME and EIBDATE—These contain the time and date at which the transaction was initiated.

2. EIBTRMID—The terminal at which the transaction is running.

3. EIBCPOSN—The position of the cursor. We initiated the transaction by entering a four-position TRANSID; therefore, the cursor ends up in screen position 4.

4. EIBCALEN—The COMMAREA length. This length is always equal to zero when a transaction is initiated by keying a TRANSID on the screen and pressing ENTER. If a program is invoked by another program which passes a COMMAREA or if it is returned to with a TRANSID and a COMMAREA, then EIBCALEN will equal the length of that COMMAREA.

5. EIBAID—This contains the hexadecimal code associated with the AID key which was last pressed. X'7D' is the code associated with the ENTER key. See App. A-3 for a list of the decimal values associated with the AID keys.

The PF keys at the bottom of the screen change for some EDF screens, but a given function is always associated with the same PF key. I will discuss the more important PF keys in succeeding EDF screen examples. ENTER: CONTINUE is displayed, above the PF key instructions. EDF progresses by pressing the ENTER key. You could keep pressing ENTER until you came to the EDF screen displayed in Fig. 18-2. Since EDF stops at every CICS command, a few intervening screens would be displayed for the ASSIGN and ADDRESS commands contained in the date and time routine shown in App. B for copy library member STPDDTTM.

ABOUT-TO-EXECUTE Command Screen

EDF displays a screen prior to the execution of a CICS command. This is illustrated by the highlighted status field on line 2 of Fig. 18-2. The highlighted CICS command about to be executed is shown on line 3. The command EXEC CICS SEND is followed on succeeding lines by its options and arguments.

```
TRANSACTION: POVB    PROGRAM: POVMBROW    TASK NUMBER 0000402    DISPLAY:   00
STATUS:   ABOUT TO EXECUTE COMMAND
EXEC CICS SEND
  MAP('MAPPOVC')
  FROM('...............01/23/86...11.22.15................................ ...)
  MAPSET('POVMBR1')
  TERMINAL
  ERASE




   OFFSET:X'00132C'    LINE:   00268       EIBFN=X'1804'

ENTER:   CONTINUE
PF1 : UNDEFINED            PF2 : SWITCH HEX/CHAR      PF3 : UNDEFINED
PF4 : SUPPRESS DISPLAYS    PF5 : WORKING STORAGE      PF6 : USER DISPLAY
PF7 : SCROLL BACK          PF8 : SCROLL FORWARD       PF9 : STOP CONDITIONS
PF10: PREVIOUS DISPLAY     PF11: UNDEFINED            PF12: ABEND USER TASK
```

Figure 18-2 EDF About-to-Execute Command Screen.

EDF sometimes displays a default option, such as TERMINAL, which was not coded in the program's CICS command. The programmer can overtype any EDF display at which the cursor stops next to when the TAB key is pressed. A command can be negated by overtyping the command function with either NOP or NOOP. The arguments for options such as MAP, MAPSET, and FROM can be altered by overtyping the existing data. The programmer can overtype in character format or can press PF2 to switch to a hexadecimal display and make the change in hex. If an argument displays a period, it is best to switch to hex if a change must be made to that field.

At the bottom of the screen above the instructions, two or three fields may be displayed:

1. OFFSET: X'00132C'—This is the program CLIST offset and may be used to locate the CICS command about to execute.

2. LINE: 0268—This is the line number corresponding to the translator printout of the CICS program. LINE will only be displayed if the program was translated using the DEBUG option. The DEBUG option generates larger program load modules because the translator line numbers must be saved in order to be displayed.

3. EIBFN='X'1804'—This is an EIB function code which is updated when a CICS command has been executed. X'1804' represents the SEND MAP command.

Program Map Display Screen

Press the ENTER key to continue the EDF session. The next screen displayed will be the program map being sent. It will be similar to the screen shown in Fig. 1-11. Data can be entered on this display of the map or you can wait until the next display of the same map. Data entered on this map will be remembered and need not be entered again on the next display of the map.

Command Execution Complete Screen

A command execution complete screen similar to that shown in Fig. 18-3 will be displayed at the completion of most CICS commands. ABEND, RE-TURN, and XCTL do not display a command execution complete screen. The EDF map displays two new fields—the response field and EIBRCODE. The response field shows RESPONSE: NORMAL. Response will usually be NORMAL unless a handle condition has been invoked, in which case the invoked condition will be displayed in the response field. A programmer can use the response field to test various conditions by overtyping the contents of the response field. A program will then follow the logic path which would have occurred if the condition had actually happened. The EIB field EIBRCODE is generally not used by an applications programmer. This field contains the response code and is usually handled in the program by the HANDLE CONDITION command. The programmer can end

```
TRANSACTION: POVB    PROGRAM: POVMBROW    TASK NUMBER 0000402   DISPLAY:  00
STATUS:  COMMAND EXECUTION COMPLETE
EXEC CICS SEND
 MAP('MAPPOVC')
 FROM('..............01/23/86...11.22.15............................'...)
 MAPSET('POVMBR1')
 TERMINAL
 ERASE




 OFFSET:X'00132C'    LINE:   00268       EIBFN=X'1804'
 RESPONSE: NORMAL                        EIBRCODE=X'000000000000'

ENTER:  CONTINUE
PF1 : UNDEFINED             PF2 : SWITCH HEX/CHAR    PF3 : END EDF SESSION
PF4 : SUPPRESS DISPLAYS     PF5 : WORKING STORAGE    PF6 : USER DISPLAY
PF7 : SCROLL BACK           PF8 : SCROLL FORWARD     PF9 : STOP CONDITIONS
PF10: PREVIOUS DISPLAY      PF11: UNDEFINED          PF12: ABEND USER TASK
```

Figure 18-3 EDF Command Execution Complete Screen.

the EDF session at any screen that displays the instruction PF3 : END EDF SESSION.

Working-Storage Display Screen

A working-storage screen similar to Fig. 18-4 would be displayed if the programmer pressed the PF5 key while Fig. 18-3 was displayed. The working-storage screen displays the highlighted starting address of main storage, followed on succeeding lines by a column of main-storage addresses, working-storage offsets, four columns of hexadecimal data, and the corresponding 16 bytes of data in

```
TRANSACTION: POVB    PROGRAM: POVMBROW     TASK NUMBER 0000402   DISPLAY:  00
ADDRESS: 0010060C                          WORKING STORAGE
00100600   000000                                    D7D6E5D4   ............POVM
00100610   000004   C2D9D6E6 E2C5E2E2 C9D6D540 C3D6D4D7   BROWSESSION COMP
00100620   000014   D3C5E3C5 C4000000 00404040 40404040   LETED...........
00100630   000024   40000000 00000000 00000000 00000000   ................
00100640   000034   00000000 00000000 00000000 00000000   ................
00100650   000044   00000000 00000000 00000000 00000000   ................
00100660   000054   00000000 00000000 00000000 00000000   ................
00100670   000064   00000000 00000000 00000000 00000000   ................
00100680   000074   00000000 00000000 00000000 00000000   ................
00100990   000084   00000000 00000000 00000000 00000000   ................
001009A0   000094   00000000 00000000 00000000 00000000   ................
001009B0   0000A4   00000000 00000000 00000000 00000000   ................
001009C0   0000B4   00000000 00000000 00000000 00000000   ................
001009D0   0000C4   00000000 00000000 00000000 00000000   ................
001009E0   0000D4   00000000 00000000 00000000 00000000   ................
001009F0   0000E4   00000000 00000000 00000000 00000000   ................

ENTER:  CURRENT DISPLAY
PF1 : UNDEFINED           PF2 : UNDEFINED          PF3 : UNDEFINED
PF4 : EIB DISPLAY         PF5 : WORKING STORAGE    PF6 : USER DISPLAY
PF7 : SCROLL BACK HALF    PF8 : SCROLL FORWARD HALF PF9 : UNDEFINED
PF10: SCROLL BACK FULL    PF11: SCROLL FORWARD FULL PF12: REMEMBER DISPLAY
```

Figure 18-4 EDF Working-Storage Screen.

character format. Any data in the program's working storage can be changed by overtyping either the hexadecimal data or the character data and pressing the ENTER key. Working storage may be scrolled through in a forward or backward direction depending on the PF key used. The programmer-defined working-storage literal END WS PROGNAME will signal the end of working storage. The EIB can be displayed from the working-storage screen by pressing PF4. The user map last displayed can be redisplayed by pressing PF6 : USER DISPLAY. Normally up to the last 10 CICS command screens are saved for possible redisplay. The working-storage screen or any EDF display which has PF12 : REMEMBER DISPLAY allows you to press this key in order to save the current screen for future display. The highlighted main-storage address at the top of the screen can be overtyped with the address of any area of main storage which is in the region or partition. Only the program's working storage can be altered; other main storage is display only. Press the ENTER key to get out of the working-storage display and to return to the current display, Fig. 18-3 for this example.

RETURN EDF Screen

Press ENTER to continue and the EDF display will move to Fig. 18-5, the return screen. The return EDF screen will only display an about-to-execute screen. As mentioned previously, there is no command execution complete screen for RETURN, ABEND, and XCTL commands. The arguments of TRANSID and COMMAREA could be overtyped if this would assist in testing.

Program Termination Screen

The program termination screen shown in Fig. 18-6 would be displayed when you press ENTER while the return screen is displayed.

```
 TRANSACTION: POVB    PROGRAM: POVMBROW    TASK NUMBER 0000402    DISPLAY:  00
 STATUS:  ABOUT TO EXECUTE COMMAND
 EXEC CICS RETURN
  TRANSID('POVB')
  COMMAREA(' 1..........')
  LENGTH(+00012)










  OFFSET:X'0012C4'    LINE:  00231       EIBFN=X'0E08'

 ENTER:  CONTINUE
 PF1 : UNDEFINED             PF2 : SWITCH HEX/CHAR      PF3 : UNDEFINED
 PF4 : SUPPRESS DISPLAYS     PF5 : WORKING STORAGE      PF6 : USER DISPLAY
 PF7 : SCROLL BACK           PF8 : SCROLL FORWARD       PF9 : STOP CONDITIONS
 PF10: PREVIOUS DISPLAY      PF11: UNDEFINED            PF12: ABEND USER TASK
```

Figure 18-5 Return EDF Screen.

```
TRANSACTION: POVB    PROGRAM: POVMBROW    TASK NUMBER 0000402    DISPLAY:   00
STATUS:  PROGRAM TERMINATION




ENTER:   CONTINUE
PF1  : UNDEFINED           PF2  : SWITCH HEX/CHAR    PF3  : END EDF SESSION
PF4  : SUPPRESS DISPLAYS   PF5  : WORKING STORAGE    PF6  : USER DISPLAY
PF7  : SCROLL BACK         PF8  : SCROLL FORWARD     PF9  : STOP CONDITIONS
PF10: PREVIOUS DISPLAY     PF11: UNDEFINED           PF12: ABEND USER TASK
```

Figure 18-6   EDF Program Termination Screen.

Task Termination Screen

The task termination screen shown in Fig. 18-7 is displayed next when the ENTER key is pressed. The programmer has the option at this point to continue or to end the EDF session. Overtype the NO next to REPLY with YES in order to continue the EDF session or just press the ENTER key with NO displayed to end the session. The browse screen shown in Fig. 1-11 will be redisplayed whether or not the session is continued and a new task will be initiated when an AID key is pressed.

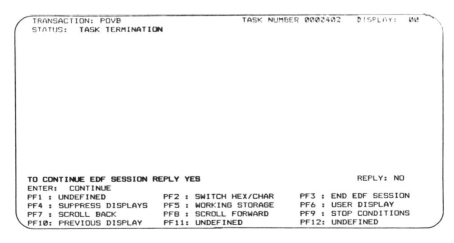

```
TRANSACTION: POVB                      TASK NUMBER 0000402   DISPLAY:   00
STATUS:  TASK TERMINATION




TO CONTINUE EDF SESSION REPLY YES                          REPLY: NO
ENTER:   CONTINUE
PF1  : UNDEFINED           PF2  : SWITCH HEX/CHAR    PF3  : END EDF SESSION
PF4  : SUPPRESS DISPLAYS   PF5  : WORKING STORAGE    PF6  : USER DISPLAY
PF7  : SCROLL BACK         PF8  : SCROLL FORWARD     PF9  : STOP CONDITIONS
PF10: PREVIOUS DISPLAY     PF11: UNDEFINED           PF12: UNDEFINED
```

Figure 18-7   EDF Task Termination Screen.

```
TRANSACTION: PQVB    PROGRAM: PQVMBROW    TASK NUMBER 0000416    DISPLAY:  00
STATUS:  PROGRAM INITIATION
   COMMAREA      = ' 1..........'
   EIBTIME       = +0112327
   EIBDATE       = +0086023
   EIBTRNID      = 'PQVB'
   EIBTASKN      = +0000416
   EIBTRMID      = 'T022'
   EIBCPOSN      = +01441
   EIBCALEN      = +00019
   EIBAID        = X'7D'                                    AT X'0013263A'
   EIBFN         = X'0000'                                  AT X'0013263B'
   EIBRCODE      = X'000000000000'                          AT X'0013263D'
   EIBDS         = '........'
   EIBREQID      = '........'
 + EIBRSRCE      , = '        '


 ENTER:   CONTINUE
 PF1 : UNDEFINED           PF2 : SWITCH HEX/CHAR    PF3 : END EDF SESSION
 PF4 : SUPPRESS DISPLAYS   PF5 : WORKING STORAGE    PF6 : USER DISPLAY
 PF7 : SCROLL BACK         PF8 : SCROLL FORWARD     PF9 : STOP CONDITIONS
 PF10: PREVIOUS DISPLAY    PF11: UNDEFINED          PF12: UNDEFINED
```

Figure 18-8   EDF Succeeding Entry Program Initiation Screen.

Program Initiation Redisplayed

The program initiation screen shown in Fig. 18-8 will be displayed if you overtyped YES on the task termination screen in Fig. 18-7 and pressed ENTER in order to continue the EDF session. This program initiation screen is similar to the screen displayed in Fig. 18-1; however, I want to point out a few significant changes. Note that the task number at the top of the screen and in EIBTASKN has changed from 402 to 416. The COMMAREA is now displayed on line 3, and its length is shown in the COMMAREA length field EIBCALEN. The cursor position (EIBCPOSN) reflects the position of the cursor on the screen before an AID key was pressed.

EDF Stop Conditions Screen

The display on condition screen shown in Fig. 18-9 will be displayed if you press PF9 on any EDF screen which lists PF9 : STOP CONDITIONS. This screen allows you to suppress the display of EDF screens you do not want to view in order to stop only at specified commands or upon encountering specific conditions. You could suppress displays of the EDF screens presented in the sample EDF session until the return screen was displayed. Just enter RETURN next to EXEC CICS in Fig. 18-9 and press the PF4 key as indicated in the instructions in order to suppress displays and continue processing. This screen allows you to enter a handle condition you wish to stop at, next to CICS EXCEPTIONAL CONDITION. You could enter conditions such as NOTFND and PGMIDERR next to this field identifier and press PF4 until one of the indicated conditions is encountered. You could continue pressing PF4 to suppress displays on any EDF screen which contained the PF4 : SUPPRESS DISPLAYS instruction.

```
TRANSACTION: POVB   PROGRAM: POVMBROW   TASK NUMBER 0000402   DISPLAY:   00
DISPLAY ON CONDITION:-

     COMMAND:              EXEC CICS
     OFFSET:                   X'.......'
     LINE NUMBER:              .........
     CICS EXCEPTIONAL CONDITION:
     ANY CICS ERROR CONDITION      YES
     TRANSACTION ABEND             YES
     NORMAL TASK TERMINATION       YES
     ABNORMAL TASK TERMINATION     YES




 ENTER:   CURRENT DISPLAY
 PF1 : UNDEFINED           PF2 : UNDEFINED           PF3 : UNDEFINED
 PF4 : SUPPRESS DISPLAYS   PF5 : WORKING STORAGE     PF6 : USER DISPLAY
 PF7 : UNDEFINED           PF8 : UNDEFINED           PF9 : UNDEFINED
 PF10: UNDEFINED           PF11: UNDEFINED           PF12: REMEMBER DISPLAY
```

Figure 18-9   EDF Stop Conditions Screen.

You could stop at specific line numbers if the program was translated with the DEBUG option which generated line numbers. The line number would be the translator listing line number and must contain six digits. It is the line number at which a command starts. The program offset corresponding to the command could also be entered.

Generally this screen is used to bypass the display of undesired EDF screens by entering a command beyond those you wish to suppress. For instance, in a browse program you would have to press the ENTER key numerous times in order to get past a series of READNEXT commands in an EDF session. You could find the command following the READNEXT command in your program and set a stop condition in order to suppress all displays until that command was reached.

Program ABEND Display

A screen similar to that shown in Fig. 18-10 will be displayed when an ABEND occurs. A common program ABEND is the ASRA, a four-character code which is displayed on the screen, denoting that a program data exception has occurred. This is generally the result of nonnumeric data's being present in a numeric field which is used in a program calculation. Normally an ASRA occurs between two CICS commands and it is difficult to determine which instruction caused the ABEND. One of two CICS commands is sometimes included in a test version of a program in order to determine where the ASRA occurred: ASKTIME and/or ENTER. Remember to remove such commands and any test data placed in working storage from a program before compiling its production version. The ASKTIME command was discussed in Chap. 10. The format of the ENTER command is

```
    EXEC CICS ENTER
                    TRACEID   (nnn)
    END-EXEC.
```

This command results in an entry to a CICS trace table and will not affect the execution of your program, but it can help you to narrow in on a program ASRA. The TRACEID entry (nnn) can be any number between 000 and 199, and it will be displayed when EDF stops at the ENTER command.

The ASKTIME and ENTER commands can be placed between other CICS commands and, unless suppressed, will display on an EDF screen as other CICS commands do. If several ASKTIME commands are placed in a program, the programmer has to keep track of which one is being executed. This may be done manually or by placing an indicative field at the beginning of working storage to signal which ASKTIME command is being executed. You can then press PF5 in order to display working storage and visually check this field. The ENTER command has an advantage over ASKTIME in that you can assign a sequence number to TRACEID which displays on the EDF screen and enables you to determine which of multiple commands is being executed. You can also move suspected data fields to the beginning of working storage in order to make them easier to find and examine when working storage is displayed.

ABEND a CICS Task

A CICS task can be ABENDed from any screen which displays PF12 : ABEND USER TASK. Pressing PF12 prompts you to ENTER ABEND CODE AND REQUEST ABEND AGAIN. You can ABEND the task with or without a

```
 TRANSACTION: POVB    PROGRAM: POVMBROW   TASK NUMBER 0000402   DISPLAY:   00
 STATUS:   AN ABEND HAS OCCURRED

      FIRTIME     = +0112215
      EIBDATE     = +0086023
      EIBTRNID    = 'POVB'
      EIBTASKN    = +0000402
      EIBTRMID    = 'T022'
      EIBCPOSN    = +00004
      EIBCALEN    = +00000
      EIBAID      = X'7D'                              AT X'0014477B'
      EIBFN       = X'0000'                            AT X'0014477C'
      EIBRCODE    = X'000000000000'                    AT X'0014477E'
      EIBDS       = '........'
      EIBREQID    = '........'
   +  EIBRSRCE    = '        '
                                        INTERRUPT: DATA EXCEPTION
    ABEND :    ASRA                      PSW: X'087C0008D013292A'

 ENTER:   CONTINUE
 PF1 : UNDEFINED           PF2 : SWITCH HEX/CHAR     PF3 : END EDF SESSION
 PF4 : SUPPRESS DISPLAYS   PF5 : WORKING STORAGE     PF6 : USER DISPLAY
 PF7 : SCROLL BACK         PF8 : SCROLL FORWARD      PF9 : STOP CONDITIONS
 PF10: PREVIOUS DISPLAY    PF11: UNDEFINED           PF12: ABEND USER TASK
```

Figure 18-10 EDF ABEND Screen.

dump. If a dump is desired, you enter the desired ABEND code you want to show up on the dump next to REPLY: which will be displayed. If no dump is needed, just enter NO and press PF12 again to ABEND the task.

Interactive Testing Tools

There are excellent interactive testing tools available which can significantly decrease the time required to test and debug CICS programs. EDF has limitations which are overcome by some of the interactive testing tools. One of the tools I have worked with does not require you to modify your program in order to stop between CICS commands. Your program can be stopped at any section or paragraph name or at various statement numbers. You can display and change most EIB and working-storage fields by reference to their symbolic names. The point at which a program is to be stopped can be altered at various break points as the execution of a program progresses and the flow of a program's logic can be altered. I use EDF along with this tool and find that they complement one another. I use EDF to trace the basic flow of a program and resort to an interactive testing tool in order to diagnose more difficult problems.

CICS Dumps

CICS dumps are often used in order to determine the cause of an ABEND which occurred in a production environment. CICS dumps are similar to batch dumps and their discussion is beyond the scope of this book.

CICS ABEND Determination Aids

There are CICS ABEND determination aids which, when available, practically eliminate the need for CICS dumps. One of these aids I have worked with allows you to display online a menu listing all ABENDS which have occurred in the test and production system. You can select the ABEND which occurred in your program and display the information and data unique to it. There is no need to wait until a dump is printed and then search through a series of dumps to find the one that is yours. The information is displayed in a user-friendly fashion and it is easy for the programmer to determine the cause of the ABEND. The online ABEND determination aid is much easier to work with and master than is the dump reading.

CICS Testing Techniques

Although it is always desirable to have files defined before testing begins, occasionally there may be a time lag between the times when a program is written and when the needed files are available. I recommend testing programs as soon as possible after they are written. Programs often contain numerous details which can be forgotten with the passing of time. If no test data is available, create some in the test version of your program. Instead of performing a section which reads a file, perform a special section written for testing which moves constant data to the fields of the required record layout. When the required file becomes available, remove the test data from your program. The program may later encounter some errors when the live file's data is used, but you will have eliminated most other errors and the program flow should be running smoothly.

SUMMARY

This chapter covered several debugging and testing techniques which I hope will be helpful as you start writing your own CICS programs. The chapter concentrated on EDF, which is a good tool available to most CICS installations. The determination and correction of program errors encountered in online systems is easier than it is in a batch environment. Several interactive testing tools and debugging aids are available. They are being enhanced, and new tools are being developed in order to make the task of online testing and debugging simpler.

You now have the knowledge and tools necessary to write and maintain most CICS programs and systems. Your mastery of CICS will come with study and practice. No single book contains all the information you need to know about CICS; start a collection of books on CICS and other data processing–related subjects. CICS, like many other subjects, *is* easy when you learn and master the fundamentals.

CONTENTS

Appendix A consists of the execute interface block (EIB), a description of commonly referenced EIB fields, and the attention identifier fields (DFHAID). DFHAID fields can be copied into working storage, and a program can compare the appropriate field against the EIB field EIBAID in order to determine which AID key was pressed.

APPENDIX A-1:
EXECUTE INTERFACE BLOCK (EIB)

The EIB COPY statement is generated by the CICS translator and copied into a program's linkage section at compile time. The EIB contains fields similar to the following:

```
Ø1  DFHEIBLK COPY DFHEIBLK.
*    EIBLK EXEC INTERFACE BLOCK
*
Ø1  DFHEIBLK.
*        EIBTIME    TIME IN ØHHMMSS FORMAT
    Ø2 EIBTIME    PIC S9(7)    COMP-3.
*
*        EIBDATE    DATE IN ØØYYDDD FORMAT
    Ø2 EIBDATE    PIC S9(7)    COMP-3.
*
*        EIBTRNID   TRANSACTION IDENTIFIER
    Ø2 EIBTRNID   PIC X(4).
*
*        EIBTASKN   TASK NUMBER
    Ø2 EIBTASKN   PIC S9(7)    COMP-3.
*
*        EIBTRMID   TERMINAL IDENTIFIER
    Ø2 EIBTRMID   PIC X(4).
*
*        DFHEIGDI   RESERVED
    Ø2 DFHEIGDI   PIC S9(4)    COMP.
*
*        EIBCPOSN   CURSOR POSITION
    Ø2 EIBCPOSN   PIC S9(4)    COMP.
*
*        EIBCALEN   COMMAREA LENGTH
    Ø2 EIBCALEN   PIC S9(4)    COMP.
*
*        EIBAID     ATTENTION IDENTIFIER
    Ø2 EIBAID     PIC X.
*
*        EIBFN      FUNCTION CODE
    Ø2 EIBFN      PIC XX.
*
*        EIBRCODE   RESPONSE CODE
    Ø2 EIBRCODE   PIC X(6).
*
*        EIBDS      DATASET NAME
    Ø2 EIBDS      PIC X(8).
*
*        EIBREQID   REQUEST IDENTIFIER
    Ø2 EIBREQID   PIC X(8).
```

APPENDIX A-2:
COMMONLY REFERENCED EIB FIELDS

EIBTIME – Time that the task was initiated.

EIBDATE – Date the task was started.

EIBTRNID – Transaction Identifier (TRANSID).

EIBTASKN – contains the task number assigned by CICS.

EIBTRMID – Terminal Identifier.

EIBCPOSN – position of the cursor on the screen before a
           Receive Map Command is executed.

EIBCALEN – length of the COMMAREA – determined by the size of
           the LENGTH ( ) field in a RETURN or XCTL command.

EIBAID   – Attention Identifier, contents are determined by
           the AID key pressed

APPENDIX A-3:
ATTENTION IDENTIFIER FIELDS (DFHAID)

A DFHAID field can be compared against the EIB field EIBAID, in order to determine which AID key was pressed by a terminal operator. DFHAID consists of fields which are similar to the following:

```
01  DFHAID    COPY    DFHAID.
01  DFHAID.
    02   DFHNULL       PIC X   VALUE ' '.
    02   DFHENTER      PIC X   VALUE QUOTE.
    02   DFHCLEAR      PIC X   VALUE ' '.
    02   DFHPEN        PIC X   VALUE '='.
    02   DFHOPID       PIC X   VALUE 'W'.
    02   DFHPA1        PIC X   VALUE '('.
    02   DFHPA2        PIC X   VALUE ' '.
    02   DFHPA3        PIC X   VALUE ','.
    02   DFHPF1        PIC X   VALUE '1'.
    02   DFHPF2        PIC X   VALUE '2'.
    02   DFHPF3        PIC X   VALUE '3'.
    02   DFHPF4        PIC X   VALUE '4'.
    02   DFHPF5        PIC X   VALUE '5'.
    02   DFHPF6        PIC X   VALUE '6'.
    02   DFHPF7        PIC X   VALUE '7'.
    02   DFHPF8        PIC X   VALUE '8'.
    02   DFHPF9        PIC X   VALUE '9'.
    02   DFHPF10       PIC X   VALUE ' '.
    02   DFHPF11       PIC X   VALUE '='.
    02   DFHPF12       PIC X   VALUE ''''.
    02   DFHPF13       PIC X   VALUE 'A'.
    02   DFHPF14       PIC X   VALUE 'B'.
    02   DFHPF15       PIC X   VALUE 'C'.
    02   DFHPF16       PIC X   VALUE 'D'.
    02   DFHPF17       PIC X   VALUE 'E'.
    02   DFHPF18       PIC X   VALUE 'F'.
    02   DFHPF19       PIC X   VALUE 'G'.
    02   DFHPF20       PIC X   VALUE 'H'.
    02   DFHPF21       PIC X   VALUE 'I'.
    02   DFHPF22       PIC X   VALUE ' '.
    02   DFHPF23       PIC X   VALUE '.'.
    02   DFHPF24       PIC X   VALUE ')'.
```

CONTENTS

Appendix B consists of copy library members common to more than one text program. It is good practice to develop copy library members for any data items or routines which are expected to be used in more than one program or system. Note the consistency of prefix usage among most data-item copy members. Similar prefixes associate data items with a particular library member.

COPY LIBRARY

The copy library entries are arranged alphabetically for ease of locating as follows:

APPENDIX B-1

```
0001*******************************************************************
0002*   'JRNLRECD'      JOURNAL RECORD          524 BYTES LONG    *
0003*   MANY PROGRAMS FORMAT A 'BEFORE' AND 'AFTER' RECORD WHEN   *
0004*   MAINTENANCE IS PERFORMED AGAINST THE FOLLOWING FILES:     *
0005*        VENDOR-MASTER-FILE       ITEM-MASTER-FILE            *
0006*             PURCHASE-ORDER-MASTER-FILE                      *
0007*******************************************************************
0008*
0009 01  JOURNAL-RECORD.
0010     05  JR-KEY.
0011         10  JR-EIBDATE          PIC S9(7)    COMP-3.
0012         10  JR-EIBTIME          PIC S9(7)    COMP-3.
0013         10  JR-SEQUENCE-NUMBER  PIC S9(5)    COMP-3.
0014     05  JR-TYPE                 PIC X.
0015         88  JR-BEFORE-IMAGE                        VALUE 'B'.
0016         88  JR-AFTER-IMAGE                         VALUE 'A'.
0017     05  JR-PREFIX               PIC XX.
0018         88  JR-VENDOR-MASTER                       VALUE 'VM'.
0019         88  JR-PURCHASE-ORDER-MASTER               VALUE 'PO'.
0020         88  JR-ITEM-MASTER                         VALUE 'IM'.
0021     05  JR-EIBTRMID             PIC X(4).
0022     05  JR-PASSWORD             PIC X(6).
0023     05  JR-RECORD-DATA          PIC X(500).
```

```
0001******************************************************************
0002*   'MAPVDTL1'   VENDOR INQUIRY & DELETE DETAIL - SYMBOLIC MAP  *
0003******************************************************************
0004*
0005 01  VM-DETAIL-MAP.
0006     05  FILLER                    PIC X(12).
0007*
0008     05  MVD-L-DATE                PIC S9(4)    COMP.
0009     05  MVD-A-DATE                PIC X.
0010     05  MVD-D-DATE                PIC X(8).
0011*
0012     05  MVD-L-TIME                PIC S9(4)    COMP.
0013     05  MVD-A-TIME                PIC X.
0014     05  MVD-D-TIME                PIC X(8).
0015*
0016     05  MVD-L-VENDOR-CODE         PIC S9(4)    COMP.
0017     05  MVD-A-VENDOR-CODE         PIC X.
0018     05  MVD-D-VENDOR-CODE         PIC X(8).
0019*
0020     05  MVD-L-VENDOR-NAME         PIC S9(4)    COMP.
0021     05  MVD-A-VENDOR-NAME         PIC X.
0022     05  MVD-D-VENDOR-NAME         PIC X(25).
0023*
0024     05  MVD-L-PHONE-AREA-CD       PIC S9(4)    COMP.
0025     05  MVD-A-PHONE-AREA-CD       PIC X.
0026     05  MVD-D-PHONE-AREA-CD       PIC XXX.
0027*
0028     05  MVD-L-PHONE-1             PIC S9(4)    COMP.
0029     05  MVD-A-PHONE-1             PIC X.
0030     05  MVD-D-PHONE-1             PIC XXX.
0031 *
0032     05  MVD-L-PHONE-2             PIC S9(4)    COMP.
0033     05  MVD-A-PHONE-2             PIC X.
0034     05  MVD-D-PHONE-2             PIC X(4).
0035*
0036     05  MVD-L-CONTACT             PIC S9(4)    COMP.
0037     05  MVD-A-CONTACT             PIC X.
0038     05  MVD-D-CONTACT             PIC X(25).
0039*
0040     05  MVD-L-STREET              PIC S9(4)    COMP.
0041     05  MVD-A-STREET              PIC X.
0042     05  MVD-D-STREET              PIC X(20).
0043*
0044     05  MVD-L-DLRS-COMMITTED      PIC S9(4)    COMP.
0045     05  MVD-A-DLRS-COMMITTED      PIC X.
0046     05  MVD-D-DLRS-COMMITTED      PIC $$,$$$,$$$.99CR.
0047     05  MVD-L-CITY                PIC S9(4)    COMP.
0048     05  MVD-A-CITY                PIC X.
0049     05  MVD-D-CITY                PIC X(18).
0050*
0051     05  MVD-L-STATE-CODE          PIC S9(4)    COMP.
0052     05  MVD-A-STATE-CODE          PIC X.
0053     05  MVD-D-STATE-CODE          PIC XX.
0054*
0055     05  MVD-L-STATE-NAME          PIC S9(4)    COMP.
0056     05  MVD-A-STATE-NAME          PIC X.
0057     05  MVD-D-STATE-NAME          PIC X(14).
0058*
0059     05  MVD-L-ZIP-CODE            PIC S9(4)    COMP.
0060     05  MVD-A-ZIP-CODE            PIC X.
0061     05  MVD-D-ZIP-CODE            PIC X(5).
0062*
0063     05  MVD-L-ATTENTION-OF        PIC S9(4)    COMP.
0064     05  MVD-A-ATTENTION-OF        PIC X.
0065     05  MVD-D-ATTENTION-OF        PIC X(20).
0066*
0067     05  MVD-L-MESSAGE             PIC S9(4)    COMP.
0068     05  MVD-A-MESSAGE             PIC X.
0069     05  MVD-D-MESSAGE             PIC X(79).
```

APPENDIX B-3

```
0001******************************************************************
0002*     'MAPVDTL2'   VENDOR ADD & CHANGE DETAIL - SYMBOLIC MAP    *
0003******************************************************************
0004*
0005 01  VM-DETAIL-MAP.
0006     05  FILLER                       PIC X(12).
0007*
0008     05  MVD-L-DATE                   PIC S9(4)    COMP.
0009     05  MVD-A-DATE                   PIC X.
0010     05  MVD-D-DATE                   PIC X(8).
0011*
0012     05  MVD-L-TIME                   PIC S9(4)    COMP.
0013     05  MVD-A-TIME                   PIC X.
0014     05  MVD-D-TIME                   PIC X(8).
0015*
0016     05  MVD-L-VENDOR-CODE            PIC S9(4)    COMP.
0017     05  MVD-A-VENDOR-CODE            PIC X.
0018     05  MVD-D-VENDOR-CODE            PIC X(8).
0019*
0020     05  MVD-C-L-VENDOR-NAME          PIC S9(4)    COMP.
0021     05  MVD-C-A-VENDOR-NAME          PIC X.
0022     05  MVD-C-D-VENDOR-NAME          PIC X(5).
0023*
0024     05  MVD-L-VENDOR-NAME            PIC S9(4)    COMP.
0025     05  MVD-A-VENDOR-NAME            PIC X.
0026     05  MVD-D-VENDOR-NAME            PIC X(25).
0027*
0028     05  MVD-C-L-PHONE                PIC S9(4)    COMP.
0029     05  MVD-C-A-PHONE                PIC X.
0030     05  MVD-C-D-PHONE                PIC X(6).
0031*
0032     05  MVD-L-PHONE-AREA-CD          PIC S9(4)    COMP.
0033     05  MVD-A-PHONE-AREA-CD          PIC X.
0034     05  MVD-D-PHONE-AREA-CD          PIC XXX.
0035*
0036     05  MVD-L-PHONE-1                PIC S9(4)    COMP.
0037     05  MVD-A-PHONE-1                PIC X.
0038     05  MVD-D-PHONE-1                PIC XXX.
0039 *
0040     05  MVD-L-PHONE-2                PIC S9(4)    COMP.
0041     05  MVD-A-PHONE-2                PIC X.
0042     05  MVD-D-PHONE-2                PIC X(4).
0043*
0044     05  MVD-L-CONTACT                PIC S9(4)    COMP.
0045     05  MVD-A-CONTACT                PIC X.
0046     05  MVD-D-CONTACT                PIC X(25).
0047*
0048     05  MVD-C-L-STREET               PIC S9(4)    COMP.
0049     05  MVD-C-A-STREET               PIC X.
0050     05  MVD-C-D-STREET               PIC X(17).
0051*
0052     05  MVD-L-STREET                 PIC S9(4)    COMP.
0053     05  MVD-A-STREET                 PIC X.
0054     05  MVD-D-STREET                 PIC X(20).
```

APPENDIX B-3   *(Continued)*

```
0055    05    MVD-C-L-CITY           PIC S9(4)    COMP.
0056    05    MVD-C-A-CITY           PIC X.
0057    05    MVD-C-D-CITY           PIC X(5).
0058*
0059    05    MVD-L-CITY             PIC S9(4)    COMP.
0060    05    MVD-A-CITY             PIC X.
0061    05    MVD-D-CITY             PIC X(18).
0062*
0063    05    MVD-C-L-STATE          PIC S9(4)    COMP.
0064    05    MVD-C-A-STATE          PIC X.
0065    05    MVD-C-D-STATE          PIC X(6).
0066*
0067    05    MVD-L- STATE-CODE      PIC S9(4)    COMP.
0068    05    MVD-A-STATE-CODE       PIC X.
0069    05    MVD-D-STATE-CODE       PIC XX.
0070*
0071    05    MVD-L-STATE-NAME       PIC S9(4)    COMP.
0072    05    MVD-A-STATE-NAME       PIC X.
0073    05    MVD-D-STATE-NAME       PIC X(14).
0074*
0075    05    MVD-C-L-ZIP-CODE       PIC S9(4)    COMP.
0076    05    MVD-C-A-ZIP-CODE       PIC X.
0077    05    MVD-C-D-ZIP-CODE       PIC X(4).
0078*
0079    05    MVD-L-ZIP-CODE         PIC S9(4)    COMP.
0080    05    MVD-A-ZIP-CODE         PIC X.
0081    05    MVD-D-ZIP-CODE         PIC X(5).
0082*
0083    05    MVD-L-ATTENTION-OF     PIC S9(4)    COMP.
0084    05    MVD-A-ATTENTION-OF     PIC X.
0085    05    MVD-D-ATTENTION-OF     PIC X(20).
0086*
0087    05    MVD-L-MESSAGE          PIC S9(4)    COMP.
0088    05    MVD-A-MESSAGE          PIC X.
0089    05    MVD-D-MESSAGE          PIC X(79).
```

APPENDIX B-4

```
0001*******************************************************************
0002*   'MAPVMCTL'  VENDOR MAINTENANCE CONTROL - SYMBOLIC MAP     *
0003*******************************************************************
0004*
0005 01  VM-CONTROL-MAP.
0006      05  FILLER                    PIC X(12).
0007*
0008      05  MVC-L-DATE                PIC S9(4)    COMP.
0009      05  MVC-A-DATE                PIC X.
0010      05  MVC-D-DATE                PIC X(8).
0011*
0012      05  MVC-L-TIME                PIC S9(4)    COMP.
0013      05  MVC-A-TIME                PIC X.
0014      05  MVC-D-TIME                PIC X(8).
0015*
0016      05  MVC-L-VEND-CD-1           PIC S9(4)    COMP.
0017      05  MVC-A-VEND-CD-1           PIC X.
0018      05  MVC-D-VEND-CD-1           PIC X.
0019*
0020      05  MVC-L-VEND-CD-2           PIC S9(4)    COMP.
0021      05  MVC-A-VEND-CD-2           PIC X.
0022      05  MVC-D-VEND-CD-2           PIC X(4).
0023*
0024      05  MVC-L-VEND-CD-3           PIC S9(4)    COMP.
0025      05  MVC-A-VEND-CD-3           PIC X.
0026      05  MVC-D-VEND-CD-3           PIC X.
0027*
0028      05  MVC-L-MESSAGE             PIC S9(4)    COMP.
0029      05  MVC-A-MESSAGE             PIC X.
0030      05  MVC-D-MESSAGE             PIC X(79).
```

```
0001**********************************************************************
0002*        'POWSVMCA'  PURCHASING SYSTEM - VENDOR COMMAREA          *
0003**********************************************************************
0004*
0005 01  WS-COMMAREA.
0006     05  CA-FUNCTION-CODE      PIC X        VALUE SPACE.
0007         88  CA-INQUIRY                     VALUE 'I'.
0008         88  CA-ADDITION                    VALUE 'A'.
0009         88  CA-CHANGE                      VALUE 'C'.
0010         88  CA-DELETE                      VALUE 'D'.
0011         88  CA-BROWSE                      VALUE 'B'.
0012*
0013     05  CA-MAP-CONTROL        PIC X        VALUE SPACE.
0014         88  CA-RECEIVE-CTL-MAP             VALUE '1'.
0015         88  CA-RECEIVE-DTL-MAP             VALUE '2'.
0016*
0017     05  CA-VENDOR-CODE.
0018         10  CA-VEND-1         PIC X        VALUE LOW-VALUES.
0019         10  CA-VEND-2         PIC X(4)     VALUE LOW-VALUES.
0020         10  CA-VEND-3         PIC X        VALUE LOW-VALUES.
```

APPENDIX B-6

```
0001*****************************************************************************
0002*  'STLNKCWA'  - COMMON WORK AREA (CWA)  - LINKAGE SECTION ENTRY *
0003*      GENERALLY USED WITH:  'STWSDTTM' AND 'STPDDTTM' COPIES     *
0004*****************************************************************************
0005*
0006 01  CWA-DATA.
0007     05  CWA-CURRENT-DATE          PIC X(8).
0008*            MM/DD/YY
0009     05  CWA-ALPHA-DATA            PIC X(18).
0010*         E.G.  SEPTEMBER 10, 1985
0011     05  CWA-DATE-MMDDYY           PIC X(6).
0012     05  CWA-DATE-YYMMDD           PIC X(6).
0013     05  CWA-COMPANY-NAME          PIC X(25).
```

APPENDIX B-7

```
0001*******************************************************************
0002*         'STPDDTTM'  - COMMON DATE/TIME FORMATTING ROUTINE        *
0003*  RETRIEVE CURRENT DATE FROM CWA - FORMAT EIBTIME TO 'HH.MM.SS'   *
0004*  COPY 'STWSDTTM' INTO WORKING STORAGE FOR REQUIRED WS- FIELDS    *
0005*  COPY 'STLNKCWA' INTO LINKAGE SECTION UNDER BLL-CELLS            *
0006*                 DEFINE:  BLL-CWA-ADDRESS                         *
0007*******************************************************************
0008*
0009      EXEC CICS ASSIGN
0010                 CWALENG (WS-CWA-LENGTH)
0011      END-EXEC.
0012*
0013      IF CWA-LENGTH  IS GREATER THAN  ZERO
0014          EXEC CICS ADDRESS
0015                 CWA (BLL-CWA-ADDRESS)
0016          END-EXEC
0017*
0018*         SERVICE RELOAD CWA-DATA
0019*
0020          MOVE CWA-CURRENT-DATE  TO  WS-CURRENT-DATE
0021      ELSE
0022          MOVE 'ERRORCWA'         TO  WS-CURRENT-DATE.
0023*
0024* FORMAT TIME TO 'HH.MM.SS'
0025      MOVE EIBTIME     TO  WS-EIB-TIME.
0026      MOVE WS-EIB-HH TO  WS-MAP-HH.
0027      MOVE WS-EIB-MM TO  WS-MAP-MM.
0028      MOVE WS-EIB-SS TO  WS-MAP-SS.
```

APPENDIX B-8

```
0001*******************************************************************
0002*          'STPDT037'    LOAD AND SEARCH STATE CODE TABLE       *
0003*      GOOD HIT:    STATE NAME IS RETURNED IN WS-STATE-NAME     *
0004*                   WS-STATE-SEARCH-STATUS = 'G'                *
0005*      NOT FOUND:  ALL  '*'  ARE RETURNED IN WS-STATE-NAME      *
0006*                   WS-STATE-SEARCH-STATUS = 'E'                *
0007*   COPY 'STWST037' INTO WORKING STORAGE FOR REQUIRED FIELDS    *
0008*   COPY 'T037STAT' INTO LINKAGE SECTION FOR STATE TABLE        *
0009*                DEFINE:  BLL-T037-STATE-TABLE-ADDRESS          *
0010*******************************************************************
0011*
0012    EXEC CICS LOAD
0013            PROGRAM ('T037STAT')
0014            SET     (BLL-T037-STATE-TABLE-ADDRESS)
0015    END-EXEC.
0016*
0017*   SERVICE RELOAD T037-STATE-TABLE.
0018*
0019    SET T037-INDEX  TO  1.
0020    SEARCH T037-STATE-ENTRIES
0021        AT END
0022            MOVE 'E'      TO  WS-STATE-SEARCH-STATUS
0023            MOVE ALL '*'  TO  WS-STATE-NAME
0024        WHEN
0025            WS-STATE-CODE  =  T037-STATE-CODE (T037-INDEX)
0026            MOVE 'G'      TO  WS-STATE-SEARCH-STATUS
0027            MOVE T037-STATE-NAME (T037-INDEX)  TO  WS-STATE-NAME.
0028*
0029    EXEC CICS RELEASE
0030            PROGRAM ('T037STAT')
0031    END-EXEC.
```

APPENDIX B-9

```
0001************************************************************************
0002* 'STWSATTR'   STANDARD ATTRIBUTE LIST USED BY THIS INSTALLATION *
0003************************************************************************
0004*
0005 01  ATTRIBUTE-LIST.
0006     05  UNPROT-NORM           PIC X       VALUE SPACE.
0007     05  UNPROT-FSET           PIC X       VALUE 'A'.
0008     05  UNPROT-BRT            PIC X       VALUE 'H'.
0009     05  UNPROT-BRT-FSET       PIC X       VALUE 'I'.
0010     05  UNPROT-DRK            PIC X       VALUE '<'.
0011     05  UNPROT-DRK-FSET       PIC X       VALUE '('.
0012     05  UNPRO. NUM            PIC X       VALUE '&'.
0013     05  UNPROT-NUM-FSET       PIC X       VALUE 'J'.
0014     05  UNPROT-BRT-NUM        PIC X       VALUE 'Q'.
0015     05  UNPROT-BRT-NUM-FSET   PIC X       VALUE 'R'.
0016     05  UNPROT-DRK-NUM        PIC X       VALUE '*'.
0017     05  UNPROT-DRK-NUM-FSET   PIC X       VALUE ')'.
0018     05  ASKIP-NORM            PIC X       VALUE '0'.
0019     05  ASKIP-FSET            PIC X       VALUE '1'.
0020     05  ASKIP-BRT             PIC X       VALUE '8'.
0021     05  ASKIP-BRT-FSET        PIC X       VALUE '9'.
0022     05  ASKIP-DRK             PIC X       VALUE '@'.
0023     05  ASKIP-DRK-FSET        PIC X       VALUE QUOTE.
```

APPENDIX B-10

```
0001*****************************************************************
0002*      'STWSDTTM'  WORKING STORAGE FOR:  DATE/TIME EDITING     *
0003*      DATE IS RETRIEVED FROM THE CWA AND TIME FROM EIBTIME    *
0004* COPY 'STPDDTTM' INTO PROCEDURE DIVISION FOR FORMATTING LOGIC *
0005* COPY 'STLNKCWA' INTO LINKAGE SECTION FOR CWA AREA            *
0006*****************************************************************
0007*
0008 01  WS-DATE-AND-TIME.
0009     05  WS-CURRENT-DATE        PIC X(8)          VALUE SPACES.
0010*
0011     05  WS-MAP-TIME.
0012         10  WS-MAP-HH          PIC XX            VALUE 'HH'.
0013         10  FILLER             PIC X             VALUE '.'.
0014         10  WS-MAP-MM          PIC XX            VALUE 'MM'.
0015         10  FILLER             PIC X             VALUE '.'.
0016         10  WS-MAP-SS          PIC XX            VALUE 'SS'.
0017*
0018     05  WS-EIB-TIME            PIC 9(6)          VALUE ZEROES.
0019     05 FILLER   REDEFINES  WS-EIB-TIME.
0020         10  WS-EIB-HH          PIC XX.
0021         10  WS-EIB-MM          PIC XX.
0022         10  WS-EIB-SS          PIC XX.
0023*
0024 01  WS-CWA-LENGTH             PIC S9(4)   COMP   VALUE ZEROES.
```

```
0001****************************************************************
0002*         'STWSSTAT'  COMMON PROGRAM STATUS FIELDS          *
0003****************************************************************
0004*
0005 01  WS-STATUS-FIELDS.
0006     05  STATUS-OF-RECEIVE     PIC X            VALUE SPACE.
0007         88  GOOD-RECEIVE                       VALUE 'G'.
0008         88  RETURN-TO-CTL-MAP                  VALUE 'C'.
0009         88  INVALID-KEY-PRESSED               VALUE 'I'.
0010         88  MAPFAIL-ON-RECEIVE                VALUE 'M'.
0011*
0012     05  STATUS-OF-SELECTION   PIC X            VALUE SPACE.
0013         88  VALID-SELECTION                   VALUE 'G'.
0014         88  INVALID-SELECTION                 VALUE 'E'.
0015*
0016     05  STATUS-OF-FORMAT      PIC X            VALUE SPACE.
0017         88  VALID-FORMAT                      VALUE 'G'.
0018         88  INVALID-FORMAT                    VALUE 'E'.
0019*
0020     05  STATUS-OF-READ        PIC X            VALUE SPACE.
0021         88  RECORD-RETRIEVED                  VALUE 'G'.
0022         88  RECORD-NOT-FOUND                  VALUE 'E'.
0023         88  END-OF-FILE                       VALUE 'F'.
0024*
0025     05  STATUS-OF-VERIFY      PIC X            VALUE SPACE.
0026         88  GOOD-VERIFY                       VALUE 'G'.
0027         88  VERIFY-ERROR                      VALUE 'E'.
0028*
0029     05  STATUS-OF-DELETE      PIC X            VALUE SPACE.
0030         88  GOOD-DELETE                       VALUE 'G'.
0031         88  RECORD-NOT-DELETED                VALUE 'E'.
0032*
0033     05  STATUS-OF-CHANGE      PIC X            VALUE SPACE.
0034         88  GOOD-CHANGE                       VALUE 'G'.
0035         88  RECORD-NOT-CHANGED                VALUE 'E'.
0036*
0037     05  STATUS-OF-EDIT        PIC X            VALUE SPACE.
0038         88  GOOD-EDIT                         VALUE 'G'.
0039         88  ERROR-ON-EDIT                     VALUE 'E'.
0040*
0041     05  STATUS-OF-WRITE       PIC X            VALUE SPACE.
0042         88  GOOD-WRITE                        VALUE 'G'.
0043         88  DUPLICATE-RECORD                  VALUE 'E'.
0044*
0045     05  STATUS-OF-ADD         PIC X            VALUE SPACE.
0046         88  GOOD-ADD                          VALUE 'G'.
0047         88  RECORD-NOT-ADDED                  VALUE 'E'.
0048*
0049     05  STATUS-OF-BROWSE      PIC X            VALUE SPACE.
0050         88  GOOD-STARTBR                      VALUE 'G'.
0051         88  BROWSE-NOTFND                     VALUE 'E'.
```

APPENDIX B-12

```
0001**********************************************************************
0002*    'STWST037'  STATE CODE AND NAME WORKING STORAGE ENTRIES     *
0003*      COPY 'T037STAT' INTO LINKAGE SECTION FOR STATE TABLE      *
0004*      COPY 'STPDT037' INTO PROCEDURE DIVISION FOR SEARCH LOGIC  *
0005**********************************************************************
0006*
0007 01  WS-STATE-CODE-SEARCH-ENTRIES.
0008     05  WS-STATE-CODE           PIC XX.
0009     05  WS-STATE-NAME           PIC X(14).
0010     05  WS-STATE-SEARCH-STATUS  PIC X          VALUE SPACE.
0011         88  STATE-FOUND                        VALUE 'G'.
0012         88  STATE-NOT-FOUND                    VALUE 'E'.
```

APPENDIX B-13

```
0001**********************************************************************
0002* 'T037STAT' - STATE CODE AND NAME TABLE - LINKAGE SECTION ENTRY *
0003*  COPY 'STWST037' INTO WORKING STORAGE FOR REQUIRED WS- FIELDS  *
0004*  COPY 'STPDT037' INTO PROCEDURE DIVISION FOR SEARCH LOGIC      *
0005**********************************************************************
0006*.
0007 01  T037-STATE-TABLE.
0008     05  T037-STATE-ENTRIES
0009         OCCURS 50 TIMES
0010         INDEXED BY  T037-INDEX.
0011         10  T037-STATE-CODE    PIC XX.
0012         10  T037-STATE-NAME    PIC X(14).
```

APPENDIX B-14

```
0001*******************************************************************
0002*    'VENDMAST'   VENDOR MASTER RECORD  -  169 BYTES LONG        *
0003*******************************************************************
0004*
0005 01  VENDOR-MASTER-RECORD.
0006     05  VM-VENDOR-CODE.
0007         10  VM-VEND-CD-1        PIC X.
0008         10  VM-VEND-CD-2        PIC X(4).
0009         10  VM-VEND-CD-3        PIC X.
0010     05  VM-VENDOR-NAME          PIC X(25).
0011     05  VM-STREET-ADDRESS       PIC X(20).
0012     05  VM-CITY-STATE-ZIP.
0013         10  VM-CITY-STATE.
0014             15  VM-CITY         PIC X(18).
0015             15  VM-STATE        PIC XX.
0016         10  VM-ZIP-CODE         PIC X(5).
0017     05  VM-TO-ATTN-OF           PIC X(20).
0018     05  VM-PHONE-NO.
0019         10  VM-AREA-CD          PIC XXX.
0020         10  VM-PHONE-1-3        PIC XXX.
0021         10  VM-PHONE-4-7        PIC X(4).
0022     05  VM-CONTACT              PIC X(25).
0023     05  VM-DOLLARS-COMMITTED    PIC S9(7)V99   COMP-3.
0024     05  FILLER                  PIC X(33).
0025*
0026*******************************************************************
0027*    WORKING STORAGE FIELDS USED FOR EDITING OF VENDOR CODE      *
0028*******************************************************************
0029*
0030 01  WS-VENDOR-CODE.
0031     05  WS-VENDOR-CD-1     PIC X       VALUE SPACE.
0032     05  FILLER             PIC X       VALUE '-'.
0033     05  WS-VENDOR-CD-2     PIC X(4)    VALUE SPACES.
0034     05  FILLER             PIC X       VALUE '-'.
0035     05  WS-VENDOR-CD-3     PIC X       VALUE SPACE.
```

BIBLIOGRAPHY

Bruno, W., and L. Bosland: *CICS Mastering Command Level Coding using COBOL*, Prentice-Hall, Englewood Cliffs, N.J., 1984.

International Business Machines Corporation Publications. (Check with IBM for latest version, release, and order number because they change periodically.) *Customer Information Control System/Virtual Storage (CICS/VS) Application Programmer's Reference Manual (Command Level)* and the *VSAM Primer and Reference*.

Jatich, Alida: *CICS Command Level Programming*, Wiley, New York, 1985.

Lee, S. David: *CICS/VS Command Level Programming with COBOL Examples*, CCD ONLINE Systems, Dallas, Texas, 1983.

Lim, Pacifico A.: *CICS/VS Command Level with ANS COBOL Examples*. Van Nostrand Reinhold, New York, 1982.

Lowe, Doug: *CICS for the COBOL Programmer Part 1: An Introductory Course*, Mike Murach & Associates, Fresno, Calif., 1984.

Lowe, Doug: *VSAM for the COBOL Programmer*, Mike Murach & Associates, Fresno, Calif., 1982.

Noll, Paul, and M. Murach: *The COBOL Programmer's Handbook*. Mike Murach & Associates, Fresno, Calif., 1985.

Noll, Paul, and M. Murach: *How to Design and Develop COBOL Programs*, Mike Murach & Associates, Fresno, Calif., 1985.

INDEX

About the Author

Joseph J. Le Bert has played a major role in the development, programming, and maintenance of numerous online and batch systems while functioning as a consultant, project leader, and senior programmer analyst at several companies. He predicts that the use of online interactive systems will grow rapidly, replacing many obsolete batch systems.